BODYMINDS
REIMAGINED

BODYMINDS REIMAGINED

(Dis)ability, Race, and Gender in Black Women's Speculative Fiction

Sami Schalk

Duke University Press Durham and London 2018

© 2018 Duke University Press
All rights reserved
Printed in the United States of America on acid-free paper ∞
Text designed by Courtney Leigh Baker
Cover designed by Matthew Tauch
Typeset in Trade Gothic Condensed and Arno Pro by
Copperline Book Services

Library of Congress Cataloging-in-Publication Data
Names: Schalk, Samantha Dawn, author.
Title: Bodyminds reimagined : (dis)ability, race, and gender
in black women's speculative fiction / Sami Schalk.
Description: Durham : Duke University Press, 2018. |
Includes bibliographical references and index.
Identifiers: LCCN 2017036970 (print)
LCCN 2018000174 (ebook)
ISBN 9780822371830 (ebook)
ISBN 9780822370734 (hardcover : alk. paper)
ISBN 9780822370888 (pbk. : alk. paper)
Subjects: LCSH: American literature—African American authors—
History and criticism. | Speculative fiction—20th century—
Women authors—History and criticism. | People with disabilities
in literature. | Race in literature. | Gender identity in literature.
Classification: LCC PS153.N5 (ebook) | LCC PS153.N5 S33 2018 (print) |
DDC 810.9/928708996073—dc23
LC record available at https://lccn.loc.gov/2017036970

Cover art: Tahir Carl Karmali, *Untitled IV*, 2014.
From the series *Jua Kali*. © 2018 Tahir Carl Karmali.

CONTENTS

PROLOGUE AND ACKNOWLEDGMENTS

This book is one grown from individual intellectual interests and a variety of collective community investments. I did not come to this topic nor these arguments simply on my own. I knew for a long time that my research would be about representations at the intersection of black feminism and disability studies. From the time I started graduate school I identified the lack of engagement between the two fields as a major issue that impacted not only my intellectual life as someone invested in both areas of research, but also my personal life as a queer, fat, black, nondisabled woman. I have written elsewhere about my entry into disability studies and my affective relationship with the field as a process of coming to identify *with* the term *crip* (Schalk "Coming to Claim Crip"). I have a similar affective connection to black feminism. Black women writers have always given me life. I have come to understand myself and my world better because of writers like Lucille Clifton, Maya Angelou, Audre Lorde, bell hooks, and Octavia E. Butler. I always knew my research would be about black feminism and disability studies. What I didn't know was that I would write about speculative fiction. What I didn't know was that I would explain to people at conferences and on job interviews how I was reading a series of paranormal romance novels about a werewolf with obsessive-compulsive disorder. This is where community comes in.

I came to speculative fiction initially as one potential chapter after my adviser, LaMonda Horton-Stallings, encouraged me to read Octavia E. Butler's *Parable of the Sower*. I was captivated by Butler's ability to create a non-realist disability that so effectively spoke to realist issues in the disability studies and disability rights communities. Later, at the Society for Disability Studies conference, I had coffee with Rosemarie Garland-Thomson and explained to her my massive plans for a study of the representation of disability in black women's writing from slave narratives to contemporary texts. I detailed my plans for each chapter, and when I began to explain the chapter on Butler, Dr. Garland-Thomson stopped me and said (essentially): *You're trying to do too much. That stuff on science fiction? No one is doing work on that. That's your project.* And so it is. I had no idea where this work would lead, but I am excited by what I have discovered in representations of disability in black women's speculative fiction with the help of various fan, artist, and activist communities, including the Black Science Fiction Society, the Carl Brandon listserv, and the Octavia E. Butler Legacy Network. I have no doubt that the lessons I have learned in the process, the ideas I have been able to foster through deep engagement with both the literature and the theory, will be beneficial for future work in not only disability studies and black feminist theory, but also literary criticism, American studies, critical race studies, and women's and gender studies as well. These are lessons, ideas, and arguments that would not exist without my multiple intellectual, artistic, and activist communities, my colleagues, my queer kinship networks, and my chosen family. I would like to thank some of these folks here. This book would not be possible without those people, groups, and organizations who have supported and guided me along the way.

First, I would like to thank my dissertation chair and mentor, LaMonda Horton-Stallings, who ushered me through graduate school, the dissertation, the job market and beyond with tough love and practical advice. Thank you to the rest of my original dissertation committee as well: Alison Kafer, whose excitement about and support of my work keeps me excited and confident too; Marlon M. Bailey, who incited me to slay and snatch on the job market; Shane Vogel, who pushed my critical engagement with American studies and literary studies; and Liz Ellcessor, who so generously came on board with my project and willingly read all those paranormal romance novels. Although not on my original committee, Margaret Price has been an incredible support, mentor, and friend throughout my career to whom I am forever grateful.

Next, I would like to acknowledge the American Association of University Women, whose generous dissertation fellowship allowed for the timely and focused completion of the first draft of this project, as well as the Huntington Library, whose short-term fellowship allowed me the incredible opportunity to explore Butler's papers there. The final version of this book manuscript was completed with the assistance of a postdoctoral fellowship in the English Department at Rutgers University, under the mentorship of Cheryl A. Wall.

I would also like to thank the many mentors, friends, and dance partners I have in the disability studies community, especially within the Society for Disability Studies. For their incredible collegiality and support, I would like to acknowledge Rosemarie Garland-Thomson, Ellen Samuels, Nirmala Erevelles, Mel Chen, Anne Finger, Eli Clare, Susan Burch, Therí A. Pickens, Brenda Brueggemann, Julie Avril Minich, Stephanie Kerschbaum, Cindy Wu, Michelle Jarman, Ann Fox, Alice Sheppard, Simi Linton, Bethany Stevens, Corbett O'Toole, Ibby Grace, Jim Ferris, Petra Kuppers, Jay Dolmage, Beth Ferri, Carrie Sandahl, Akemi Nishida, Juliann Anesi, Ally Day, Aimi Hamraie, Kate Caldwell, Jina B. Kim, Lezlie Frye, and everyone else who has joined me on the SDS dance floor. Special thanks to Kathy McMahon-Klosterman and Jean Lynch for first introducing me to disability studies when I was a sophomore at Miami University and for continuing to mentor and support me many years later.

I would also like to thank my current colleagues in the Department of Gender and Women's Studies at the University of Wisconsin–Madison as well as my former colleagues in the English Department at the University at Albany, especially Tamika Carey, Robert Miller, Randy Craig, and Michael Leong. Thank you to my mentor Jennifer Wilks, and everyone from the Duke University Summer Institute on Tenure and Professional Advancement. I have an incredible amount of love and gratitude for the Octavia E. Butler Legacy Network, especially Ayana Jamieson, Moya Bailey, and Cassandra Jones for the community they have provided me. Further thanks to my mentors, colleagues, and friends from my time at Indiana University, especially Denise Cruz, Melinda Brennan, Krystal Cleary, and Heather Montes Ireland. Additionally, thank you to Duke University Press, especially my editor, Elizabeth Ault, who remained incredibly kind, attentive, and generous throughout the long and difficult process of turning the dissertation into a book.

I must further extend my gratitude to my network of personal support in Bloomington, Indiana; Albany, New York; and beyond, including Terry Flynn, Dru Miller, Megan Albertz, Katie Hu, Kavita Patel, Nicholas Belongie, Avery Smith, Greta Lind, Beth Lodge-Rigal, Whryne Reed, Annie Stephens, Maeve Kane, James Mallek, John Person, Britney Johnson, Julia Cadieux, Maya Washington, Ashaki Jackson, Drea Brown, the Shade Room, all the lovely weirdos of F&L, all the fierce women of Queer Ladies Night, and all the bartenders at Uncle Elizabeth's, The Back Door, Oh Bar, and the Speakeasy 518.

To the incomparable Jess Waggoner, thank you for being so brilliant, kind, talented, and loving—you are everything I could ever want in a colleague, best friend, and love all rolled into one fabulously accessorized package. I look forward to our many adventures together. To Jeremy Nottingham, thank you for your unwavering love and support; I remain continually in awe of what we have created together. I am forever yours.

Of course, I have to also thank my mother, Beverly Schalk, for her years of support. Mom, I am so grateful that you helped give me the confidence and freedom to discover what I love and do it with gusto, even when it took me farther and farther away from home. Finally, this book is dedicated to Sydney and Jonathan Schalk, the best little weirdos I know. You both continue, without even realizing it, to give me hope for a better future.

INTRODUCTION

Nothing happens in the "real" world unless it first happens in the images in our heads. — GLORIA ANZALDÚA, "La conciencia de la mestiza: Towards a New Consciousness"

Confession: I was not initially a fan of speculative fiction. There. I said it. Of course, I now know the error of my ways, the misconceptions I held about the geeky male whiteness of the genre. I now know how ill-informed I was in my belief that speculative fiction was escapist fluff that had nothing to do with my real-world investments in fighting oppression in order to find or create new, freer ways of being in the world. Then I read Octavia E. Butler and quickly realized that this genre I had dismissed, this genre I had been able to avoid throughout most of my educational career, was far more diverse, compelling, and politicized than I had ever imagined.

Reading *Parable of the Sower,* I began to understand how politically astute speculative fiction can be, how it can comment on our world and make us imagine alternative possibilities: the good, the bad, the ambivalent, and the downright terrifying. I quickly consumed everything Butler had written — every novel, every short story. I even bought an expensive copy of her out-of-print book *Survivor* after getting my first check at my first tenure-track job. Reading Butler changed the way I read as well as the way I think about texts and the world. I never met her, but her fiction is now as familiar to me as my own memories. And now that I have spent time in her archives at the Huntington Library, she has become a long-lost friend whose complicated life, incredible drive, and exquisite prescience has often brought me to tears.

Reading Butler led me to the worlds of black speculative fiction and Afrofuturism, to feminist speculative fiction and queer speculative fiction, to new conferences, new colleagues, new friends, and ultimately to writing this book. Butler's work also led me to ask questions like: What might it mean to imagine disability differently? Differently from the stereotypical stories of pity, helplessness, and victimhood, of evil, bitterness, and abjection, of nonsexuality and isolation, of overcoming and supercrips? What would it mean to imagine disability differently than these dominant cultural narratives we typically encounter? What might it mean to imagine blackness differently? Womanhood differently? Sexuality differently? If, as Gloria Anzaldúa claims, "nothing happens in the 'real' world unless it first happens in the images in our heads," then changing the narratives of (dis)ability, race, and gender, changing the way marginalized people are represented and conceived in contemporary cultural productions, can also change the way such people are talked about, treated, and understood in the "real" world ("La conciencia de la mestiza" 385).

Speculative fiction allows us to imagine otherwise, to envision an alternative world or future in which what exists now has changed or disappeared and what does not exist now, like the ability to live on the moon or interact with the gods, is suddenly real. For marginalized people, this can mean imagining a future or alternative space away from oppression or in which relations between currently empowered and disempowered groups are altered or improved. Speculative fiction can also be a space to imagine the worst, to think about what could be if current inequalities and injustices are allowed to continue. Marie Jakober writes that "the great gift of speculative fiction [is that] it makes us think, and specifically, it makes us think *differently*. It makes us examine things we have never examined. Even better, it makes us *re-imagine* things we thought we knew" (30; original emphasis). The black women writers in this book have made me think differently, examine texts differently, and imagine and reimagine (dis)ability, race, and gender in ways I never had before. In honor of Butler and the many writers her work eventually lead me to, I begin this book with the often-stated (and hashtagged) assertion that representation matters in material, concrete, and life-affirming—life-changing—ways. Representation matters.

CONTEMPORARY BLACK WOMEN'S speculative fiction reimagines the possibilities and meanings of bodyminds, particularly in regard to (dis)ability, race, and gender.[1] This reimagining changes the rules of interpretation, requiring modes of analysis that take into account both the relationships between (dis)ability, race, and gender and the contexts in which these categories exist. Contemporary black women's speculative fiction changes the rules of reality to create worlds with new or different genders, races, disabilities, and other forms of life, and in doing so these texts also require a change in how we read and interpret these categories.

Bodyminds Reimagined is the first monograph to focus on the representation of (dis)ability by black authors. At the heart of it all, this book is a loving, critical intervention into black feminist theory and disability studies. Black feminist theory is an approach to interpreting, acknowledging, and tracing the effects of interlocking oppressions, particularly from the perspective of black women. Black feminist theory is an academic field and mode of literary criticism that emerged out of black feminist movements and groups who found their presence, experiences, and concerns being excluded or ignored within white mainstream feminism and black power and civil rights movements. Disability studies is the interdisciplinary investigation of (dis)ability as a socially constructed phenomenon and systemic social discourse which determines how bodyminds and behaviors are labeled, valued, represented, and treated. While the field began as primarily a social-science-based one in the 1980s, disability studies has now become a field infused with the humanities. Due to its later emergence as a field, disability studies has benefited immensely from theories and approaches in women's and gender studies and race and ethnicity studies. While both black feminist theory and disability studies are academic projects with firm social justice roots and investments, the scholarship in each of these fields rarely becomes scholarship in the other.

While black feminist theorists have done much to demonstrate the relationship of various oppressions, (dis)ability is rarely accounted for in black feminist theory. Of course, even though (dis)ability is often not acknowledged as a vector of power in black feminist theory, it is absolutely not the case that black feminists have done no work on issues of disability.[2] In fact, issues of disability have appeared in numerous moments in black feminist theory and activism over time; black feminist scholars have just not generally undertaken this work from an explicitly disability studies perspective or directly connected their work to the disability rights movement. Concomitantly, disability studies scholars have generally not recognized black feminist work on health activism, illness, and access to medical care as properly disability studies.[3]

The field of disability studies, while often attentive to gender and sexuality, has often avoided issues of race, remaining centered on white experiences and representations of disability. That said, the area of race and disability studies has seen dramatic increase and exciting development in recent years.[4] I build on the work of scholars such as Ellen Samuels and Julie Avril Minich who have demonstrated how incorporating a disability studies perspective is key to understanding the racial and gendered implications of a text and how attention to race and gender similarly helps reveal the operation of ideologies of ability in texts seemingly not "about" disability at all. In this book, therefore, analysis of the role of (dis)ability in speculative fiction by black women illuminates issues of race and gender that might otherwise be obscured.

Both black feminist theory and disability studies have provided insights that have fueled my personal and intellectual development in innumerable ways. *Bodyminds Reimagined* is my effort to bring them together, demonstrating both their overlapping interests and the ways in which each field has theories and insights that are valuable to the other. This book is a call to black feminists to include (dis)ability in our work and investigate both ableism (discrimination toward people with disabilities) and ability privilege (the personal, social, and structural advantages given to the nondisabled in our society) in our intellectual and activist communities. It is an exhortation to disability studies scholars to not merely include race, but to allow black feminist and critical race theories to transform the field. More specifically, *Bodyminds Reimagined* intervenes in disability studies literary criticism, which has often been based on more canonical, realist, and/or white-authored texts. By offering alternative theories for interpreting (dis)ability in literature in conjunction with race and gender, particularly in the context of nonrealist texts, I intend to change the way we read and analyze literature in disability studies. This occurs even at the level of language.

Language Choices: Bodymind and (Dis)ability

There are two key terms I use throughout this book that may be unfamiliar to readers: *bodymind* and *(dis)ability*. While both terms have some established history within disability studies, they are not necessarily used widely in the field. Bodymind and (dis)ability, however, are essential terms for my work on black women's speculative fiction. In her foundational article "The Race for Theory," Barbara Christian argues that the language of black feminist theorists and literary critics ought to be based on and inspired by the language of the texts under study. In this case, the black women's speculative fictional texts I analyze in this book particularly demand terminology that can account for the nonrealist representations of new or altered people, societies, and worlds. A major argument of *Bodyminds Reimagined* is that interpreting the reimagining performed by black women's speculative fiction requires modes of analysis that take into account both the relationships between social systems of privilege and oppression as well as the context in which categories of (dis)ability, race, and gender exist and are given meaning. One of these modes of analysis is finding language that can effectively express the theoretical insights of these texts.

As indicated by the title, the first essential term for this book is *bodymind*. Bodymind is a materialist feminist disability studies concept from Margaret Price that refers to the enmeshment of the mind and body, which are typically understood as interacting and connected, yet distinct entities due to the Cartesian dualism of Western philosophy ("The Bodymind Problem and the Possibilities of Pain" 270). The term *bodymind* insists on the inextricability of mind and body and highlights how processes within our being impact one another in such a way that the notion of a physical versus mental process is difficult, if not impossible to clearly discern in most cases (269). Price argues that bodymind cannot be simply a rhetorical stand-in for the phrase "mind and body"; rather, it must do theoretical work as a disability studies term. *Bodymind* is an essential concept in chapter 3 in my discussion of hyperempathy, a nonrealist disability that is both mental and physical in origin and manifestation. *Bodymind* generally, however, is an important and theoretically useful term to use in analyzing speculative fiction as the nonrealist possibilities of human and nonhuman subjects, such as the werewolves discussed in chapter 4, often highlight the imbrication of mind and body, sometimes in extreme or explicitly apparent ways that do not exist in our reality.

In addition to the utility of the term *bodymind* in discussions of speculative fiction, I also use this term because of its theoretical utility in discussions of race and (dis)ability. For example, *bodymind* is particularly useful in discussing the toll racism takes on people of color. As more research reveals the ways experiences and histories of oppression impact us mentally, physically, and even on a cellular level, the term *bodymind* can help highlight the relationship of nonphysical experiences of oppression—psychic stress—and overall well-being.[5] While this research is emergent, people of color and women have long challenged their association with pure embodiment and the degradation of the body as unable to produce knowledge through a rejection of the mind/body divide. *Bodymind* provides, therefore, a politically and theoretically useful term in discussing (dis)ability in black women's speculative fiction and more.

The second key term for this book is *(dis)ability*. I use this term to reference the overarching social system of bodily and mental norms that includes ability and disability. I use (dis)ability because unlike terms such as *gender*, which references man, woman, genderqueer, transgender, and other gender identities, disability without the parenthetical adjustment merely references disability and impairment. The term *(dis)ability* also highlights the mutual dependency of disability and ability to define one another. While other scholars use *dis/ability* or *ability/disability* to similar effect, I believe the parenthetical curve as opposed to the backslash better visually suggests the shifting, contentious, and contextual boundaries between disability and ability.[6]

Throughout this book, I use *(dis)ability* when referencing the wider social system and I use *disability* or *ability* when referring to those specific parts of the (dis)ability system. While I recognize that there may be moments in which the line between disability and (dis)ability may be blurry, it's important to linguistically differentiate as best as possible in this work for a number of reasons. First, (dis)ability allows me to better highlight the important relationship of hyperability or "powers" and disability in speculative fiction. Second, in speculative fiction the function and meaning of (dis)ability does not necessarily comply with our realist understanding of what constitutes ability and disability and therefore must be explained for each text. Third, as my approach to interpretation is highly informed by theories of intersectionality, there is real critical utility in having a linguistic corollary when talking about (dis)ability and other vectors of power like race and gender. This change in terminology, therefore, is both important for capturing the nuances of the nonrealist worlds in speculative fiction and necessary for having shared, parallel language in bringing together black feminist theory and disability studies. Both of my key terms, *(dis)ability* and *bodymind*, are used and developed in relationship to the theoretical frameworks I engage in this book as well.

Theoretical Foundations: Intersectionality and Crip Theory

Throughout *Bodyminds Reimagined,* I use a genre-attentive and text-specific approach to (dis)ability, race, and gender that is informed by both black feminist theory and disability studies. This approach is first informed by Barbara Christian's insistence that theory does not have to look a particular way or use a prescribed language to produce knowledge, but can take narrative forms in literature (Christian, "Race for Theory" 41). Christian writes that black feminist literary critics do not have to find or create theories to apply to literature, but instead should try to understand the theories being expressed or embodied in the texts themselves through close reading because "every text suggests a new approach" (50). I've already discussed how this approach influences my use of the terms *bodymind* and *(dis)ability,* but it also shapes how I engage with current theories in black feminist theory and disability studies. Since there is still only a small body of scholarship on (dis)ability in black women's literature, it is particularly necessary that I take the literary texts in this study as productions of theories which will aid in understanding their representations of (dis)ability, race, and gender. Black women writers' reimagining of the possiblities and meanings of bodyminds is a form of theorizing about social categories, identities, and oppressions which operates in conversation with existing theories rather than replicating theory wholesale or being pure expression that must be theorized by the critic. There are two key theoretical conversations that inform my interpretations of the insights of black women's speculative fiction: intersectionality and crip theory.

Intersectionality is a term generally used to describe both how people experience multiple social systems at once and a scholarly approach to analyzing and researching this multiplicity of identities, oppressions, and privileges. Although the specific word comes from Kimberlé Crenshaw, the concept has its roots in black and woman-of-color feminisms that address the ways women of color deal with both racism and sexism in their daily lives—even within feminist and antiracist organizations that sometimes ignore, downplay, or even perpetuate one oppression in the effort to fight another.[7] Typically, *intersectionality* is used to reference major social identities that are created within systems of privilege and oppression, including race, class, gender, sexuality, (dis)ability, age, nationality, and ethnicity. However, the term can also be used more liberally to include any intersecting identity, even those that are not typically viewed as major social markers but may be especially salient in particular contexts, such as religion.

In my use of *intersectionality* in this book, I read (dis)ability, race, gender, and sexuality as simultaneously identities, experiences, systems of privilege and oppression, discourses, and historically situated social constructions with material effects. I understand intersectionality as an epistemological orientation and practice that is invested in coalition building and resistance to dominant structures of power.[8] I trace the relationships between systems of power in the United States, historically and contemporarily, and explore how black women writers of speculative fiction change the rules of reality in their texts to contest oppressive systems of thought and behavior.

My intersectional approach takes into account recent critiques of the term without abandoning the concept altogether.[9] I acknowledge that the term *intersectionality* is too often used only in the context of multiply marginalized people, especially black women. Intersectionality is also too often assumed to only apply to minority identity positions or understood in purely additive and ever-expanding terms. But what is important about these statements is that they are about problems with how intersectionality is being used and not necessarily issues with intersectionality itself as a theoretical approach. This is where I differ from scholars who are encouraging a move toward other terms and methods. I am personally still invested in the potential of intersectionality and I find power in its particular women-of-color lineage even as I am aware and critical of how it has been used in limiting, static, and even regressive ways. Intersectionality does not mean the same thing to all scholars nor is it used in a uniform way. As a dynamic form of matrix (as opposed to single-axis) thinking, intersectionality provides an important means for untangling the mutual constitution of oppressions such as racism, ableism, and sexism and for understanding how systems of power work within and beyond identity claims alone. My approach to intersectionality, therefore, responds to critiques of it while also incorporating work by scholars such as Cathy J. Cohen, who calls for a destabilization and radical politicization of identities rather than their destruction because identities can be used for survival and collective action (36–37, 45; see also Moya). In particular, the incorporation of (dis)ability into intersectional frameworks where it is often left out helps highlight the necessity of including identity, but not being limited to identity alone in intersectional analyses because of the way discourses of (dis)ability have been used to justify discrimination and violence against other marginalized groups (Baynton).

My use of intersectionality is directly informed by the way I read the relationship of identities and oppressions interacting within black women's speculative fiction. The texts I discuss in this book are ideologically complex. The genre of speculative fiction particularly lends itself to such complexity because its nonrealist conventions can be used to highlight the socially constructed, and therefore mutable, nature of concepts like (dis)ability, race, and gender. By reimagining the meanings and possibilities of bodyminds, speculative fiction can alter the meanings of these categories, requiring readers and critics alike to adapt our modes of reading, interpretation, and analysis or develop new ones. The black women authors in this study take up the possibilities of speculative fiction in order to depict ableism, racism, and sexism as intersecting, mutually constitutive forces which often collude with one another as well as act in place of one another.[10] Through nonrealist conventions such as time travel, futuristic settings, and nonhuman characters, these authors make evident the often-occluded ways that racism and sexism can be enacted through discourses of (dis)ability and how ableism can take effect through concepts of race and gender in the real world. These texts depict how discursive and material enactments of ableism, racism, and sexism are interactively deployed in social, political, and interpersonal arenas. At the same time, these texts refuse to reduce such moments of codeployment to a single oppression or to suggest that these moments only impact those who are multiply marginalized. The black women's speculative fiction in this book relishes in intersectional complexity, possibility, and change.

The second theoretical foundation of this book is crip theory, a relatively recent theoretical turn in disability studies.[11] Although mentioned by scholars like Carrie Sandahl early in the development of the field, the term *crip theory* was popularized by Robert McRuer in his book by the same name, establishing it as an approach to disability studies, similar to queer theory, which seeks to destabilize and contest, but not entirely dismantle, disability identity (Sandahl, "Queering the Crip or Cripping the Queer?" 53). More recently, Alison Kafer argues that crip theory expands and enriches disability studies by "including within disability communities those who lack a 'proper' (read: medically acceptable, doctor-provided, and insurer-approved) diagnosis for their symptoms" and by "departing from the social model's assumption that 'disabled' and 'nondisabled' are discrete, self-evident categories, choosing instead to explore the creation of such categories and the moments in which they fail to hold" (*Feminist, Queer, Crip* 36, 18). The potential failure and flexibility of the label *disability* is critical to reading speculative fictional texts that do not represent (dis)ability in traditional or expected ways. This crip theory understanding of disability as a category also dovetails with my approach to intersectionality, which emphasizes understanding (dis)ability, race, and gender as socially constructed and mutable social systems of oppression, identity, discourse, and experience.

Crip theory is especially important when discussing the work of racially marginalized writers because the social system of (dis)ability has a different impact on and meaning for such populations due to race. A crip theory approach to race and disability studies requires an expansion of the category of disability to include illness, disease, and secondary health effects.[12] This is because people of color and the poor are more likely to have experiences on the borders or outside of able-bodiedness and able-mindedness due to violence and failures of society to provide access to affordable, quality insurance, housing, and medical care.[13] I believe crip theory is fundamental to the incorporation of race into disability studies and to the incorporation of disability studies into race and ethnicity studies as well.

The history of race in disability studies is a vexed one that I should acknowledge, particularly because early work in race and disability studies has several direct relationships to my focus on black women's speculative fiction. The name that typically appears first in discussions of race and disability is Chris Bell and his infamous, ubiquitously cited essay "Introducing White Disability Studies: A Modest Proposal." This essay is often referenced as proof of the whiteness of disability studies. However, while Bell's critique is valid—disability studies was and is very white and often insular—his essay is too often taken to mean that there was zero work on race and disability prior to this modest proposal for change. This assumption is false.

Rosemarie Garland-Thomson was one of the first disability studies scholars to provide sustained race and disability analysis in the final chapter of her book *Extraordinary Bodies*, published in 1997. Analyzing work by Ann Petry, Toni Morrison, and Audre Lorde, Garland-Thomson contends that these writers infuse "the traditionally mute, static spectacle of otherness with voice, gaze, and power to act—all without normalizing the extraordinary body" (*Extraordinary Bodies* 133). This refusal to normalize is what differentiates these texts from the others Garland-Thomson analyzes and is the reason why she concludes her book with them. It is important to both the field and my work that one of the earliest studies of disability and literature ends with writing by black women as the space that offers the most celebratory, complex, and politicized possibilities for representing disability.

Even before Garland-Thomson's book, however, other scholars also acknowledged the need for developing work on the impact of race on experiences of disability,[14] and a few key disability studies articles and books appeared in the 1990s and early 2000s which discussed disability and race.[15] Furthermore, many of the texts to initially engage the intersection of disability and race did so through analysis of the American freak show and its position at the center of multiple oppressive discourses. The role of the freak show in early work on race and disability is important for this book because the decline of the American freak show in the 1940s coincides with the emerging popularity of speculative fiction and the so-called Golden Age of Science Fiction. Recognizing this concurrent rise and decline as connected, Jeffery A. Weinstock argues that "with the freak show's waning hold on American culture, along with society's moral reevaluation of exhibiting real-world non-Western or disabled people for amusement, a psychic *need* for freaks found expression in SF fiction and film" (328; original emphasis). The suggested cultural replacement of freak shows with science fiction geneologically and theoretically connects early work on race and disability to my work here on (dis)ability, race, and gender in contemporary black women's speculative fiction.

While this brief genealogy of race in disability studies could be interpreted as a too-generous reading of the early racial politics of the field, I think it's important to acknowledge rather than dismiss or ignore this scholarship, even if it does not fit perfectly within current expectations of what research on race and (dis)ability "should" look like. To erase this history is to deny disability studies' vexed history of engagement with race, which provides the foundation for recent work to be more intersectional and nuanced, particularly recent work in crip theory that challenges the way we understand disability and disability politics specifically through engagement with race.

Drawing on the theoretical resources outlined here, this book models methods of readings and interpretation which allow me—and hopefully other readers and critics—to understand each text's own ways of theorizing and reimagining bodyminds. In turn, I consider how these texts require us to change our modes of reading, interpreting, and analyzing (dis)ability, race, and gender. Black women authors' reimagined bodyminds are made particularly possible by the nonrealist conventions of speculative fiction. To further demonstrate this approach, I'd like to turn briefly to a recent example from popular culture. Although neither fiction nor written by a black woman, the speculative thriller film *The Girl with All the Gifts,* released in the United Kingdom in 2016 and in the United States in 2017, provides a useful demonstration of the importance of terms like *bodymind* and *(dis)ability* as well as the need for intersectionality and crip theory in the analysis of (dis)ability, race, and gender in nonrealist representations. Set in a near future England, *The Girl with All the Gifts* is a modern take on the zombie apocalypse genre. The film opens by introducing the audience to Melanie, a young black girl who is confined in an institution for reasons initially unknown.

Melanie wears an orange hooded sweatshirt and sweatpants reminiscent of a prison jumpsuit and sleeps in a bare, locked cell with only a cot; a wheelchair; and two personal photos, which she keeps hidden. When Melanie is taken out of her cell, two guards appear, one who keeps a gun pointed at her at all times and another who straps her into the wheelchair across her legs, hands, and head. Melanie's cheerful, kind greetings to each adult she encounters stands in stark contrast to the fear and hatred directed at her and the other children in the institution. Twice an offscreen guard calls them "friggin' abortions" and later another refers to them as "creepy," questioning how the teacher, Ms. Justineau, can stand to be so close to them. The children in the institution, seemingly all white boys besides Melanie, wear the same attire and are strapped into wheelchairs in the same fashion.[16] They are all taken and left strapped in their wheelchairs in a classroom. Ms. Justineau is the only person who seems to regard the children with any compassion, and she is particularly fond of Melanie.

At one point, after Melanie shares a story she wrote, Ms. Justineau reaches out and gently caresses the top of Melanie's head. Melanie's closed eyes and deep breath in response suggests that she is rarely, if ever, touched. In this moment, however, the head guard, Sergeant Parks, bursts in to yell at Ms. Justineau for breaking the rules by touching Melanie. He cautions her that they are not truly children at all. To demonstrate his point Sergeant Parks lifts his sleeve, spits on his arm, and rubs.[17] He then places his arm in front of a boy in the class, who begins to respond in an animal-like fashion, growling and straining to bite Parks's arm. Quickly the other children on that side of the room respond in the same way. This is the audience's first indication of what is going on in the world of the film.

After this scene the film slowly reveals increasing details about the situation outside of the institution. We learn that much of humanity has been wiped out by a parasitic fungal disease that takes over the brain, creating "hungries" who roam abandoned cities and attack living creatures, human and animal alike. Hungries have gray, decaying skin, are mostly dormant, and seemingly lack self-awareness. They stand still in large groups for extended periods of time until they are awakened, so to speak, primarily due to the smell of noninfected beings nearby, as well as when there is sudden movement or loud sound. When awakened, hungries are both fast and strong and spread their disease through bodily contact.

The institution where Melanie and the children are kept is at once a military base to protect uninfected humans and a research facility. The children there, we eventually learn, are being monitored and studied in order to understand the fungal disease. This includes killing some of the children to dissect their bodies in the hopes of using their brains and spinal fluids to create a cure. Unlike the hungries, who roam mindlessly, these children were born with the disease and their brains have a more symbiotic relationship with the fungus. So while they are carriers and need to eat raw meat of some sort (in the institution we see Melanie fed a bowl of worms, later she eats a cat and a bird), children born with the disease are otherwise able to speak, learn, move, and behave like other humans.

Not long into the film the institution is attacked by hungries. Melanie escapes with Ms. Justineau, Dr. Caldwell, Sergeant Parks, and a guard named Kieran. While Parks and Kieran wish to leave Melanie behind, Ms. Justineau and Dr. Caldwell insist on taking her with them—the former because she truly cares about Melanie and the latter because she needs Melanie's body to create a cure. The rest of the film involves this group travelling through the dystopian wasteland. As they travel, Melanie learns more about her disease, its effects, and how to survive.

Bodymind is a useful term in analyzing *The Girl with All the Gifts*. Melanie's brain—what we would consider the home of the mind—is covered with this fungus which causes her to crave flesh and, when hungry, temporarily lose self-awareness and self-control. While her body remains externally unchanged, she appears to be faster and stronger than a typical child. It is impossible to refer to her disease as merely physical or mental alone when hunger, typically considered a very physiological process, results in dramatic mental effects for her. Melanie's bodymind is holistically affected by the fungus.

Similarly, *(dis)ability* as an overarching term for disability and ability and the contestable borders in between is also appropriate for discussions of the film, particularly from a crip theory perspective, which includes illness, disease, and discourses of (dis)ability in its approach. If not for the institutional setting and the way the adults in the film treat her, Melanie would mostly appear nondisabled and in some ways even hyper-able. She is smart, observant, and physically strong and agile. As the film progresses she better understands that when she becomes hungry she needs to eat raw meat quickly to avoid harming people around her. Melanie is essentially the heroine of the film. To the majority of the adults around her, however, she is too different and too threatening; she must be confined, studied, treated, and cured—or used as a cure for others. People around Melanie question her very humanity and her status as "alive," conjecturing that she may be merely mimicking human behaviors instead of being a true human. For example, the head researcher, Dr. Caldwell, tells Ms. Justineau that "they present as children" but "the fungus does their thinking for them." In the world of the film Melanie is treated as disabled and dangerously so because she poses the threat of both death (if she were to eat someone) and contagion (if she were to bite or touch them). The fear of contagion here is very much about disability, as the disease is incredibly disabling to adults. The tension between Melanie's fresh-faced innocence and her danger to the adults is palpable throughout the film.

The unclear and shifting (dis)ability status of children with the disease, however, becomes particularly evident when Melanie discovers a group of them who roam as a feral pack to attack people and animals. While the children are dirty and lack language since they had no education as Melanie did, they appear to be able to communicate with and take care of one another. What constitutes disability in this context? It becomes increasingly evident that the world is changing and Melanie and children like her are much more likely to survive. The world the adults once knew—our realist world—is all but gone. As the world changes, what is and is not a disability changes as well, revealing an essential part of reading (dis)ability, race, and gender in speculative fiction: the importance of context and interpreting a text within its rules of reality—something I will say more about in the reading methods section of this introduction.

But *The Girl with All the Gifts* is not exclusively about disability. We cannot understand the nuances and registers of this nonrealist representation if we do not read intersectionally. The immense militarized fear of these children and their disease is racialized via the choice to make Melanie our protagonist.[18] She is the only child of color depicted and one of three people of color in the film with speaking lines. She is a black girl surrounded by white people as she is imprisoned for medical research in a military compound and then treated as a prisoner as she travels with the others. While her race is never directly commented on, her disease and the fear it invokes in others comes across as a metaphor for racialized fear. Shortly after their escape, Parks insists that Melanie be handcuffed, muzzled, and strapped to the gun turret on the roof of their military vehicle rather than ride inside. Ms. Justineau exclaims, "She's got a muzzle on her face and her hands tied behind her back and you're still afraid of her?" Park replies, "Yeah, and you should be too." Although this film is set and was produced in the United Kingdom, its allusion here to antiblack police/military violence—which is far from exclusive to the United States—is striking. Numerous incidents of police violence have been justified through claims of police officers fearing for their own lives, even when the person who was injured or murdered was handcuffed, restrained, outnumbered, and/or significantly smaller than the police officer(s) involved.

We cannot separate fear of Melanie's disease from fear of her blackness. The frequent expressions of her being not truly human gesture toward a long history of dehumanizing black people around the world, to say nothing of the history of medical experimentation on black bodies. Yet our compassion for her, I argue, is also in response to her age and gender. As a prepubescent child Melanie is presumed innocent by viewers.[19] She is also soft-spoken, polite, and a girl, whereas the other children in the institution are boys, and the feral children are all long-haired and dirty in a way that occludes their sex/gender identities. The gentle innocence the audience is encouraged to perceive in Melanie via casting and acting choices would be more difficult if she were played by a young black boy. Many black children are read as older than they are;[20] but in the context of the institutional setting, the handcuffs, and so on, Melanie's gender softens the explicitness of the film's commentary on antiblack police violence since much of that discourse is focused on the targeting of black men and boys.[21] Melanie's age and gender therefore work to counterbalance the threatening nature of her race and (dis)ability in the world of the film.

As the film moves toward its end Dr. Caldwell makes a desperate attempt at creating a cure by playing on Melanie's emotions, telling her that if she agrees to the dissection she can save Ms. Justineau's life. Melanie seems ready to agree, but first asks what will happen to the other children. When Dr. Caldwell doesn't respond Melanie asks if she still thinks that children with the disease merely mimic human behavior. Dr. Caldwell says no and they have the following exchange:

MELANIE. We're alive?

DR. CALDWELL. Yes, you're alive.

MELANIE. Then why should it be us that dies for you?

In this moment Melanie refuses to sacrifice herself and the other children. This explicitly flips a frequent trope in horror, thriller, and action films in which characters of color regularly act as martyrs, dying valiantly to save the white protagonists. The scene also rejects the trope of disabled people dying or being cured at the end of a film or novel. Instead of sacrificing herself to save Ms. Justineau, the only person who has ever shown her love, Melanie leaves the trailer they are hiding out in and goes to set a large plant of the fungus on fire, which will release the infectious spores, creating a massive if not worldwide epidemic. By releasing the spores Melanie initiates a new world in which she will no longer be considered disabled, dangerous, or abnormal due to her disease. This choice allows for an undetermined future for Melanie and the children like her, yet it also means sacrificing the lives and freedom of the adults with her. Dr. Caldwell and Sergeant Parks both die chasing after Melanie, and Ms. Justineau must live permanently in the air-locked trailer or she will become infected. Melanie's decision to release the spores is represented as an emotional one for her, but one she makes with clear determination.

The final scene begins with a close-up of Ms. Justineau's face as she lies in bed crying. There is a knock and she gets up. Outside the trailer Melanie organizes the children from the institution and from the feral group they encountered earlier in the film. The children sit in rows on the ground outside facing a large windowed area so that Ms. Justineau can teach them via a loud speaker from inside. When Ms. Justineau tells the children that she will tell them a story if there is time, Melanie speaks the final words of the film. With the sun and a smile on her face, she responds, "There'll be lots of time." The film ends here with a young black girl who was considered dangerous and disabled by the adults around her now beginning a new world for herself and people like her in which their bodymind differences will not be considered disabling, dangerous, or animalistic. At the end of the film, it appears Ms. Justineau will have to spend the rest of her life in that trailer, and it is unclear how and if this group of children will create a lasting society for themselves. The film thematically draws on discourses of disability as well as, more subtly, discourses of race and gender to create empathy for both Melanie and Ms. Justineau in this simultaneously dark and hopeful ending.

The Girl with All the Gifts is a useful popular culture example which demonstrates the utility of my key terms, *bodymind* and *(dis)ability*, and my primary theoretical frameworks, intersectionality and crip theory, in interpreting (dis)ability, race, and gender in nonrealist representations. Throughout the rest of *Bodyminds Reimagined* I explore how black women writers of speculative fiction reimagine the possibilities of bodyminds and thereby change not only the rules of reality in these nonrealist worlds, but also the rules of interpretation, requiring modes of analysis that consider both the relationships of (dis)ability, race, and gender and the contexts in which these terms are given meaning. While the intersectional relationship of (dis)ability, race, gender, and other vectors of power are important to explore in representations of all kinds, speculative fiction provides a particularly interesting and important avenue for interrogating the social construction and mutual constitution of these systems of privilege and oppression.

Why Speculative Fiction?

In this book I use the term *speculative fiction* to reference any creative writing in which the rules of reality do not fully apply, including magical realism, utopian and dystopian literature, fantasy, science fiction, voodoo, ghost stories, and hybrid genres. By "rules of reality," I mean culturally and historically specific social narratives of the possibilities and meanings of bodyminds, time, space, and technology, as well as our constructed notions of what constitutes a "real" disability, gender, race, and so on. For example, in terms of technology, air travel would have defied the rules of reality for people in the Middle Ages and yet it is an accepted possibility today even for those who have never experienced this type of travel themselves. To take a (dis)ability specific example, the learning disability Attention-Deficit/ Hyperactivity Disorder (ADHD) is a contemporary diagnosis that did not exist as a "real" disability before being defined by psychological professionals and accepted by society at large. On the other hand, homosexuality was once considered a psychological disorder by the American Psychological Association, but is no longer categorized as such.[22] Drawing from several examples from *The Girl with All the Gifts* that have been previously noted in this introduction, reading within the rules of the reality of the film means understanding the fungal infection as a real disease with potentially disabling effects in the narrative. While crip theory problematizes diagnosis as the sole parameter for defining disability, these examples serve to illustrate what I mean by historically and culturally specific rules of reality. Since speculative fiction includes stories in the future, other worlds, altered pasts, and altered present periods, this genre can shift, challenge, and play on what readers expect of bodyminds and reveal how such expectations shape definitions of (dis)ability, race, and gender. *Bodyminds Reimagined* analyzes how representations of (dis)ability, race, and gender in speculative fiction force readers to question the ideologies undergirding these categories. I contend that questioning the ideologies of (dis)ability, race, and gender in black women's speculative fiction allows for a challenge to the attitudes, biases, and behaviors that result from them, as well as an exploration of their relationships to one another.

I use *speculative fiction* as my umbrella term because the novels in this study do not collectively fit under any other single genre label, nor do they all comfortably fit within other critical terms. For example, Mark Dery's *Afrofuturism* is primarily concerned with racialized uses of technology and the future, while Marleen S. Barr's *feminist fabulation* focuses on expressions of postmodern feminist critique (Dery 8; Barr *Lost in Space* 11–12). Likewise, Ingrid Thaler's term *Black Atlantic speculative fictions* is primarily concerned with race and nonnormative notions of time, while *utopian literature* refers to ideal or (nearly) perfect imagined societies and *dystopian literature* references its opposite: undesirable, nightmare fictional worlds (2).[23] While issues of technology, feminism, time, and better and worse imagined futures will all be a part of the chapters to come, none of these are my exclusive focus. My work here engages major issues in Afrofuturism, feminist fabulation, Black Atlantic speculative fiction, utopias, and dystopias—and hopefully has important insights for scholars of these areas—but the texts analyzed in this book are not encompassed by any one of these terms alone. The focus of *Bodyminds Reimagined* is on representations of (dis)ability, race, and gender in nonrealist texts by black women. Speculative fiction is therefore the most appropriate broad, umbrella term for this work, one that allows me to include a wide variety of texts which may not otherwise be read together. Further, my use of speculative fiction allows me to mostly circumvent discussions of genre boundaries, genre histories (including histories of exclusion), and canon building which are not essential to my arguments.[24] On the whole, I am less concerned about genre labels and more concerned with how a variety of nonrealist tropes and devices influence the representation of (dis)ability, race, and gender in these black women's texts.

Black women's speculative fiction has social and political importance because of how the texts shift our understanding of the meanings of and relationships between (dis)ability, race, and gender. Despite its potential, speculative fiction is generally an undertheorized genre. Jewelle Gomez discusses the reason for this undertheorization, writing that speculative fiction "is thought of as 'fun' rather than as serious writing worthy of critical discussion. . . . [It is this] idea that speculative fiction is somehow an indulgence or that it is trivial that seems the more probable reason for its dismissal by literary critics" (950). Both disability studies and black feminist theory have historically focused more on realist texts for a number of practical and political reasons that ought to be understood.

In disability studies there is an emphasis on the need for less ableist representations of people with disabilities that has produced a strong investment in life writing and realism.[25] G. Thomas Couser writes that disability life writing is a response to traditional misrepresentation in Western culture which can allow people with disabilities to move from object to subject and consciously counter ableist stereotypes and ignorance.[26] Although Couser does not claim that the realism of life writing is the only method through which such changes in social perception can occur, his work is reflective of the field's leanings toward realism as an effective way to create cultural change.[27] Life writing emphasizes notions of the real and the authentic in opposition to a history of negative and skewed portrayals of people with disabilities by nondisabled people. Along these lines, Sara Hosey writes that "many [disability studies] critiques implicitly (and at times, explicitly) call for a more realistic, more sophisticated, and perhaps more ethical disability representation" (37). Here Hosey's connection between realism, sophistication, and ethics implies that these elements go hand in hand.[28] I, however, question whether the relationship of realism with authenticity, ethics, and sophistication is as inherent or clear cut as some work in disability studies might suggest.

Black women writers also have a history of critical engagement with the real-world repercussions of fictional representations. As Ann DuCille notes, early black women's literature was primarily concerned with combating negative stereotypes of black women by representing black women characters who were infallibly good and who could fit within the cult of true womanhood via the politics of respectability (13–30).[29] Early black feminist literary criticism often focused on recovering these writers from the late nineteenth and early twentieth centuries in an attempt to bring their work out of the shadows of history and create a genealogy of black women's writing.[30] The realist emphasis and political practicality of much early black women's fiction, however, had its limits, particularly from a disability studies perspective. As Ellen Samuels writes, throughout early African American literature generally there is "an emphasis on wholeness, uprightness, good health and independence" (*Fantasies of Identification* 30). These concepts, which appeared regularly in early black women's writing, make drawing attention to disability quite difficult because the disabled bodymind is typically considered in opposition to these terms—though more disability studies scholars are finding outliers and challengers to this general trend.[31]

The expectations of what literature can or should do for black people shifted as time passed, and there was an increase in complexity of representations which began to include issues of sexuality and violence, particularly intracommunity violence. Although the Harlem Renaissance witnessed early black speculative fiction by men, such as W. E. B. Du Bois's "The Comet," published in 1920, and George Schuyler's *Black No More*, published in 1931, the majority of African American texts still worked within the confines of realism. Like disability rights communities, many black people believed and still believe that the primary purpose of black-authored literature was/is to combat racism by offering positive, realistic representations that do not perpetuate stereotypes or create negative associations with black people.[32] Butler experienced such expectations for her work, stating, "When I began writing back in the 60s, my writing of anything but utter reality was considered some kind of, almost betrayal, a waste of time at best. I was supposed to, according to some people, be contributing to the struggle and not writing things that weren't real" (quoted in Hampton 137). As the Black Women Writers Renaissance emerged in the 1970s, however, this emphasis on realism began to shift.

The focus on realism as the proper or preferred avenue for politically effective literature for marginalized groups like black women and disabled people overlooks the immense possibilties of speculative fiction as well as the limits of realism. Several black feminist scholars have critiqued this faith in realistic representations. Madhu Dubey, for example, contends that models of characterization that imply there is a real, knowable black subject or community to properly represent prevent appreciation for nonrealist characterizations that attempt to destabilize a humanist model of identity and reality (*Black Women Novelists and the Nationalist Aesthetic* 4). Wahneema Lubiano also argues against prioritizing realism, writing, "Deployed as a narrative form dependent upon recognition of reality, realism suggests disclosure of the truth (and then closure of the representation); realism invites readers/audience to accept what is offered as a slice of life because the narrative contains elements of 'fact'. . . . Realism used uncritically as a mode for African-American art implies that our lives can be captured by the presentation of enough documentary evidence or by insistence on another truth" (262–63).

Black women novelists have been central in the "effort to interrupt the realist legacy" of African American literature (Dubey, *Black Women Novelists and the Nationalist Aesthetic* 5). Authors such as Toni Morrison and Alice Walker were some of the earliest contemporary black women authors to present challenges to this legacy with their uses of magical realism, ghost stories, dream sequences, and other nonrealist literary devices, while still operating within a relatively realist framework. Much has been written about these authors, both within and outside of black feminist literary criticism, but substantially less has been written about black women speculative fiction writers, especially in regard to their representation of (dis)ability.

I fully acknowledge the importance and impact of disability life writing and other realist modes of representing disability that have been the focus of much disability studies literary criticism. However, the arguments of Dubey and Lubiano about the limits of realist representations for black subjects also apply to disabled subjects. Emily Baldys argues, "We must be critical not only of depictions that seem obviously overdetermined and fantastical, but also of those that seem realistic or believable . . . by challenging representations that offer ideologically limited versions of the 'reality' of disability" (139).[33] By focusing on ideology, Baldys makes clear that problematic fictional representations of disability occur not because of inherent issues with realism or nonrealism, but because of ableist understandings of people with disabilities. Authors *can* create anti-ableist representations that are not necessarily primarily dependent on realism, claims to authenticity, or even writers who explicitly identify as disabled. In particular, speculative fiction offers an opportunity for new, complex representations of (dis)ability that can provide possibilties and advantages distinct from, yet related to, the possiblities and advantages of disability life writing.[34]

An important difference between speculative fiction and realist fiction is that speculative fiction does not purport to directly reflect reality; rather, speculative fiction brings *aspects* of reality into newly constructed worlds in which realist rules regarding time, space, bodyminds, abilities, and behaviors need not be followed. Critics of feminist science fiction argue that speculative fiction offers women writers a freedom of style and content that is not restrained by patriarchal realities, and thus these writers can better explore alternative gender identities, roles, and relations (Barr, *Alien to Femininity* xi; Lefanu 2). Critics of black speculative fiction have similarly contended that by rejecting verisimilitude and linear representations of time, speculative fiction opens up "a unique set of imaginative possibilities for a [black American] literary tradition that has long been burdened by the demands of realist social protest" (Dubey, "Speculative Fictions of Slavery" 779).[35] Although criticism on speculative fiction has only recently included (dis)ability, several disability studies scholars have noted that the speculative fiction genre—and science fiction in particular—seems quite concerned with (dis)ability.[36] As scholars of science fiction have similarly argued in regard to race, in many ways issues of (dis)ability are fundamental to the genre.[37] Criticism on speculative fiction that does not consider (dis)ability tends to be based on ableist assumptions of bodyminds even though speculative fiction texts often challenge such assumptions. Disability studies can provide speculative fiction critics additional language and frameworks to discuss the multiple ways in which texts challenge normative assumptions about the possibilities and meanings of bodyminds.

The freedom afforded speculative fiction authors through the rejection of verisimilitude, the use of nonmimetic devices, the disruption of linear time, and other tropes which subvert our expectations of reality are all beneficial to writers who wish to represent a world not restricted by our contemporary racist, sexist, ableist, homophobic, and classist realities. Without a doubt, speculative fiction representing marginalized groups can achieve the utilitarian goals of disability life writing and black feminist fiction noted above. Speculative fiction can move people with disabilities, black women, and disabled black women from objects to subjects by making them the main characters, resisting stereotypes, and providing controlled, selected access into the various experiences of these populations. Speculative fiction can do all of this while representing such characters in worlds not restricted by the weight of realism, which limits the parameters of representation. As Lubiano argues, "A marginalized group needs to be wary of the seductive power of realism, of accepting all that a realistic representation implies because of its inclusion of some 'facts.' The reasons for 'real' as a positive evaluation are tied, of course, to scarcity, the paucity of . . . *facts* and *representations* as well as the desire for more" (263–64; original emphasis). Speculative fiction can help fulfill the desire for more facts and representations of marginalized groups while also offering a distinctly different way of challenging ableism, racism, and sexism because the author sets the new rules of their fictional worlds.

Within these new worlds of speculative fiction (dis)ability, race, and gender do not have to have the same physical and mental manifestations nor the same social connotations and regulations. Returning again to *The Girl with All the Gifts,* in the world of the film disability takes on a shifting meaning as initially the children with the fungal infection are treated as disabled and dangerous, but as the infection spreads at the end of the film it becomes clear that the bodyminds of the children will become the norm and no longer be regarded as disabled. In this case, viewers bear witness to the ways that social standards and expectations of bodyminds and behaviors (like whether or not one should or should not eat raw flesh) are major determinants of the definition of disability in a particular society or culture. To take another example, in Butler's *Lilith's Brood* series (also referred to as the *Xenogenesis* series), no major character is disabled in any explicit, realist sense of the term. However, the aliens in the novel are particularly interested in humans due to the genetic possibilities of their cancerous cells which, when adapted by the aliens through interbreeding, allow for fast healing, shapeshifting, and limb regeneration. In this series, what we would consider a potentially disabling condition of the human species is actually something loaded with positive potential—even though accessing that potential means breeding with an alien species and possibily the end of the human race as we know it. Here cancer has a different meaning than it does in our contemporary reality, but this new meaning is real and important within the context of the narrative. As I demonstrate in chapter 4, speculative fiction can defamiliarize (dis)ability, race, and gender in ways that are intellectually and politically productive. By shifting our taken-for-granted social norms, speculative fiction makes unconscious preconceptions about (dis)ability, race, and gender more readily apparent, challenging readers to think outside of the accepted definitions of these categories. The nonnormative nature of the representation of (dis)ability, race, and gender in speculative fiction, however, often requires similarly nonnormative methods of reading and intepretation.

Reading Methods:
Interpreting (Dis)ability, Race, and Gender in Speculative Fiction

As I mentioned in my discussion of the theoretical foundations of this book, my method for reading and interpreting (dis)ability, race, and gender in speculative fiction is genre-attentive, text-specific, and informed by theories of intersectionality and crip theory. There are three major aspects of my reading method including: rejection of good/bad binaries, going beyond exclusively character analysis, and, perhaps most importantly, reading within the rules of a reality of a text. I will discuss each of these in turn.

First, my reading method refuses the simplistic binary of good representations and bad representations, acknowledging that adherence to norms of one system of privilege and oppression may defy norms of another.[38] For example, women, especially black women, are highly sexualized, yet people with disabilities are often denied sexual expression. When interpreting the representation of a sexualized black disabled woman, then, an intersectional analysis must balance attention to each of these oppressive histories rather than singularly celebrating or condemning such a representation as inherently empowering or regressive, respectively. This reading method also operates from the understanding that the experience of intersectional categories cannot be understood as simplistically good or bad either. Tobin Siebers argues that "disability studies needs to account for both the negative and positive valences of disability, to resist the negative by advocating the positive and to resist the positive by acknowledging the negative" (5). Siebers's argument here is particularly important for the analysis of disability in regard to people of color since purely celebratory approaches to disability identity ignore the fact that people of color and poor people are more likely to acquire disabilities through violence and lack of access of quality medical care.[39] My approach to reading black women's speculative fiction, therefore, understands disability as what Tobin Siebers calls complex embodiment.[40] Understanding disability as a complex experience means remaining attentive to positive, negative, and ambivalent aspects of disability (physically, mentally, and socially) as well as the relationship between all three. My inclusion of the mental in my approach to the complex experience of disability—an aspect that can be lost when using Siebers's original term *complex embodiment*—is particularly important when addressing the social construction of able-mindedness as I do in chapter 2 and nonapparent disabilities as I do in chapters 3 and 4.

Second, my reading method does not focus solely on character analysis.

As discussed above, my use of intersectionality understands (dis)ability, race, and gender to operate simultaneously as identities, experiences, systems of privilege and oppression, discourses, and historically situated social constructions with material effects. By not focusing on identity alone, my analysis throughout this book is similarly not exclusively focused on the disabled women protagonists that populate the majority of my primary texts. While I do perform character analysis, I also build my arguments on plot, narrative structure, and the setting of the constructed nonrealist worlds in which these characters live. This is evident in my reading of *The Girl with All the Gifts* in that the space of the institution/military compound, Melanie's prison-like attire, and the fear, anger, and disgust directed at her by the adults around her are just as important to understanding the racial implications of the film as anything Melanie says or does herself. Recent scholarship on speculative fiction and race has revealed how race operates in explicit and implicit ways in the genre. Isiah Lavender writes, "Science fiction often talks about race by not talking about race" (*Race in American Science Fiction* 7). He asserts that the genre "is actually transmitting assumptions of racism even in stories that are ostensibly envisioning a future where race has become irrelevant" and explicitly racialized characters are absent (20).[41] Similarly, Michael Bérubé argues that taking a disability studies approach to the acts of reading and interpretation "*need not involve any characters with disabilities at all.* It can involve *ideas about* disability, and ideas about stigma associated with disability, regardless of whether any specific character can be pegged with a specific diagnosis" (*The Secret Life of Stories* 19; original emphasis).[42] Analyzing multiple aspects of a text allows me to demonstrate how cultural concerns of (dis)ability, race, and gender appear even when disabled, racialized women and gender-nonconforming characters are not actively present or central to the narrative.

One specific way I move beyond character analysis alone is through my approach to metaphor, especially disability metaphor. (Dis)ability, race, and gender often operate as mutually constitutive discourses that inflect texts even in the absence of explicit embodied representations of these categories. As a result, these concepts can be used as metaphors without negating their physical, mental, and social materiality. This is especially important within disability studies. Following the lead of disability studies scholars such as Ato Quayson, Clare Barker, and Amy Vidali, I read for the metaphoric and material meanings of (dis)ability as well as its intersectional relationship to other vectors of power which may be deployed in opposition to or conjunction with it. In *The Girl with All the Gifts* Melanie's disease is understood as a disability for the bulk of the film, and yet the way she is treated because of her disease gestures toward a history of dehumanization of and medical experimentation on black bodies. This history is made palpable through Melanie's disability and race in a way that insists on both the material and metaphoric significance of the fungal disease in the film. It can indeed be read as a metaphor of this racialized history, but such a reading must not evacuate the material role of disability in this history as well. I will elaborate on disability metaphors further in chapter 1, as this is foundational to many of my later arguments. Like Julie Avril Minich, my work seeks to expose "the ideology of ability in situations that do not appear immediately to be about disability" because sometimes the texts, events, and issues that seem to be less about disability and more about race are also the ones that most clearly demonstrate "the most violent consequences of the ideology of ability" (*Accessible Citizenships* 98, 121). (Dis)ability operates beyond identity alone and functions to uphold and define (as well as be upheld and be defined by) race and gender.

Lastly, my method of reading black women's speculative fiction grounds analysis within the constructed reality of the individual text and not by current cultural or personal standards of the real or unreal. In other words, I generally accept the rules which structure the text, its characters, and its society rather than reading these aspects of the texts only through or against the rules which structure our contemporary reality. As Isiah Lavender insists, "We cannot assume anything about the world of the sf text because its rules are most likely different from those in our experience of narrative realism—that is to say, we have to first recognize and understand the innate conditions of the sf text before we can grasp the story itself" (*Race in American Science Fiction* 59). While clearly the sociohistorical context of production will influence the nonrealist worlds of speculative fiction, it is important to not allow this influence to reduce the possibilities of interpretation. As with all criticism, there is room for various interpretations, but if a basic premise of the text includes something dramatically opposed to our reality—such as the presence of a disease that makes people need to eat flesh—then we must take such a premise as an important material context for character development and plot. In short, the rules and methods of interpretation must change alongside the rules of reality in a text.

This approach to speculative fiction can become difficult when analyzing (dis)ability, race, gender, and other vectors of power because these terms may not mean the same thing in our current reality as they do in the world of the text. In some ways this parallels the concern in gender studies, queer theory, and disability studies with attempting to locate a universal woman, gay, lesbian, queer, or disabled subject/identity across all time periods and cultural locations.[43] I similarly suggest that critics of speculative fiction must take a culturally aware, contextualized approach to deploying these terms in regard to the reimagined bodyminds in these texts. As much as possible I use the terms and concepts employed in the text when describing a character's identity positions and explain how such positions relate to our more recognizable cultural categories.

In this book, I primarily reference the categories of gender, race, and (dis)ability. I use the word *gender* to refer to the social categories men, women, transgender, and genderqueer as determined by the character's self-identification or, in cases where the character is not granted interiority or does not communicate their gender identity, how the character is read or represented by the narrating voice. The use of this category in the texts I analyze is consistent with American contemporary realist notions of gender except in the fantasy texts discussed in chapter 4, which feature nonhuman characters. I use the word *race* to refer to the social categories of African American/black, white/Caucasian, Latino/a/x, Asian, South Asian, Middle Eastern, and Native American/Indigenous as typically determined by a person's genetic background, community of origin, skin tone, hair, and other phenotypical features as well as a character's self-identification when available. In the first three chapters of this book, the category of race is relatively stable and consistent with contemporary American notions of race. Again though, in chapter 4, race as we understand it cannot be applied to speculative fictional worlds with completely new racial, ethnic, and species categories. I will discuss the issues of applying gendered and racial terms to speculative fiction texts with dramatically different racial, gender, and species categories in that chapter.

When interpreting (dis)ability in speculative fictional contexts, I adapt Kafer's model of disability, which resists the hard distinction between disability and impairment and understands disability as both relational, meaning that it is "experienced in and through relationships; it does not occur in isolation," and political, meaning that it is "contested and contestable" (*Feminist, Queer, Crip* 8, 10). As I began to model in my reading of *The Girl with All the Gifts,* disability in my analyses will be determined by a combination of physical, mental, and social factors. I read a character as disabled if the character experiences their bodymind as different from others and that difference cannot be better interpreted as gendered, racial, or another type of difference;[44] if that character's bodymind is interpreted from a medical or psychological perspective in the text as nonnormative and in need of treatment or cure; and if a character's bodymind variation is considered nonnormative or deviant by the text's fictional society at large. Note that, as mentioned in my discussion of crip theory, within this wide definition of disability in my work, disease and illness are included, particularly when the disease or illness has extended or permanent effects on a character.

In sum, my approach to interpreting (dis)ability, race, and gender in black women's speculative fiction is grounded in intersectionality and crip theory and is based on three main methods: rejecting positive/negative representational binaries, not being limited to character analysis alone (including engagement with disability metaphors), and reading within the rules of reality of a text as much as possible. I lay out these methods in order to model an approach based in both black feminist theory and disability studies which can be used by scholars within both fields. These reading methods allow me to best demonstrate how black women's speculative fiction reimagines the possibilities and meanings of bodyminds and thereby changes the rules of interpretation in regard to (dis)ability, race, and gender.

Chapter Overview

While the implications of *Bodyminds Reimagined* extend into fields such as critical race and ethnicity studies, women's and gender studies, African American and black diaspora studies, American studies, cultural studies, science fiction studies, and literary criticism, in writing the book, I primarily address black feminist theorists and disability studies scholars (and black feminist disability studies scholars), knowing that, like me, the people in these groups are also working and teaching in the above-mentioned fields and departments. The multiplicity of my audiences shapes the layout and tone of the book. Each chapter spends a significant opening section detailing the major theoretical and thematic issues with which it is concerned before delving into the close readings, using one to three concrete examples to illustrate my arguments. The chapters build on one another, using the theories and arguments developed in the previous ones; however, I have written each chapter so that it can be read and understood on its own as well. This style is intended to be useful for students and nonacademics interested in specific ideas, texts, or authors I discuss. Further, I have included frequent signposting and numerous footnotes, the latter of which are intended to serve as pedagogical devices to point readers from various educational and disciplinary backgrounds to additional reading in case a particular topic or idea I mention in passing sparks their interest. In terms of tone, I attempt to use accessible, plain language as much as possible and to explain how I am using academic terms when they first appear. I have worked to keep my sentences direct and clear because I hope that this book is useful to a range of individuals, including artists, fans, and activists.

In addition to using accessible language, style, and tone, I also frequently use the first-person perspective. This book did not write itself. The ideas did not come from thin air. They come from me, the work I have done, and the people who have pushed and encouraged my thinking. My use of the first-person perspective claims these arguments as my own, knowing at times they may fail to be as clear, correct, or strong as I want. Relatedly, I also often use the words *we* or *us*. Sometimes *we* means disability studies scholars; sometimes *we* means black feminists; sometimes *we* means the readers of these texts; sometimes *we* means black people; sometimes *we* means any and all scholars, students, artists, and activists invested in understanding how oppressions manifest in our world and how we can resist them in creative, critical, and concrete ways. I use both *I* and *we* because I do not work in isolation; I belong to multiple communities of thinkers who have shaped me and my work. I use *I* and *we* because I am a fat, black, queer, nondisabled woman who identifies with people with disabilities and who hopes to bring my communities together in conversation with one another through my work. If you, reader, do not yet identify as part of this *we*—as part of any of these multiple *we's*—then I hope that you may begin to as you read this book.

Bodyminds Reimagined contains four chapters and a conclusion. Each chapter begins with theoretical and thematic framing and then moves to close readings of one or more texts as illustrative examples. My discussion of the texts in this study does occur in a relatively chronological pattern; however, this is not meant to indicate a linear progressive narrative of representation. I have grouped the texts thematically and arranged the chapters in order to build my overall argument about how the reimagining of bodyminds in black women's speculative fiction changes the rules of interpretation, requiring new modes of analysis that take into account the relationships between (dis)ability, race, and gender and the contexts in which these categories exist.

The first chapter, "Metaphor and Materiality: Disability and Neo–Slave Narratives," argues that fictional representations of disability in slavery expand the neo–slave narrative's ability to represent what was previously unable to be represented within the specific historical and pragmatic contexts of the traditional slave narrative. While black feminist and other literary scholars have traditionally read these representations of disability as metaphors for the long-lasting impact of the violence of racism, disability studies scholars have argued against reading disability as primarily or exclusively a metaphor for trauma. Using Butler's *Kindred* as my example, I demonstrate that by historicizing these representations within the material conditions of slavery, we can read disability in neo–slave narratives simultaneously as metaphors for the legacy of racial violence and as more literal references to the multiple ways in which black people were impaired in the antebellum period.

Chapter 2, "Whose Reality Is It Anyway? Deconstructing Able-Mindedness," discusses how, due to the fact that the world is experienced differently by everyone, reality can be subjective. However, those who actively claim to experience realities considered drastically different from the majority are labeled mentally disabled and potentially forcibly medicated, institutionalized/incarcerated, or harmed as a result.[45] Using the example of Phyllis Alesia Perry's *Stigmata,* I argue that in rejecting realist norms, black women's speculative fiction can reveal how able-mindedness is socially constructed and upheld through racial and gendered norms and how this social construction impacts the practices of the psychiatric medical-industrial complex and American culture at large. By insisting on the socially constructed nature of able-mindedness, black women's speculative fiction also offers up new modes of historical and institutional knowledge that stem from the perspective of multiple marginalized groups and honors their experiences of the world. In the conclusion to this chapter I connect these ideas to the role of able-mindedness in contemporary violence against black people.

Chapter 3, "The Future of Bodyminds, Bodyminds of the Future," further builds the claim that black women's speculative fiction theorizes new possibilities and meanings of the bodymind by focusing on representations of diverse bodyminds in the future. Many futuristic texts create worlds in which certain realist oppressions and/or social identities have been erased. In particular, speculative fiction often depicts futures in which disability no longer exists due to advancements in technology and race no longer matters because of racial mixing. In this chapter, I explore how, through the representation of the nonrealist disability hyperempathy, Butler's *Parable* series imagines how diverse bodyminds might exist in the future. In particular, this series resists ableist assumptions about a technologically created, disability-free future by emphasizing the importance of context to understanding a person's experience of disability and the possibility of pleasure from/through disability. This chapter also shows how a disability studies–grounded analysis can help illuminate a text's theoretical implications for issues of race, gender, and class as well.

Chapter 4, "Defamiliarizing (Dis)ability, Race, Gender, and Sexuality," analyzes speculative fictional fantasy texts with nonhuman characters, including N. K. Jemisin's *The Broken Kingdoms*, which features a blind demon protagonist who can see magic, Shawntelle Madison's *Coveted* series about a werewolf with obsessive-compulsive disorder, and Nalo Hopkinson's *Sister Mine* about two formerly conjoined twins born from human and demigod parents. These texts defamiliarize concepts of (dis)ability, race, gender, and sexuality in varying ways, thus demonstrating how black women's speculative fiction challenges the supposedly fixed and knowable nature of these categories. In particular, these texts defamiliarize realist disabilities and give them new meanings in their fantastical worlds with nonhuman characters, while also creating new races/species and new or altered gender and sexuality categories. This defamiliarization forces readers to forgo their outside knowledge of these real-world categories and learn about them anew through the perspective and experiences of the protagonists.

Finally, in the conclusion I reflect on the importance of this work to black feminist theory and disability studies. I reassert my central argument and provide suggestions for future research, performing my own reimagining of a speculative fictional academic future for the ideas and topics that this book addresses. I end with a reflection on the role of pleasure in research, writing, reading, and living as a multiply marginalized person.

METAPHOR AND MATERIALITY

Disability and Neo–Slave Narratives

"I lost an arm on my last trip home. My left arm" (Butler, *Kindred* 9). Octavia E. Butler's *Kindred* opens with this line, with the amputated arm of a speaker whose gender, race, sexuality, class, and other identities are not yet known. What readers first know about the narrator of *Kindred* is that they are a disabled person.

In her analysis of the opening of the novel, Katherine McKittrick writes that this lost arm is "hauntingly reminiscent of Sojourner Truth's working arms, through which Truth claimed her black femininity to white slave abolitionists" (35). McKittrick's connection between *Kindred*'s narrator, Dana, and Sojourner Truth is apropos, but perhaps not—or not exclusively—in the way she intends. McKittrick connects Dana and Truth as two black women who experienced slavery and whose arms are a reflection of this experience: Truth's "working" arms and Dana's disabled one. "Working" here can be read as suggesting arms that are able to perform manual labor and arms that "work" in the sense of being able to function in the socially expected way. Dana's amputated arm could indeed be read as an allusion to Truth who infamously bared her arms and supposedly asked "Ain't I a woman?" in order to challenge the notion that women are weak and therefore undeserving of the vote.[1] But Dana is also more literally similar to Truth in that they were both disabled. Truth's hand was disabled in an accident, and she often hid this hand in photos and paintings and never mentioned her injury in speeches (Minister). It is possible, therefore, to follow McKittrick's reading metaphorically and interpret Dana's missing, disabled, or *non*working arm as symbolic of Truth's visible, able, working arm that helped suffragists gain the right to vote. It is also possible to read the connection between Dana and Truth more literally and materially as two black women disabled in slavery. Is it possible, however, to read disability in *Kindred* as simultaneously metaphor and materiality?

In this chapter, I argue that disability can take on both metaphorical and material meaning in a text—an argument that provides an important foundation for the entirety of this book. Reading for both the metaphorical and material significance of disability in a text allows us to trace the ways discourses of (dis)ability, race, and gender do not merely intersect at the site of multiply marginalized people, but also how these systems collude or work in place of one another. In this chapter, I argue that within the historical and cultural context of American slavery, ableism worked for racist ends against all black people, not merely the ones disabled in ways we would now consider disability. Understanding how the collusion of oppressions plays out in various historical and cultural moments—and the representations which emerge from or about these moments—is key to integrating disability into black feminist theory and vice versa. For these reasons, then, this broad theoretical argument about reading disability as both metaphor and materiality is foundational to this book's specific arguments about how black women's speculative fiction reimagines bodyminds and changes the rules of interpretation as well as its larger intervention into my two main fields of research.

By making this argument about interpreting disability metaphors, I challenge the "methodological distancing" from disability that occurs in much scholarship on black women's writing (and on racial and ethnic literatures generally) through critical interpretation of disability as metaphor (Mitchell and Snyder 2). I also, however, critique the disability studies position against most metaphorical uses of disability. I argue that refusing to read disability as a metaphor ignores the mutual constitution of (dis)ability, race, and gender as social categories and cultural discourses which have material effects on people's lives. Reading disability as both metaphor and materiality, therefore, is essential to a black feminist disability studies approach to analyzing texts, especially those produced by people of color. Using the history of slavery as my example, I contend that scholars must read representations of disability in neo–slave narratives as constitutive of both the discursive use of (dis)ability to justify the enslavement of black people *and* the physically and mentally disabling repercussions of racism for black subjects in the antebellum period and beyond. I argue that neo–slave narratives allow for an understanding of the representation of disability as simultaneously material experience and as metaphor for other mutually constitutive and intersectional experiences of oppression, both in the past and today. I develop these arguments through an analysis of Butler's *Kindred*.

Kindred is the story of Dana Franklin, a twenty-six-year-old black woman living in California in 1976. While moving into her new home with her white husband, Kevin, Dana feels dizzy and is inexplicably pulled back in time to antebellum Maryland where a young white boy is drowning. Dana saves the child only to be threatened by his father with a gun, the sight of which causes Dana to pass out and return to 1976. Throughout the novel this pattern continues: whenever Rufus Weylin, whom readers eventually learn is Dana's great-great-grandfather, feels his life is in danger, Dana gets pulled back in time; whenever Dana feels her life is at risk, she inexplicably returns to 1976. This bond is complicated by the fact that despite Rufus's position as a slaveowner and future rapist of Dana's black great-great-grandmother, Alice, whom she befriends, Dana feels she cannot kill Rufus or allow him to die before the birth of Alice's daughter, Hagar, who will continue Dana's family line. To do so would potentially alter the future and risk the lives of Dana and her forbearers, according to the time travel logic to which Dana adheres.[2]

In what follows, I first provide an overview of the neo–slave narrative genre, especially in regard to nonrealism and (dis)ability. Second, I discuss how disability studies scholars have critiqued metaphors of disability before then arguing for the importance of historicizing metaphors, especially in regard to race. In this second section I also survey the historical relationship of (dis)ability and slavery in order to provide the foundation for my literary analysis. In the third section, I examine how disability in *Kindred* has been previously interpreted and then go on to provide my own reading of the text, one that acknowledges the metaphorical power of disability as well as the more concrete meanings and implications of disability in the book. Finally, in the conclusion, I reemphasize that representations of disability must be read as metaphorical and material in an overlapping fashion, an argument that provides a theoretical foundation on which I build later arguments in this book. This proposed approach is important for analyzing the relationship of (dis)ability, race, and gender, especially in black women's literature and literature from other marginalized groups.

The Neo–Slave Narrative Genre

In order to understand the neo–slave narrative, one must first understand traditional slave narratives as the genre which neo–slave narratives respond to, revise, and expand on.[3] Traditional slave narratives were texts written by former slaves with the specific purpose of trying to convince readers to oppose slavery. Narrators of these texts attempted to do this by insisting on the humanity of black people and revealing the inhumanity of the slave system. In order to achieve this goal, slave narratives were typically preceded by letters of support from white benefactors who assured readers that the writer was a truthful person who indeed wrote or dictated the story on their own. In the narratives themselves, former slave authors often avoided topics which would upset or offend readers, gesturing toward the horrors of slavery without providing too much detail. Ultimately, slave narratives were used to support abolition and encourage others to support it as well. They were not intended to be particularly literary or radical because their central purpose would be undermined by such qualities.[4] Many authors of neo–slave narratives based their work on slave narratives and other historical records of slavery. Butler's papers at the Huntington Library reveal that she read numerous historical monographs about slavery and the antebellum South as well as the slave narratives of Frederick Douglass, Solomon Northup, Charles Ball, William Wells Brown, Harriet Jacobs, and Harriet Tubman (Octavia E. Butler Papers, "OEB 274," 1975; "OEB 3036," 1993).

I use the term *neo–slave narrative* to refer to a broad range of post-Emancipation fictionalized representations of slavery. Unlike traditional slave narratives, which sought to use consciously constructed personal narratives to promote the abolitionist cause, neo–slave narratives are often viewed as attempts to recover or rediscover aspects of slaves' experiences that were not included in traditional slave narratives. Neo–slave narratives, therefore, use history to (re)construct experiences of slavery and affectively (re)connect contemporary individuals to slavery in ways that the less literary, nongraphic, and highly pragmatic traditional slave narratives often cannot. Despite this recovery element, neo–slave narratives also recognize that due to the marginalized position of slaves and lack of access to independent publishing and education, traditional historical methods of archival research do not necessarily produce new information. As Madhu Dubey argues, neo–slave narratives "situate themselves against history, suggesting that we can best comprehend the truth of slavery by abandoning historical modes of knowing" ("Speculative Fictions of Slavery" 784). In fact, many neo–slave narratives blur fact and fiction in order to comment on and challenge our ability to read any history of slavery—including slave narratives—as unadulterated truth, encouraging us instead to consider history, especially histories of marginalized people, as inherently partial, flawed, and filtered through human interpretation. The use of metaphor and nonrealism are both essential to this counter- (rather than anti-) historical task of the neo–slave narrative genre.

Since the publication of *Kindred* in 1979, which "set the tone for much subsequent fiction about slavery," this reconstructive task of reading against the historical grain is often performed through a variety of nonrealist devices, including the disruption of traditional linear narrative, ghost stories, and time travel (Ryan 18).[5] The change to nonrealist representations of slavery is an important difference between neo–slave narratives and traditional slave narratives because the traditional narratives relied on realism to underscore the authenticity, truthfulness, and trustworthiness of the narrative and narrator.[6] Hayden White writes that both history and fiction depend on the distinction between the real and the imaginary. She contends that in order for a text, like a traditional slave narrative, to be understood as true and real in modern discourse, it must "possess the character of narrativity" (H. White 10). As a result of this connection between traditional forms of narrative and truth, our notions of the real, both in historical and fictional texts, depend on concepts of continuity, chronology, and causality. Neo–slave narratives, however, use speculative fictional devices to refuse traditional narrative modes and thus also reject traditional notions of what constitutes the real. These literary devices that disrupt temporality and narrativity "are designed to convey certain truths about slavery that are inaccessible through the discipline of history" (Dubey, "Speculative Fictions of Slavery" 791). Speculative fictional neo–slave narratives therefore work to reclaim lost voices, to critique traditional historical methods associated with white, nondisabled men, and to use fiction and nonrealism to expose many of the untruths and absences of the historical record and cultural memory of slavery.

In addition to being nonrealist, contemporary neo–slave narratives also have a different relationship to (dis)ability than traditional slave narratives. Sherryl Vint writes that traditional "slave narratives aimed to show their black protagonists' humanity, they required the demonstration of bodily suffering to guarantee authenticity and to spur the reader into sympathy, yet they also needed to avoid reducing the narrating subject to his or her suffering body" ("'Only by Experience'" 244). The desire to demonstrate suffering without being reduced to such suffering in a traditional slave narrative depends on keeping the possibility of recovery, healing, and redemption (through the ending of slavery) open and viable.[7] This distinction between the suffering, but recoverable black subject versus the suffering black subject reduced to a suffering (and thus irrecoverable) bodymind can be read as a distinction between nondisabled and disabled black people. Here, only a nondisabled slave narrator presents the possibility of recouping black subjects by ending slavery because the suffering and otherwise disabling circumstances are represented as solely resulting from the slave system. A disabled narrator could easily be interpreted by readers as evidence of the permanent damage done to black people by slavery (or their inherent inabilities regardless of enslavement or not) and the impossibility of incorporating black people into full citizenship, a concept that is traditionally imbued with assumptions of ability.[8] A traditional slave narrative could not, therefore, fully detail the violence of slavery, which disabled so many people without jeopardizing its pragmatic purpose.

In the antebellum period, a slave narrator could not, within the discursive limits of that sociopolitical context, make a claim to rationality, morality, and citizenship while also claiming disability. Since disability and intellectual and moral capacity were viewed in opposition, even if an author had a disability it would not be represented in a traditional slave narrative as central to their personhood or experience. The two major exceptions to this representational absence are, one, when disability is represented as an effect of slavery on another person who is not the author and is then used as an example of the evils of the slave system, and, two, when disability is represented with the narrator, but cured, erased, or overcome in freedom.[9] Even then, however, such representations had to be limited since emphasizing the disablement of black people at large could, once again, limit collective group claims to the rationality, morality, and citizenship denied black subjects during this period. Contemporary neo–slave narratives do not have the same pragmatic, discursive, or editorial limits and are therefore able to represent disability both as part of the reality of slavery and as a central aspect of an individual's lived bodymind experience. In addition to *Kindred*, other neo–slave narratives that represent disability include Alex Haley's *Roots*, Toni Morrison's *Beloved*, Phyllis Alesia Perry's *Stigmata*, Margaret Walker's *Jubilee*, Edward P. Jones's *The Known World*, James McBride's *Song Yet Sung*, and Marie-Elena John's *Unburnable*. Despite the fact that disability in neo–slave narratives could be read as evidence of the violence against black people in the antebellum period, representations of disabled body-minds in neo–slave narratives are primarily interpreted as metaphors for the impact of racism, whether historically, contemporarily, or both.

Critiquing and Historicizing Disability Metaphors

The relationship of (dis)ability to race, gender, sexuality, class, and other social systems of privilege and oppression is often explored in scholarly writing as symbolical rather than literal, in the form of what I refer to as ableist metaphors, oppression analogies, and disability metaphors. Ableist metaphors, also sometimes referred to as ableist rhetoric, are common phrases and sayings, such as, "She is blind to that issue" or "Their call fell on deaf ears," which use disability to imply limitation, damage, or other negative concepts. Ableist metaphors, especially within feminist writing, have been critiqued by a number of disability studies scholars.[10] Oppression analogies, on the other hand, compare experiences of, for example, racism and ableism. These analogies have typically been regarded as problematic linguistic moves that attempt to validate one oppression while devaluing or distorting another.[11] Scholars have argued that rather than dispose of oppression analogies altogether, however, we ought to be specific about where these comparisons fail. Critics of oppression analogies encourage scholars and activists to recognize, in Chris Ewart's words, "the importance of considering their constitutive, imperfect parts," and to use this recognition, as Mark Sherry puts it, "to unpack the power dynamics which link the two experiences [of oppression], both in practice and in rhetoric" (Ewart 153; Sherry 16). Ableist metaphors and oppression analogies are different from what I call *disability metaphors*, which have been the subject of much criticism and debate in disability studies.

In their pivotal book of disability studies literary criticism, *Narrative Prosthesis: Disability and the Dependencies of Discourse,* David T. Mitchell and Sharon L. Snyder use the term *narrative prosthesis* to refer "to both the prevalence of disability representation and the myriad meanings ascribed to it" (4). The concept of narrative prosthesis has since become the primary way in disability studies to critique a representation for negatively relying on disability to further a narrative's plot or theme at the expense of abstracting disability out of material existence. Others in the field have built on Mitchell and Snyder's work to similarly critique the tendency to interpret disability as a metaphor.[12] Lennard Davis writes that "metaphorization can be problematic in terms of identity because it disembodies disability and makes it a template for something else" (*The End of Normal* 20). He argues that unless a film or text is about disability, the inclusion of a disabled character is assumed to have symbolic significance and can actually distract viewers/readers from the narrative, almost like mentioning a gun that is never used. Davis asserts, "In an ableist culture disability can't just *be*—it has to *mean* something. It has to signify. . . . In this sense disability is allegorical—it has to stand for something else—weakness, insecurity, bitterness, frailty, evil, innocence, and so on" (37; original emphasis). This critique of disability as metaphor, symbol, allegory, and so on has been useful in revealing the ableist tendencies of various representations such as canonical American and English literature and mainstream films. In some instances, however, this now-standard critique of using disability symbolically has prevented critics from exploring how representations can be at once material and metaphorical, obscuring how disability as metaphor, in and of itself, is not inherently a bad thing.

More recently, the conversations in disability studies have shifted to respond to and challenge this general resistance to reading disability as metaphor, particularly among those who work on race and disability.[13] My arguments here are indebted to these existing critiques, and I build on them in a way that particularly emphasizes why reading disability as metaphor and materiality is essential to work on blackness and disability. In her work on disability in postcolonial literature, Clare Barker argues that "vilifying disability metaphors across the board only serves to entrench disability as a form of difference that requires singular treatment," and disallows critics to be open to "the multiple forms disability representation might take even within one text" (20, 21). Writing about these multiple forms of disability representation, Ato Quayson argues that they oscillate between abstraction and material circumstances (23). This oscillation, I argue, results from the sociohistorical ways in which (dis)ability as a systemic ideology about the expectations and standards for bodyminds, behaviors, and health has, according to Nirmala Erevelles, undergirded, naturalized, and rationalized oppressive race, gender, class, and sexuality systems ("In Search of the Disabled Subject" 104–5). In other words, because (dis)ability has been used by dominant social discourse to reference, define, and regulate other social systems, it is imperative from an intersectional perspective to read for the possible metaphorical, allegorical, or otherwise abstract ways in which the fictional representation of disability alludes to race, gender, class, and sexuality as well. At the same time, to read the representation of disability as primarily a metaphor for race, gender, class, or sexuality would be to ignore (dis)ability's role in the historical realities of these mutually constitutive social systems and to erase the presence and importance of disabled people within other marginalized groups. As Alice Hall argues in her work on William Faulkner, Morrison, and J. M. Coetzee, "Metaphor and materiality are inextricably linked: to read disability as a metaphor is not to eclipse its physical implications entirely. Instead, a varied and shifting constellation of literal and metaphorical depictions of the disabled body become central" to the ways authors can explore ethical, narrative, and political concerns (174). I argue that black women's speculative fictional representations of disability engage a variety of ethical, narrative, and political concerns about (dis)ability, race, and gender that requires reading disability as metaphor and materiality, directly changing a common interpretive trend in disability studies.

In interpreting the representation of disability in black women's literature and other representations by marginalized groups, therefore, we cannot divorce images of disability from the other oppressive systems also operating within the texts and within the cultures and histories within which these texts are created. Erevelles argues that disability is a condition of becoming that must be theorized in its historical and material context (*Disability and Difference in Global Contexts* 26). In particular, responding to the call for positive representations of disability and the general trend toward celebratory pride narratives in disability studies, Erevelles asks, "How is disability celebrated if its very existence is inextricably linked to the violence of social/economic conditions of capitalism?" (17). Close and careful consideration of the real-world relationship of disability to gendered, racialized, sexual, and economic violence, such as slavery, is essential to interpreting representations of disability because this relationship impacts the creation and reception of representations of disability by groups impacted by such violence. As Dan Goodley argues, "Modes of ableist cultural reproduction and disabling material conditions can never be divorced from hetero/sexism, racism, homophobia, colonialism, imperialism, patriarchy and capitalism" (34). Writers and artists can use disability metaphors to reference this inextricable relationship. Disability studies, black feminist, and other scholars invested in social justice must therefore work to parse the metaphorical and material meanings of disability, remembering that the literal and the figurative impact and shape each other as well.

The relationship of discourse, history, and representation to the material realities of (dis)ability, race, and gender are of particular importance for this book's interventions in disability studies and black feminist theory. The racist violence of slavery and the following Jim Crow era haunted, and indeed still haunts, black bodyminds with continued threats to physical and psychic well-being.[14] The relationship of blackness to systemic disabling violence in the past impacts the relationship of blackness and disability today.[15] My argument about reading disability as metaphor and material existence extends beyond representations of slavery or even literature. However, here I use the neo–slave narrative as a useful example of how disability can appear in literature metaphorically and materially to underscore the mutually constitutive relationship of disability and blackness, historically and contemporarily. Before discussing the representation of disability in *Kindred,* therefore, it is necessary to first understand the specific material and metaphorical (or discursive) relationships of blackness and disability in American slavery. This process of contextualizing and historicizing the metaphorical use of disability in a text is essential to the study of representations of disability and blackness as well as disability and other systems of oppression.

Throughout the antebellum period, the concept of (dis)ability was used against black people in the United States as a method of proving inferiority and justifying enslavement. As Douglas Baynton writes, "Disability arguments were prominent in justifications of slavery in the early to mid-nineteenth century and of other forms of unequal relations between white and black Americans after slavery's demise. The most common disability argument for slavery was simply that African Americans lacked sufficient intelligence to participate or compete on an equal basis in society with white Americans.... A second line of disability argument was that African Americans, because of their inherent physical and mental weaknesses, were prone to become disabled under conditions of freedom and equality" (37).

To provide examples of these types of arguments, Baynton cites medical literature from the period which claimed that "drapetomania" was "a condition that causes slaves to run away" because their masters had treated them with too much familiarity and equality, while "dysaestheia aethiopis" was an "ailment," supposedly most common among freed slaves, which "resulted in a desire to avoid work and generally cause mischief," also colloquially called "rascality" (38).[16] When reading about these kinds of historical examples, Ellen Samuels reminds us that doctors and anthropologists of the nineteenth and early twentieth centuries didn't "distinguish between characteristics ascribed to race and those ascribed to physical or mental ability as we do today"; therefore, antebellum white writers were not analogizing race and (dis)ability so much as they were "merging the two into a flexible category of mental immaturity and incapacity" (*Fantasies of Identification* 178). This flexible discursive merging of blackness and disability is an example of the deployment of ableism for racist means and may be one reason why black people today can be resistant to associations with disability; indeed, this association has been used historically to justify the infliction of numerous acts of social, political, economic, and physical violence against African Americans including psychiatric institutionalization or imprisonment, medical experimentation, insurance policy discrimination, and exclusion from the military.[17]

Resistance to association with disability, however, reinforces ableist notions that disability can be equated with inferiority and serve as a justifiable reason for oppression, discrimination, and other forms of unequal treatment. Disability has been a discursive factor in the oppression of other groups as well. Snyder and Mitchell contend "that disability has become the keystone in the edifice of bodily based inferiority rationales built up since the late eighteenth century" and that most marginalized groups have distanced themselves from disability at one point or another in order to gain their civil rights (*Cultural Locations of Disability* 12, 17). Samuels argues that to critique the way scholars and activists have attempted to use "real" disability to demonstrate how "false" disability was ascribed to people of color "is not to deny the pervasively destructive scientific racism directed against people of color . . . [nor] to claim for disability some kind of originary or hierarchical status as the ultimate, grounding category of oppression. Rather it is to foreground the necessity of a fully integrated analysis that proceeds from the central understanding that race and disability are mutually constitutive and inseparable" (*Fantasies of Identification* 113). While I agree with Samuels generally, disability studies critiques of the ways disability has been used in civil rights discourses often seem to assume that the groups in question simply do not want to be thought of or categorized as disabled.[18] Rarely do these critiques consider how some oppressive systems, such as slavery, literally disabled many people.

The particular collective physical and mental trauma of slavery cannot be separated from the discursive elements used to support a violently oppressive system. That is, we cannot talk about how supposed "false" disability was used intellectually and discursively in medical, scientific, legal, and other cultural venues as a reason for enslaving black people without also talking about how that very enslavement threatened and often actually created mental and physical disability for black subjects. As Erevelles argues, we cannot pose "a simply causal effect (viz. that slavery produces disability) . . . [because] both disability/impairment and race are neither merely biological nor wholly discursive, but rather are historical materialist constructs" ("Crippin' Jim Crow" 87). This is why reading representations of disability as simultaneously metaphor and materiality is so essential—disability oscillates between abstraction and material meanings due to its social history. In other words, because (dis)ability has been used by dominant social discourses to reference, define, and regulate other social systems, it requires reading for the metaphorical, allegorical, or otherwise abstract ways in which its fictional representation is implicated in gender, race, class, and sexuality concerns as both discursive signifier and material effect.

The material effects of discourses of (dis)ability on African Americans in the United States is exemplified in the slave system. Slavery, which was justified through recourse to ableist discourses, was a traumatic and often lifelong experience for black people that physically produced disability through hard labor, malnutrition, violence, and lack of effective medical care and psychologically through fear of physical and sexual violence, disruption of families and communities, and general inhumane treatment.[19] Extreme scars, missing fingers, missing ears, and mishealed bones were all likely impairments resulting from enslavement. Even free blacks were not protected from this threat due to poor free labor situations, racial violence, and the constant threat of reenslavement or false enslavement. These issues are material facts supported by a variety of historical sources, *not* metaphors for the oppression slaves and free blacks faced. The disabled slave was typically considered a slave of little to no worth because they were assumed to be unable to produce (enough) labor for an owner and could not be sold on the market for a profit. The pain and trauma inflicted on black bodyminds during slavery was regular and often condoned—if not actually inflicted—by law.[20] This social situation that allowed black people to be regularly, violently disabled or killed did not end with the Emancipation Proclamation.[21] When disability studies scholars dismiss metaphorical uses of disability in relation to racial oppression, particularly slavery, we dismiss this history. When black feminist and other critical race scholars read representations of disability as only metaphors for past or continued racial oppression, we disregard this history. However, if part of the purpose of neo–slave narratives is to incite us to never forget what occurred and to represent what could not be represented before, then we must not only remember slavery as the oppression of black people, both enslaved and free, but also remember it as a systemic racial violence that often produced black disabled bodyminds via ableist discourses of blackness.

In fact, we might consider disability to be one of the major issues that the neo–slave narrative can address in order to understand the continued impact of the history of slavery on black people today. The American slave system, and the Jim Crow laws that followed, produced many of the concrete material conditions that continue to keep black people disproportionately impoverished, incarcerated, and disenfranchised. By understanding the role of (dis)ability in slavery, discursively and materiality—how, as Erevelles claims, "black bodies become disabled and disabled bodies become black"—we might also then be able to better understand and trace how disability and blackness continue to be imbricated categories, how ableism and racism continue to collude and work in place of one another in the lives of all black people and all disabled people, not merely black disabled people alone ("Crippin' Jim Crow" 87). When I refer to the materiality of disability, then, I mean the ways these representations of disability engage with the societal and individual impact of ableism on bodyminds, historically, contemporarily, or both. When I refer to metaphors of disability, I mean uses of the discourse or image of disability in a text which can be interpreted as referencing something that is not exactly or exclusively about the lives and experiences of people with disabilities. In the next section I provide a reading of Butler's *Kindred* that acknowledges the relationship of disability and slavery in both its metaphorical and material forms as an example of how such an approach works and why it matters so much in the context of interpreting neo–slave narratives specifically and African American literature more broadly. My focus on *Kindred* as a speculative fictional neo–slave narrative also thereby builds this book's overarching argument about how black women's speculative fiction changes the rules of interpretation and analysis.

Kindred

I focus on *Kindred* for this argument about (dis)ability in neo–slave narratives due to the influence this novel has had on the genre. In his book on fictionalized representations of slavery in the United States, Tim A. Ryan writes that although "few scholars or writers seemed to pay much attention to *Kindred* when it first appeared, the majority of slavery novels published since 1980 use strategies and conventions similar to those of Butler's work" (144). I also focus on *Kindred* because of the centrality of disability to both the text and the numerous scholarly interpretations of it. In their discussion of previous scholarship on *Kindred,* Susan Knabe and Wendy Gay Pearson write, "Much critical work has attempted to think through the relationship between Dana's encounter with history and the loss of her arm, yet none of the arguments about it are wholly compelling" (68). Indeed, *Kindred* has been interpreted many times by critics of different backgrounds and theoretical perspectives, yet Dana's amputated arm has generally been interpreted in one of only three ways: as symbolizing the impact of history, the loss of self, or the disruption of black kinship. The language in these interpretations tends to use—often through puns—words associated with disability without ever acknowledging disability as a material experience. I will provide an overview of the various metaphorical interpretations of Dana's amputated arm before using close reading to argue that disability in *Kindred* is simultaneously metaphorical and material due to the historical mutual constitution of race and (dis)ability.

Most frequently, Dana's disability is interpreted as a metaphor for the impact or "hold" of the history of slavery on the present, especially for African American people. [22] In this first vein of interpretation, Dana's amputation is considered a metaphor for "the permanent, disabling wound that slavery leaves on individuals today," according to Lisa A. Long; for how "both black and white Americans have been scarred by the institution and legacy of slavery," according to Angelyn Mitchell; for how "even in the present, racism is still crippling" according to Isiah Lavender; and for how, according to Nadine Flagel, "history can disarm the present" (Long 470; Mitchell 70; Lavender, *Race in American Science Fiction* 69; Flagel 224). [23] Second, Dana's loss of an arm is also read as a metaphor for the part of herself lost in the past—as a symbol of how she returns "unwhole" due to her interaction with history (Flagel 232). This particular interpretation appears in the work of Flagel, Anne Donadey, Gregory Jerome Hampton, and Patricia Melzer, the latter of whom states, "The experience took a part of her—literally" (Melzer, *Alien Constructions* 100). This second reading generally aligns with a comment Butler herself made in an interview, stating that she could not allow Dana to "come all the way back" or "come back whole" (quoted in Steinberg 473). Finally, Dana's disability is also read as a metaphor for the disruption of black kinship and the generally fraught nature of black family histories due to rape, lost records, and forcibly changed names. Donadey writes that "Dana's severed arm can also be interpreted as a reference to limbs that were broken off family trees through the discontinuities caused by slavery" (72).[24] In a related vein, explicitly emphasizing metaphor, Knabe and Pearson argue that "the most powerful way of understanding Dana's amputation might be to consider it as a corporeal metaphor for the ways in which black kinship has been dis-membered by the past and black people, through their unrecognizability as kin, deprived of recognition as fully human" (68). These three interpretations—disability as impact of history, disability as loss of self, and disability as disruption of black kinship—collectively represent the predominant ways in which Dana's disability in *Kindred* has been previously read.

As the examples above illustrate, these interpretations are primarily metaphorical, focused on the symbolic meanings of Dana's disability while hardly considering the materiality of disability, not only on Dana's bodymind, but also within the American slave system itself. Lisa Yaszek, for example, insists on the importance of metaphor to appreciate or make sense of the novel, stating, "Butler shows us that while Dana's literal situation may indeed seem like something out of a fantastic sci-fi scenario, metaphorically it makes perfect sense" (1063). Interestingly, critics typically offer not one, but multiple metaphorical readings of Dana's disability or the moment of her impairment, indicating that a single moment or aspect of the text can have different meanings even for an individual scholar. Yet only a few of these scholars appear to regard disability in the text as an actual state of being, meaningful in its materiality as well as its metaphorical significance.

Scholars who attempt to provide some material analysis of disability include Sarah Eden Schiff, who notes that Dana's amputation "is typical of a Civil War injury," and Sarah Wood, who argues that "Dana bears the visual scars of slavery" literally from being whipped (Schiff 121; Wood 95). A. Timothy Spaulding also argues that Dana's disability should not be read as "an abstraction" because *Kindred* "forces us to interrogate not only the discursive legacies of slavery in our contemporary moment but also the concrete and material connections between American slavery and late-twentieth-century culture" (29). Spaulding does not, however, suggest what those concrete and material connections might be. All three of these scholars attempt to connect Dana's disabled bodymind to the materiality of disability in the antebellum period; however, such readings are rare overall and in each of these examples, the materiality of disability is not the focus of the larger arguments. Only Therí A. Pickens has analyzed *Kindred* from an explicitly disability studies approach. She argues that Dana's "disability remains tethered to historical black experiences of enslavement in America . . . [and therefore] disability moves beyond metaphor or narrative prosthesis to foreground Dana's embodiment" ("Octavia Butler and the Aesthetics of the Novel" 170). As a black disability studies scholar, Pickens insists on the materiality of Dana's embodiment while also refuting Dana's disability as narrative prosthesis because Dana's disability is not merely a device to move along the plot or develop character; rather, it is a material reference to experiences of slavery. Building on Pickens's argument, in my reading of *Kindred*, I argue that disability is used both metaphorically and materially to demonstrate not only the connection between the past and present, but also the connections between disability and slavery, between ableism and racism. I locate these connections in the prologue, the rationale for time travel, the moment Dana is physically disabled, and the epilogue.

First, however, a brief aside. Readers familiar with *Kindred* may wonder why I have not included Carrie, the young slave girl (and later woman) with a speech disability who uses hand gestures to communicate. My analysis here focuses on Dana because of the way disability structures Dana's experience in the text and because of Dana's role as the contemporary person impacted by the legacy of slavery—a role fundamental to the purpose of neo–slave narratives. Carrie, however, is clearly part of the way Butler emphasizes how nonnormative bodyminds were devalued and mistreated in slavery. Carrie is the only child of Sarah's whom the Weylins have not sold because, as Sarah states, "Carrie ain't worth much as the others 'cause she can't talk. People think she ain't got good sense" (*Kindred* 76). In addition to Carrie, other references to disabled slaves include Alice's husband Isaac whose ears are cut off for running away, "old and crippled" Aunt Mary, and an unnamed slave woman "whose former master had cut three fingers from her right hand when he caught her reading" (147, 91). The multiple representations of disability beyond Dana's missing arm underscore the importance of disability to the text and Butler's awareness of the materiality of disability during the antebellum period. However, as discussed in the introduction, a disability studies approach can and should look beyond explicitly disabled characters to understand how (dis)ability as a social system operates in a text, especially within speculative fiction. As a result, I do not include Carrie, Isaac, Aunt Mary, and the unnamed slave woman in my analysis in order to focus on how disability operates at structural and plot levels in the text in addition to these more brief yet explicit representations of black disabled people.

The importance of disability to *Kindred* is suggested immediately at the beginning of the novel. Readers first encounter Dana in a hospital, her arm amputated. She states, "I was almost comfortable except for the strange throbbing of my arm. Of where my arm had been . . . I moved my head, tried to look at the empty place . . . the stump" (10; ellipses in the original). At the hospital, police officers and doctors ask questions of Dana's husband, Kevin, suspicious about the circumstances surrounding her injury. As readers, we are not granted any more information in the prologue than the doctors and police because, according to Dana, if Kevin tells the truth of what happened he would "be locked up—in a mental hospital" (11). All that readers initially know is that Dana lost her arm on her "last trip home" and that when pushed to explain how, both she and Kevin insist they don't know (9). From here, the first chapter, "The River," moves the text temporally to what could be considered the beginning of the plotline, to when a nondisabled Dana first experiences time travel. I write "could" and "plotline" here because the idea of a "timeline" in *Kindred* is complicated. Technically, the plotline begins with Dana moving into the house and the first moment she traveled back in time, even though the text begins with her in the hospital (an event that is actually toward the end of the plotline). The plotline then continues until Dana stops time-traveling and ends when she visits the site of the Weylin plantation in the present. While a traditional timeline following a linear notion of time would begin in 1815 and continue through 1976, a timeline in terms of the trajectory of the plot would move between 1976 to 1815 to 1976 and so on, since throughout her journey Dana travels to the 1800s and back. As a result, the term *timeline* does not quite work for this novel, and *plotline* is a more appropriate term that privileges Dana's experience of time and space rather than traditional Western notions of time. L. H. Stallings suggests that scholars should develop "new conceptualizations of time and space in order to change the trajectory of future discourses about race and racial identity. Standard, western, or straight time may be useful for charting the representations or performances of blackness, but they have often failed to fully delineate the experience of being black" (190). If black feminist literary criticism understands texts as not merely representations to be interpreted through theory, but productions of theory in and of themselves, then *Kindred*'s representation of black experiences of time challenge notions of linearity and causality, emphasizing instead circularity and mutual constitution of events and meaning.

The prologue also does important temporality work by challenging cultural narratives of disability. Typically, disabilities are categorized as congenital (occurring from birth) or as acquired (occurring after birth). As Kafer notes, people with acquired disabilities "are described (and often describe themselves) as if they were multiple . . . the 'before disability' self and the 'after disability' self (as if the distinction were always so clear, always so binary). Compulsory nostalgia is at work here, with a cultural expectation that the relation between these two selves is always one of loss, and of loss that moves in only one direction" (*Feminist, Queer, Crip* 42–43). In *Kindred*, this before and after self is not so clear since readers are first exposed to Dana's "after" self. The unidirectional understanding of disability as loss that Kafer theorizes is, therefore, challenged through the novel's structure, which begins with Dana as disabled and then moves to Dana as nondisabled before she is disabled again.[25] Through the threat of disablement set up by the prologue and the uncertain nature of Dana's time travel, it is possible to read Dana as always already disabled with no "before" self to even reference. That is, if Dana's arm is lost in the past or if her disablement occurs somewhere between the past and then present, then Dana never really was nondisabled in the present. This is particularly true for readers because within the timeline of the story, it begins and ends with Dana disabled. Although Dana appears nondisabled throughout most of the novel, we know that she is, was, and will be disabled (again). *Kindred's* temporality of disability therefore refuses to follow simplistic and ableist conventions of a before and after binary constructed as single directional loss.

It is important that the text begins with disability of an inexplicable and mysterious nature, with disability that has already existed and will exist again. The unaccounted-for injury at the start of the novel causes disability to haunt the text because it is already present in the reader's consciousness after the prologue. For the rest of the narrative readers know that at some point Dana will have her arm amputated—we just don't know how or when. Instead, readers anticipate and expect that disablement could occur at any moment in the text, an experience that psychologically gestures toward the vulnerability of slaves to disability at any moment as well. For most enslaved people, impairment of some sort was fairly inevitable given their living and working conditions; the question was not if, but when. The notion that everyone will be disabled if they live long enough is a truism in disability studies. Disability is sometimes jokingly referred to as an equal opportunity minority category—the only one anyone can join instantly at any moment. When we make such claims in disability studies, however, we should also be attentive to the fact that disability was and is a more likely facet of life for particular populations.[26] The inevitability of disability for Dana is thus established in *Kindred* with the set-up of the prologue, and, as a result, disability becomes a sometimes occluded, but ever-present part of the text through its assured return. In the novel, disability is both presence and possibility, literal embodiment and abstract threat/promise readers know will come true.

This temporally unbounded, inevitable disability in *Kindred* impels time travel in the text. I diverge slightly from the typical assumptions about the impetus for Dana's time travel and contend that due to the impending presence of disability in the text from the prologue, Dana's time travel is initiated by not only the threat of death, but also the threat of disablement. Critics have generally interpreted Dana's travel in time as tied to the threatened lives of herself and Rufus.[27] Marisa Parham writes that Dana is "transported between two distinct times and places by the fear of her own death," via actual violence on her bodymind and the possible premature death of Rufus, which would theoretically disallow her birth in the future (1324). Early in the book Dana herself comes to believe that it is Rufus who brings her back in time, stating, "So he had called me. I was certain now. The boy drew me to him somehow when he got himself into more trouble than he could handle" (*Kindred* 26). Without a doubt, time travel for Dana typically occurs in relation to incidents which produce or threaten bodily harm to either Rufus or Dana. Over the course of the novel Dana is brought to antebellum Maryland when Rufus is drowning, when he sets a fire in his room, when he breaks his leg falling out of a tree, when he is losing a fistfight, and when he nearly drowns in a puddle while passed out drunk. Dana returns to 1976 when threatened with a gun by Rufus's father, when beaten and almost raped by a patroller, when being whipped, when threatened with a gun by Rufus, when she slits her own wrists, and when Rufus tries to rape her. These incidents that pull Dana between the 1800s and 1976 vary in their severity. Some do indeed seem to bring characters close to death and others seem to bring them closer to disablement. It is important to remember the historical specificity of these moments and the difference between medicine in the twentieth and twenty-first centuries and medicine in the "primitive age" of the 1800s, as Dana refers to it (42). Indeed, Dana remains keenly aware of the difference in medical care between her time and Rufus's, as indicated in her interaction with a condescending white doctor and her decision to bring both painkillers and sleeping pills back in time with her. In the antebellum period, the line between an incident causing disability (like a broken leg that might not set right and thus cause a limp) and an incident causing death (like drowning) is much thinner than the line between disability and death today for most people in the United States, despite ableist notions to the contrary.

Dana's ability to travel in time is not only impelled by disability, but it can also be read as a nonrealist disability itself. Traditionally, time travel is associated with science fiction texts in which a character builds a time machine and willingly, excitedly moves back and forth in time. As Sherryl Vint explains, "In many time-travel narratives, the emphasis is on control of the timeline, on ensuring that the dominance of one's 'kind' persists into a future associated with progress. . . . This attitude can be associated with the Western paradigm of science as a relation to the world of dominance and mastery. African Americans have a quite different relationship both to science and to the idea of the future" ("'Only by Experience'" 243).

Indeed, for Dana, time travel is not facilitated by her mastery of a technological device, but rather by an unnamed psychic connection to her forebears. For her, time travel is not voluntary or fun. It is a difficult and painful experience that constantly endangers her. Some scholars, such as Benjamin Robertson, have read Dana's forced moves through time as "enhanced physical abilities" which give her power over history, albeit power she cannot, or refuses to, use (370). This reading, however, does not reflect how Dana seems to experience time travel. She is constantly returning with injuries and pain from her interactions with the past. She also experiences fear and anxiety about when the pull through time will happen again and if she will be able to survive and return to 1976 relatively safely once more. This fear causes Dana to refuse to leave the house, afraid of pulling a total stranger back in time with her, or hurting people if she were to time travel while driving her car (*Kindred* 116).

The experience of time travel does not empower Dana so much as it disables her or, at the very least, continually threatens disablement. Dana acknowledges that she is being forced to live in a time when blacks are considered "subhuman" and women considered "childlike" (68). As a black woman, Dana is put at increased risk for disablement by involuntary time travel and she seeks to be free of it. *Kindred*'s representation of time travel reveals this speculative fictional device to be highly racialized, gendered, and ability-centric since only certain individuals, such as Dana's white, male, nondisabled husband, Kevin, who survives several years in the past without her, could retain their contemporary rights and privileges when moving into the past. As Jennifer E. Henton argues, *Kindred* is "a striking refutation of time travel as techno-advancement" for all people (108). Thus time travel in *Kindred* is structured by disability in multiple ways: Dana's moves through time are impelled by the threat of disability, the involuntary experience of these moves is disabling, and her place as a black woman in the antebellum past puts her at additional risk for disablement.

This reading of disability as a major structuring element of time travel in *Kindred* is reinforced when we consider that the culminating moment of the text, the moment when the time travel apparently ceases, is the moment of Dana's disablement—the moment when disability returns as material, embodied presence and when, as she kills Rufus for attempting to rape her, she returns to the present with her arm "flesh joined with plaster" in her living room wall (261). Critics have, in addition to their interpretations of Dana's disability more broadly, tended to read this moment as both traumatic and liberating. Flagel writes that Dana "gains more by killing Rufus than she ever did by saving him. Though she does not escape unharmed, she regains physical and emotional freedom," while Schiff argues that "by sinking the knife into his side, Dana—fantastically—rewrites, possibly even unwrites, the narrative of her ancestor's primary trauma" (Flagel 223; Schiff 122). Without a doubt, this moment is traumatic and painful. First, it is mentally and emotionally traumatic because Dana experiences attempted rape and is forced to kill. This then is another way in which the possibility of disability haunts the text in the form of the potential mental disability that could result from sexual assault and having to kill to protect oneself. Second, it is physically traumatic and painful when she returns to the present with her arm stuck in a wall (or stuck in the past, as Rufus held on to her). Dana describes the experience of wrenching her now amputated arm from the wall as "an avalanche of pain, red impossible agony" (261). It is symbolically significant that the culminating moment of the text, when Dana's time-traveling relationship with slavery presumably ends as Rufus dies, is also the moment of disability's material return. The three predominant readings of Dana's resulting disability from this moment—disability as the impact of history, loss of self, or disruption of black kinship—are not incorrect, but this moment also supports my claim that the dual material presence and threat of disability is a structuring element of the entire novel. Here the prologue's indication of inevitable disability comes to fruition, and Dana, like many slaves in American history, experiences pain, trauma, and eventually disability. She does not simply embody the relationship between these concepts metaphorically, she literally experiences it.

The metaphorical readings of Dana's disability do make sense, but the materiality of her amputation refuses to be denied and a black feminist disability studies reading of the novel must acknowledge both valences. The materiality of disability is further emphasized by the fact that the novel does not end with the moment of Dana's disablement, but rather continues into the brief but potent epilogue. In this final portion of the novel, "as soon as [her] arm was well enough," Dana and Kevin travel to Maryland to locate where the Weylin plantation had been (262). In the countryside, they find that Rufus's house is gone and the farmer living on the land has never heard of the Weylins. Nothing physical remains except a few old newspapers that indicate Rufus died in an accidental house fire. After his death, all the slaves were sold, though several slaves, including Dana's ancestor Hagar, do not appear in the sale list. After their search for information finds nothing more than these few details, Kevin tells Dana she will likely never know what happened to everyone. In response, Dana touches first the scar on her face from where Rufus's father once kicked her and then her empty sleeve. Here we are reminded of Dana's *disabilities* via her touching both the place where her arm once was and her scarred face, which can be read as a stand-in for her scarred back. When Dana speaks after this moment of physical ritual remembrance, she questions why she wanted to come back in the first place, to which Kevin replies, "To try to understand. To touch solid evidence that those people existed. To reassure yourself that you're sane" (264).

On the one hand, this final scene refuses to answer any questions, leaving not only Dana and Kevin, but also readers to wonder what happened in the past and what will happen now. On the other hand, this scene also depicts Dana as a disabled woman continuing her life. This is important for two reasons. First, it is important that the book does not end with disablement and pain, with the only representations of Dana's disabled bodymind as bloody and screaming after injury or confused and aching in the hospital. The novel represents Dana in the end as healed and disabled at the same time. Her bodymind is different, yes; it has clearly been impacted by her experience of slavery. Nevertheless, Dana continues on past the moment of disablement and, as Henton claims, "can again live as a normal, non–time traveling woman," a normal, *disabled,* non-time-traveling woman that is (108). Second, this ending is important for the neo–slave narrative genre. As previously stated, neo–slave narratives are supposed to be able to represent what could not be included in traditional slave narratives. Traditional slave narrative authors needed to represent themselves as normatively as possible, making moral and rational pleas for the sympathy of the reader. As the narrator of a neo–slave narrative, Dana is allowed to be a disabled woman whose disability is readily, yet nonspectacularly displayed. Dana's amputated arm has clearly impacted her, but her disablement is not mourned in the text as emblematic of the horrors of slavery, as many critics have argued; rather, Dana seems most impacted by her inability to recover historical evidence of her experience and the experiences of her ancestors. As Pickens writes, "The book simply ends. Its denouement is neither tragic nor triumphant" ("Octavia Butler and the Aesthetics of the Novel" 175). If anything, the epilogue seems to be a critique of history and the paucity of the archive when it comes to finding the voices and experiences of marginalized people.

While the epilogue is only a brief explicit representation of disability compared to the sustained impending possibility of disability that operates throughout the majority of the novel, this final portion of the text further demonstrates how disability is integral to the structure of *Kindred.* From the prologue, which sets up disability as inevitable; to Dana's time travel compelled by the possibility of disability; to the moment of Dana's disablement, which brings the prologue to fruition; to the epilogue, which represents Dana as a disabled woman looking for answers to her traumatic and painful experience, disability is a consistent and guiding aspect of the book. Disability is not a metaphor for Dana; it is part of her embodied existence, and yet the (im)materiality of her missing limb is intimately tied to and thus a symbol of her particular experience of slavery.

Disability even plays a prominent role in Dana's last words in the book. She states, "If we told anyone else about this, anyone at all, they wouldn't think we were so sane" (264). Here Dana acknowledges the nonrealist nature of her experience and how claims to sanity or able-mindedness in contemporary culture are dependent on rationally explained experiences understood as real—a topic that I will discuss at length in the next chapter. Disability studies scholars argue our culture tends to narrativize disability, wanting a story and explanation for nonnormative bodyminds.[28] This urge to narrativize disability is encapsulated in the common ableist question

"What happened to you?" In *Kindred,* as noted earlier, the before and after temporality typically assumed of disability cannot be adequately applied. In her present context, Dana's disability cannot have a story attached, at least not a temporally linear, culturally recognizable, and rationally acceptable story. Here, just as disability structures the novel as a whole, disability or, more precisely, ableism structures what Dana can and cannot say about her experience.

From start to finish, literally from Dana's first sentence to her last, disability structures *Kindred.* Disability in the text is at once a metaphor for racial oppression *and* a reference to or reflection of the material prevalence of disability for black people during the antebellum period. This simultaneity of representational modes is essential to the novel's impact as a neo–slave narrative. *Kindred* relies on both metaphor and materiality to connect the past and the present, to reveal what could not previously be revealed in traditional slave narratives, and to demonstrate how these historically lost elements are essential for understanding the legacy of slavery today.

Conclusion

In response to both disability studies scholars who criticize the use of disability as a metaphor and black feminist and other critics who almost exclusively interpret disability as a metaphor for other oppressions and thematic concerns, I have demonstrated how a contextualized and historicized perspective allows critics to trace both the metaphorical and material uses of disability. This approach to disability metaphors requires being particularly attentive to the relationships of disability to racial, gendered, economic, and sexual violence, such as that which occurred in American slavery. Although disability studies scholars have been rightfully critical of how disability is often interpreted as a metaphor for trauma or other oppressions, we cannot dismiss outright all metaphorical uses of disability, especially when these metaphors are connected to or blended with material issues of disability and impairment, either in the text itself or in the referent of the metaphor—in this case, slavery. In *Kindred,* disability is not exclusively metaphorical, despite previous critical readings to the contrary. Dana is literally disabled by her experience with the physical, emotional, sexual, and discursive violence of slavery, and disability haunts and propels the novel throughout. As a result, we must read this representation of disability for both metaphorical and material meanings. I intend for my approach to reading disability as metaphor and materiality to be useful and applicable not only in regard to black women's speculative fiction, but also with respect to any representation of disability in texts produced by or focused on people of color, women, gender-nonconforming people, and lesbian, gay, bisexual, trans-, and queer people, who each have histories of discourses of (dis)ability being used to justify their oppression.

The discussion of the relationship of disability and slavery in this chapter also demonstrates the neo–slave narrative's ability to represent what was previously unable to be represented within the specific historical and pragmatic context of the traditional slave narrative. Disability is one of the major things neo–slave narratives can represent that traditional slave narratives could not. In particular, the metaphorical and material representations of disability that appear in *Kindred* and other neo–slave narratives are made possible by the context of speculative fiction. Mark Bould argues that "critical treatments of the neo–slave narrative have typically neglected the significant use made of fantastic devices so as to trouble and confront the history of slavery in the New World (which includes its ongoing legacies)" (183). The use of speculative fictional devices is integral to the representation of disability in *Kindred*. Only nonrealist representations can create the circumstances in which slavery has a real, direct bodily impact on contemporary individuals. In the twenty-first century, there are no survivors of slavery remaining to speak about their experiences, and thus, as Long contends, "experiential and bodily connection to slavery has been lost. No one alive bears the physical scars of African American enslavement" (460). Speculative fictional neo–slave narratives can intervene in this lost connection, using nonrealist narrative devices such as time travel to make what was once a reality real again, to, as Dubey writes, "rupture narrative realism in order to offer an immediate bodily experience of the trauma of slavery" ("Speculative Fictions of Slavery" 788). Through a historicized approach that incorporates disability studies and black feminist theories, representations of racialized and gendered (dis)ability can be understood in their metaphorical and material intersectional complexity. In the next chapter, I continue to read disability as metaphor and material experience in another neo–slave narrative, Phyllis Alesia Perry's *Stigmata*. There I extend this chapter's arguments on the importance of disability to the neo–slave narrative genre's goal of exploring the lingering effects of slavery, this time in connection with the social construction of able-mindedness.

WHOSE REALITY IS IT ANYWAY?

Deconstructing Able-Mindedness

Sanity is that combination of perceptions,
interpretations, teachings, and beliefs that we
share with others of our community.

Sanity is the tool with which we build worlds
around ourselves. The smoother our interface
between our personal worlds and those of others,
the more sane, the more human we perceive
those others to be.
—OCTAVIA E. BUTLER, unpublished verse from *Earthseed:
The Books of the Living* (Octavia E. Butler Papers)

"Reality" is promiscuous, at the very least.
—WAHNEEMA LUBIANO, "But Compared to What?"

The short-lived television series *The Tomorrow People* (a 2013 remake of
the British television series that aired from 1973 to 1979) focuses on a high
school student, Steven Jameson, who, viewers are initially led to believe, is
a young man with a mental disability who hears voices and sleepwalks.[1] In
the opening of the first episode, viewers see Steven taking medications at
the behest of his mother because Steven's now-absent father also had a similar mental disability. By the end of the first episode, however, Steven learns

he is not disabled, but is instead one of the Tomorrow People, a group of genetically evolved superhumans, or "homo superiors," with the powers of telepathy (thus Steven's hearing voices), teleportation (thus the "sleep-walking"), and telekinesis. Very swiftly, therefore, the series erases any sem-blance of Steven as disabled by his experience of an often frightening, con-fusing, and stigmatized differing reality. Instead, the show positions Steven as not only hyper-able, but also as part of a community of superhumans. This quick transition from potential disability to super ability is common in speculative fiction, particularly within the superhero genre. This type of representation also occurs in the comic and film versions of the *X-Men* series in which individual mutants are initially represented as feared, pit-ied, or isolated due to their abilities, perceiving themselves as "freaks," until they are brought into the mutant family fold by Professor X or Magneto, who help them harness and control their abilities.[2] But what if Steven and the X-Men's differing experiences of reality did not include abilities that are later valued by the rest of the world or that give them the ability to better protect themselves and others? What if these characters lacked a commu-nity of others with the same experiences or abilities, people with similar re-alities? What if Steven Jameson, white, male, heterosexual, hyper-able cho-sen one of the Tomorrow People, was black and female and alone in this particular experience of reality? How would the story be different?

Phyllis Alesia Perry's *Stigmata* is the story of Lizzie DuBose, a black woman in her thirties living in the American South in the 1990s. The book switches between this present setting and the past to relay Lizzie's narrative. The timeline of the text begins when a fourteen-year-old Lizzie receives the trunk of her deceased grandmother, Grace, and begins to have flash-backs to the experiences of her ancestors, including a former slave, Ayo. As the text progresses and the flashbacks become more vivid, readers come to understand that Lizzie is experiencing what Lisa A. Long calls multiple or communal consciousnesses (470–71). That is, the spirits (or souls or disembodied subjects) of Grace and Ayo each reside within Lizzie's body-mind alongside Lizzie's own separate mental existence. As Lizzie struggles to come to terms with her multiplicity, she begins to physically experience parts of Grace's and Ayo's past lives, including Ayo's wounds from slavery. When Lizzie experiences these particular wounds, her parents interpret them as suicide attempts and institutionalize her. Indeed, the book opens with an immediate representation of disability, as an adult Lizzie sits in her psychologist's office about to be released after fourteen years of forced institutionalization. *Stigmata* further demonstrates how disability can take on both metaphorical and material meanings in a text in equally compelling and complex ways. Disability in this novel is an allusion to the historical legacies of slavery. Lizzie's disability is also a real and, at times, incredibly painful experience impacting her bodymind and the trajectory of her life. The novel uses disability as metaphor and materiality to critique the racist, sexist, and ableist construction of able-mindedness and the racist, sexist, and ableist practices of the psychiatric medical-industrial complex.

In my discussion of the epilogue of *Kindred* in chapter 1, I briefly explored how the book's multiple references to mental hospitals and sanity suggest that if Dana were to tell the real story of how she lost her arm, she would risk being labeled as mentally disabled and potentially institutionalized.[3] This is because those who do not claim to experience time and space within the rules of our contemporary reality may be considered mentally disabled due to their claims of living in a differing reality from others—as viewers see briefly in the first episode of *The Tomorrow People*. A label of mental disability in contemporary culture, with its accompanying stereotypical associations with threat, violence, and instability, can cause an individual to be subjected to discrimination, violence, and possibly institutionalization or forced treatment. As Sherryl Vint writes, however, "Butler's novel reminds us that there is more to truth and sanity than what survives in the official historical record" ("'Only by Experience'" 254). *Kindred* gestures toward the fact that our contemporary notions about able-mindedness—and the privileges and oppressions which result, depending on which side of the binary one falls—are influenced by cultural context and time period, as well as by gender, race, class, and sexuality. What *Kindred* suggests, *Stigmata* makes explicit. As another speculative fictional neo–slave narrative, *Stigmata* continues *Kindred*'s insistence on the metaphorical and material relationship of (dis)ability, race, and gender both historically and contemporarily, while focusing more specifically on critiquing the social construction of able-mindedness and the practices of the psychiatric medical-industrial complex. By able-mindedness, I mean the socially constructed norm of mental capacity and ability that is typically posed in binary opposition to mental disability. Able-mindedness includes concepts such as rationality, reasonableness, sanity, intelligence, mental agility, self-awareness, social awareness, and control of thoughts and behaviors. Though I use the terms *able-mindedness* and *mental disability* throughout this chapter, I do so only to acknowledge and engage how these concepts are understood in society at large. I still assert that the bodymind is not two separable entities, as is indicated even by the fact that physical behaviors (such as the ability to control actions) are considered indicative of able-mindedness.

In this chapter, I argue that by challenging the rules of reality—particularly the assumption that there is only a single reality—black women's speculative fiction has the potential to deconstruct able-mindedness, revealing how this (dis)ability concept is deeply dependent on racial and gendered norms. I demonstrate not only how race and gender are often embedded in metaphoric uses of mental disability, but also how people who experience realities considered dramatically unlike the realities of the majority are labeled and treated differently, depending on their race, gender, and (dis)ability statuses. Using the example of *Stigmata,* I contend that black women's speculative fiction can engage our cultural association of differing realities with mental disability in order to critique the ableism, racism, and sexism that socially construct able-mindedness with real material consequences, especially within the psychiatric medical-industrial complex.

By making arguments about how black women's speculative fiction can deconstruct able-mindedness, I am neither claiming that mental disability does not exist nor denying the realities of people with mental disabilities. Instead, I am doing two things. First, I insist that race and gender are important factors in who gets labeled mentally disabled and how a person is treated as a result of such a label. Second, in line with approaches from postpsychiatry and various mental disability rights movements, I challenge the notion that mental disability is a purely biological and readily apparent phenomenon of the bodymind.[4] I fully recognize that for some people psychiatric labels and treatments are useful and that, as my example of *Stigmata* will demonstrate, the experience of differing realities can be frightening or painful and thus something that an individual may seek to be rid of or experience less. Through the deconstruction of able-mindedness, black women's speculative fiction insists that the possibilities and meanings of bodyminds are experienced—and thus must be interpreted—in the context of race, (dis)ability, gender, and other vectors of power. In particular, *Stigmata* demonstrates how these discourses, systems, and identities impact our experiences of reality and how a lack of recognition for differing realities has more punitive and dangerous results for some populations than others. The novel draws attention to these issues in order to critique the psychiatric medical-industrial complex and its frequent pathologizing denial of how experiences of oppression can have a material, nonmetaphorical impact on the bodyminds of people of color, women, trans- people, gender-nonconforming people, and disabled people, especially those who fit into more than one of these categories.

Race, Gender, and the Social Construction of Able-Mindedness

In order to understand how *Stigmata* deconstructs and critiques able-mindedness and the psychiatric medical-industrial complex, it is important to first understand how race and gender have historically been enmeshed with the concepts of able-mindedness and mental disability, thereby shaping psychiatric practices. Again, I define able-mindedness as a socially determined label of mental ability that broadly encompasses a wide range of concepts such as rationality, intelligence, social awareness, self-control, and more. The concept of able-mindedness shifts based on not only time and place, but also the identities of the individuals considered to be within or outside of that category. As Bradley Lewis argues, "Models of madness frame and select certain aspects of a perceived human reality and make them more salient than others. . . . the choice of model or frame depends not on science but on the perspectives and values of the person and persons involved" (107–8). Mental disability is framed as the outside or opposite of able-mindedness. As a result, understanding the gendered and racialized histories of mental disability also helps us understand the social construction of able-mindedness. After all, as black feminist theorist bell hooks asserts, the margins define the center.

The marginalized space of mental disability, which defines the center space of able-mindedness, is currently officially constructed in the psychiatric medical-industrial complex with the *Diagnostic and Statistical Manual of Mental Disorders* (DSM). Work by scholars of the history of medicine and science demonstrates, however, that "no diagnosis is actually unproblematic or freed from social and cultural issues" (Davis, *The End of Normal* 82–83). Since the DSM was originally published in 1952, in an attempt to standardize the practice of psychiatry, categories and labels of mental disabilities have appeared, shifted dramatically, and sometimes disappeared entirely. Some changes in diagnostic criteria have occurred due to changes in socially accepted behaviors and norms around sexuality, gender, and race, as well as through lobbying by activists. For instance, activism by those both within and outside of psychiatry removed homosexuality from the DSM and, more recently, changed the diagnosis of gender identity disorder to gender dysphoria—neither of which was without controversy. Even as practitioners and researchers attempt to remove bias from the manual, they cannot account for all the ways cultural and individual bias impacts the perception of behaviors and states of mind in the diagnosis and treatment of mental disability. Due to the conflicting social norms and stereotypes of various genders and races, certain behaviors and states of mind are interpreted in divergent ways when expressed and interpreted by differently situated individuals. In other words, a black woman behaving in one way is likely to be interpreted differently than a white man behaving the same way. Further, interpretations of a black woman's behavior may also vary depending on the identity of the interpreter, whether that person is another black woman, a black man, a white woman, and so on.

There are many historical examples of racial and gendered bias in the creation of categories of mental disability. Take, for instance, the flexibility of the term *feebleminded* in American eugenics. While the term may now connote mental disability, Wendy Kline writes that in the early twentieth-century United States, feeblemindedness was often used to describe anyone whose behaviors were thought to be "inappropriate," "threatening," or otherwise deviating from social norms, particularly those regarding race, gender, and sexuality (22). For example, one supposed indication of feeblemindedness in white women in the 1920s was the lack of an appropriately adverse response to overtures or kindness by black men (Roberts 69). A more recent example is the history of schizophrenia. Jonathan Metzl details how until the 1960s schizophrenia was considered a primarily white, female, and relatively benign mental disability, but after the civil rights movement "research articles from leading psychiatric journals asserted that schizophrenia was a condition that also afflicted 'Negro men,' and that the black forms of the illness were marked by volatility and aggression" (xii). Several leading psychiatrists in the period began conflating schizophrenia with the perceived anger and instability of groups such as the Black Panthers and Nation of Islam, sometimes going so far as to claim that participation in "black liberation movements literally caused delusions, hallucinations, and violent projections in black men" (100).[5] These examples illustrate how deviance from social norms, especially norms of race and gender, has historically been construed as mental disability, with its related material consequences such as institutionalization, incarceration, social exclusion, and forced treatment. Only those who adhere to social norms are considered able-minded. Able-mindedness, however, does not exist merely in the absence of an official psychiatric diagnosis. Able-mindedness and mental disability are also constructed in more unofficial and quotidian spaces.

While it may seem simplistic or obvious to say, our experiences of reality within a shared time and place vary significantly by our cultural locations within the systems of (dis)ability, race, gender, class, sexuality, and more. Experiences of differing realities, however, are often denied and dismissed through discourses of able-mindedness. Katherine McKittrick argues that even "the built environment and the material landscape are sites that are intensely experiential and uneven, and deeply dependent on psychic, imaginary work"—work structured by history, identity, and experience (2). Black women's speculative fiction suggests the possibility that individuals, such as black women and others with extended histories of oppression, may experience time, events, interactions, space, and place in distinctly different ways than people without such histories. In other words, the experience and interpretation of reality by a racial, gender, sexual, or (dis)ability minority may dramatically differ from those in the majority.

The history of cultural bias in psychiatric diagnosis extends into the everyday when marginalized people speaking about their experiences of differing realities are positioned outside of able-mindedness. While marginalized people may not (always) be explicitly or officially labeled mentally disabled when discussing their differing experiences of reality, they are often threatened with such labeling. Ashley Taylor argues that "the specter of the disabled mind is deployed against those who fail to conform to dominant gendered and racialized roles and behaviors, and used as a way to bring dissenters back in line" (188). This is illustrated time and time again when marginalized individuals are accused of overreacting to, being too sensitive about, or reading too much into the actions and behaviors of those around them; when marginalized people who attempt to call out, name, and share their experiences with oppression are told that the way they experienced an event is not the way it really happened or the way that others experienced it, that they are missing something, that their interpretation was not what was intended, and so on and so on. The line between able-mindedness and mental disability is not stable. Accusations of being "too sensitive" can easily become labels of "paranoia." Allegations of being "too emotional" can swiftly move into categorizations of "hysterical" and "volatile." The dismissal of marginalized people's individual and collective experiences, contemporarily and historically, often positions us in an able-mindedness borderlands of sorts, close to being pushed even further into the margins.[6] In other words, both disabled and nondisabled people from marginalized groups are accused of behaving outside the realm of able-mindedness as a way of denying or erasing marginalized experiences of the world.

To take an example, in her extensive history of the medical abuse of black people, Harriet A. Washington writes, "Historically, African Americans have been subjected to exploitative, abusive, involuntary experimentation at a rate far higher than other ethnic groups. Thus, although the heightened African American wariness of medical research and institutions reflects a situational hypervigilance, it is neither a *baseless* fear of harm nor a fear of imaginary harms. A 'paranoid' label is often affixed to blacks who are wary of participating in medical research. However, not only is *paranoid* a misnomer but it is also symbolic of a dangerous misunderstanding [of this history of African American experiences with medical professionals]" (21; original emphasis). Washington argues there is a cultural misunderstanding of the historically valid reasons why African Americans may not trust doctors and hospitals; however, in his history of schizophrenia, Metzl writes that in the 1950s doctors "reflexively read mistrust of medical authority as a symptom of mental illness" in black men (87). These two quotes illustrate how marginalized people's reactions toward institutions which have historically inflicted violence on them have not only been dismissed, but have also been used as indicators of mental disability. It is only possible for this racist tactic to be effective if ableism, which discriminates against and devalues those considered to be disabled, is also in effect. That is, labeling black people's distrust of medical authority as mental disability can only be a dismissal of the legitimacy of this distrust if mental disability is, via ableism, understood as something that negates the validity of an individual's experience of the world. This then is how both able-mindedness and mental disability (and the borderlands in between) are shaped not only by ableism, but also racism, sexism, and other oppressions. I want to be clear here that I am not equating race and gender with (dis)ability, nor am I denying that experiences of oppression can cause or exacerbate mental disability; rather, I am arguing that these categories mutually inform one another.[7] Ableism is used discursively in the name of racism and sexism against nondisabled people of color, women, trans- individuals, and gender-nonconforming people so that "racialized and gendered bodies are marginalized by norms of able-mindedness and used as markers against which able-minded normalcy is upheld" (Taylor 183). When black feminist, critical race, and gender studies scholars leave unchallenged the social construction of able-mindedness, accepting that able-mindedness is a necessary precursor to having racialized and gendered experiences of reality validated and recognized, we leave intact the very ableism being used against us. [8]

Like the discursive use of (dis)ability in antebellum scientific racism, the deployment of mental (dis)ability in contemporary discourses of race and gender also has material effects on bodyminds, including, as *Stigmata* suggests, subjection to the psychiatric medical-industrial complex, and, as I will discuss more in the conclusion, the use of extreme force by police when encountering black people. By representing a variety of differing realities, speculative fiction has the ability to critique the denial of individual experiences of reality without suggesting that mental disability is not real and without denying that different experiences of reality can be painful, frightening, or otherwise difficult. As my reading of *Stigmata* demonstrates, black women's speculative fiction can engage cultural associations between differing realities and mental disability in order to critique the ableism, racism, and sexism that collectively socially construct able-mindedness with real material consequences.

Stigmata

Stigmata has received very little critical attention in comparison to texts like Butler's *Kindred* and Toni Morrison's *Beloved*—likely because Perry has not published work since *Stigmata*'s prequel, *A Sunday in June*, came out in 2004. When scholars have engaged the text, however, it is typically in connection to these other two major black women's speculative fictional neo–slave narratives. Similar to the interpretations of *Kindred* discussed in chapter 1, the main character Lizzie's disability has been frequently interpreted as a metaphor for the impact of slave history on contemporary black people and on black women in particular.[9] Some scholars, however, emphasize the material nature of Lizzie's scars. Camille Passalacqua, for example, contends that "Lizzie's body and its scars are concrete" and not "merely symbols of traumatic memory," while scholars such as Lisa A. Long, Pamela B. June, and Stefanie Sievers have each drawn attention to the nonmetaphorical role of medicine and psychiatry in the text (Passalacqua 115). In this section, I respond to and build on this existing scholarship by bringing the role of (dis)ability to the foreground of the analysis.

In my interpretation of *Stigmata,* I focus primarily on Lizzie, but also include discussion of her ancestors Ayo and Grace. I argue that disability here takes on a multilayered representational pattern that cycles between metaphor and materiality. First, Lizzie's multiple consciousnesses are symbolic of the legacy of slavery on contemporary African Americans, *and* they are, in the speculative fictional context of the novel, literally real within and upon her bodymind. In this literal sense, Lizzie experiences her multiple consciousnesses as disabling, but unlike *Kindred*'s Dana, who loses an arm and knows she cannot tell anyone how, Lizzie tries to explain her experiences and is read as delusional, as disabled in a different way. Lizzie is then interpreted as mentally disabled by those around her and institutionalized. As a result, in this second layer of metaphor and materiality, Lizzie's experience of a psychiatric institution provides an additional metaphor for the dismissal of historical knowledge and the afterlife of oppression as well as a direct material critique of the social construction of able-mindedness and the ableist, racist, and sexist practices of the psychiatric medical-industrial complex. My reading of the novel is divided into two parts: the first part briefly addresses Lizzie's experience of multiple consciousnesses and its consequences, and the second part more fully details outsider interpretations of Lizzie's experience of multiple consciousnesses and their consequences.

Lizzie's experience of being mentally and physically inhabited by her ancestors and experiencing moments from their previous lives has been referred to by critics in various ways: as reincarnation, stigmata, "communal consciousness," "simultaneity of experiences," "re-embodiment," and even "supernatural powers" (Long 471; Sievers 136; June 51; Duboin 295). I choose to refer to Lizzie's experience as multiple consciousnesses because Lizzie is neither Ayo nor Grace, but Ayo and Grace are within Lizzie as something akin to spirit or souls, multiple and separate within one bodymind. That said, there is a fluid connection, an unstable blending and separating of consciousnesses that occurs throughout the novel. At times, Ayo, Grace, and Lizzie seem distinct and at other moments, they seem to be one, or at least have influence on each other. For example, at times Lizzie speaks to and behaves in a motherly way toward her own mother, who is Grace's daughter. The word *multiple* within the term *multiple consciousnesses* therefore represents not only when Lizzie, Grace, and Ayo exist as three distinct entitites, but also when they blur together, and thus the multiple ways in which their consciousnesses exist separately *and* together.

Lizzie's experience of multiple consciousnesses also includes *rememory,* a term that originally comes from Morrison's *Beloved* and has been taken up as a theoretical concept for understanding both fictional and real-life experiences. Ashraf H. A. Rushdy defines rememory as "a mental-spatial structure where what happened in one place at one time to one person becomes experientially available at another time for another person" (*Remembering Generations* 6). While in *Beloved* rememory represents something a bit less tangible, more internally visual and emotional, in *Stigmata* rememory becomes more literal, direct, and physical.[10] After receiving a trunk containing a quilt once owned by her grandmother, Grace, and journals once owned by her great-great-grandmother, Ayo, Lizzie begins inexplicably to have vivid visions of Grace's and Ayo's life experiences (though she does not realize that they are specific to these women initially). As mentioned above, Lizzie also hears the voices of Ayo and Grace speaking to her as if inside her head. Each of these ancestors experienced multiple consciousnesses as well, so this nonrealist disability is hereditary, although it skips a generation, only appearing in the next individual after the last ancestor with multiple consciousnesses has died. At first Lizzie fights to make the visions and voices disappear as she begins to experience their fear and anxiety, but later she starts to physically relive experiences, which leaves fresh bruises and cuts on her body. I refer to these experiences collectively, the visions, voices, emotions, and physical moments, as *rememories* both because I think the term is particularly appropriate to describe a connection across generations that cannot be explained in religious, spiritual, psychological, or metaphysical terms alone and because using rememory emphasizes how Perry draws on a genealogy of black women's speculative fictional neo–slave narratives to construct her novel. When Lizzie experiences a rememory, she recognizes the experience as that of Ayo's life or Grace's, but once Lizzie has lived through the rememory, the experience is also now hers as well. Similarly, even after death, Ayo and Grace gain new experiences through Lizzie. In *Kindred* only Dana and, inadvertently, Kevin, travel back and forth in time between two specific periods. Through Perry's take on rememory, however, Lizzie, Ayo, and Grace all move in multiple ways among and between their three respective time periods and lives. This representation of time travel is not only multidirectional, but also simultaneously psychic and physical. Although Lizzie and Grace have the rememories of Ayo's past, they do not live through it themselves. Instead, they reexperience it as Ayo did, with no ability to act different or change it, inevitably enduring the physical consequences of this reliving as well.

Lizzie experiences her multiple consciousnesses and psychic time travel as disabling. From her first rememory in the form of a dream to her experience of Ayo's slave chains on her wrists which causes her parents to institutionalize her, Lizzie experiences pain, memory loss, lack of control or awareness of her behavior, terrifying feelings of being trapped, damaged relationships, and disruption of life activities, such as her inability to finish college or hold a job. These effects of Lizzie's multiple consciousnesses lead me to read her experience as a disability in the text. It is a mental difference with physical, emotional, and social effects that Lizzie experiences as impeding her daily life activities. As will be discussed, Lizzie's multiple consciousnesses are also medicalized and pathologized by many people around her and considered a nonnormative way of being in her society (the American South between 1974 and 1996). The pathologization and institutionalization of Lizzie is foreshadowed by Grace's narrative. In portions of the novel devoted to Grace, readers learn that once Grace began having her rememories from Ayo she was so afraid that she was losing her mind and that her husband would institutionalize her that she ran away from home, leaving her three small children behind (57).[11]

Throughout the rest of my analysis I will refer to Lizzie's multiple consciousnesses as her disability, which is later misread and pathologized by other characters in the text as a different, unnamed mental disability. In calling Lizzie's multiple consciousnesses a disability and not putting disability in scare quotes to trouble or discount it, I am taking the speculative fictional world of *Stigmata* on its own terms and recognizing the reality of Lizzie's experience in the text, even though this experience breaks the rules of our contemporary reality. As discussed in the introduction to this book, this approach is an important part of reading speculative fiction, particularly nonrealist representations of (dis)ability in which bodyminds do not adhere to our expectations in a variety of ways. It is completely plausible that Lizzie's experience of multiple consciousnesses *could* have been represented as simply exciting or indeed as a sort of superpower, but it's not. It is represented as a disability with mental, physical, and social manifestations, and in order to understand Lizzie's disability in all its complexity, we must read within the representational structure and rules set up by the text. Note here that I am referring only to Lizzie's experience of multiple consciousnesses as a disability. For Grace, during her life, sharing consciousness with Ayo was also disabling, but it seems that in afterlife, both she and Ayo share consciousnesses with Lizzie in ability-enhancing ways. Grace and Ayo do not seem to automatically reexperience their past pain when Lizzie experiences one of their rememories—though at one point Grace is described as stepping in to take a blow for Lizzie during an Ayo rememory (125). Further, Grace uses her shared consciousness with Lizzie to obtain forgiveness from her daughter—Lizzie's mother—for leaving her. Ayo and Grace are able to communicate and connect with their family members through this shared multiple consciousness even as Lizzie experiences it as a disability. By calling Lizzie's specific experience a disability I am not marking her with a medical or pathological label; rather, I am acknowledging the materiality of her experience without claiming that this experience is inherently negative or should automatically be subject to outside treatment. Further, this label of disability does not preclude my ability to similarly recognize the metaphorical power of Lizzie's experience of multiple consciousnesses. Like Dana's amputated arm, Lizzie's disability can also be understood to represent how present-day African Americans are impacted by the legacy of slavery—a history that is deeply undergirded, as discussed in chapter 1, by the mutual constitution of blackness and disability.

In addition to the concrete disabling experience of multiple consciousnesses in the text, Lizzie also has to endure how her disability and its symptoms are interpreted by those around her. When Lizzie manifests on her wrists the wounds of Ayo's experience of being chained, her parents believe she has attempted to kill herself. Lizzie is subsequently institutionalized at age twenty and not released for fourteen years. She is read and labeled as disabled in a different way than she is actually disabled, resulting in forced psychiatric institutionalization and treatment. This is not to say that if the doctors had recognized her disability for what it was—if her diagnosis was "correct," as it were—that institutionalization would have been appropriate. Lizzie's experience of multiple consciousnesses is denied and dismissed because it does not fit into societal understandings of reality in regard to time and subjectivity. Lizzie's disability can only be understood by others in the text when it is labeled as mental disability. As a result, Lizzie is not given support in a way that could have been beneficial for coping with her multiple consciousnesses since her reality is presumed to not actually exist. The possibility of treatment here is not the issue; rather, the problem is the inability to understand differing realities as anything but insanity that must be contained and eradicated through institutionalization, isolation, and forced pharmaceutical treatment. Lizzie's narrative commentary throughout the novel provides an ironic and wry response to the consistent misrecognition and outright denial of her multiple consciousnesses and her resulting differing reality, creating a critique of the psychiatric medical-industrial complex and the social construction of able-mindedness.

Lizzie's fourteen years of institutionalization, between November 1980 and June 1994, are not frequently represented in the text. Only four of twenty-six chapters depict Lizzie during her institutionalization.[12] Of the twenty-two-year span of Lizzie's life represented in the novel (ages fourteen through thirty-six), twelve years go unrepresented, and eight of those twelve years take place during her time in psychiatric hospitals. This relative quiet about Lizzie's experience in institutions is not mentioned in other critical work on the novel, although Duboin has claimed that the narrative disruptions in time are "suggestive of Lizzie's failing memory" (296). I argue, however, that the narrative structure and gaps in timeline emphasize not Lizzie's faulty memory, but rather the difficulty of or hesitancy toward representing her experience of institutionalization since the majority of the gaps are from that period of her life. These narrative gaps then are not disruptions, but purposeful silences that replicate Lizzie's choice to not speak for several years while in the psychiatric hospitals. Further, the structure of the novel creates a nonlinear narrative that, as Sievers argues, "blurs the distinctions between normalcy and insanity by placing Lizzie's thoughts before, during, and after her hospitalization next to each other" (134). Similarly, Passalacqua contends that "Lizzie's first-person narration makes it difficult for readers to believe that she is as crazy as the doctors in the mental hospitals suggest" (144). I argue, therefore, that the silences and nonlinear timeline together demonstrate how both the narrative structure and content of Stigmata critique the psychiatric medical-industrial complex and the social construction of able-mindedness. Additionally, similar to the way Kindred's narrative structure represents Dana as disabled, then nondisabled, and disabled once more, the narrative structure of Stigmata also allows for a disruption of a linear conceptualization of disability as unidirectional loss.

From the four chapters that do represent Lizzie's institutionalization, readers learn some important information. During her time in three different hospitals, Lizzie spends two years not speaking. At some point during those two years, she has a rememory of Ayo being whipped and manifests those wounds on her back. After this rememory occurs, its effects are interpreted as another suicide attempt and Lizzie is given four shots of an unnamed drug per day while being supervised twenty-four hours a day for two weeks (Stigmata 175). Also during her period of silence Lizzie receives recognition of her multiple consciousnesses from another institutionalized woman who says she saw Lizzie "leave" and another woman take her place when Lizzie experiences a rememory (162–63). Multiple times during her institutionalization Lizzie is represented as not being believed by the doctors and being angry about the way they treat and talk to her. Finally, at one hospital Lizzie meets a visiting priest who introduces her to the concept of stigmata, the manifestation of the wounds of Christ on the bodyminds of true believers. While Lizzie is not religious, she relates to the concept of having bodily effects from a deep psychic and affective connection with the traumatic and painful experiences of another. It is then implied that the concept of stigmata helps Lizzie begin to understand and live with her disability better since she brings it up to her doctors as an explanation for her experience that she finds more acceptable than their psychiatric diagnoses.

Critics of *Stigmata* have found the pathologization of Lizzie's experience by her family and doctors to be representative of larger social and theoretical issues, particularly regarding race and gender. These black and women-of-color feminist approaches insist on what disability studies scholars might resist: an understanding of *Stigmata*'s representation of the treatment of Lizzie's disability as a metaphor for the experiences of black and female bodyminds within medical discourses historically. For example, Duboin argues that Lizzie's father and doctors "epitomize the hegemonic scientific mind, the patriarchal will to control one's environment through 'objective' and reassuring rationalization," and that the nonrealist elements of the text allow it to challenge this "gendered Cartesian discourse that tends to 'hystericize' rather than 'historicize' the uncontrollable black female body that remembers" (285). June contends that the doctors' refusal to believe Lizzie's explanation of her experiences "may be indicative of a systematic white guilt and/or denial of the severity of slavery and its legacy" (57). Similarly, Long's interpretation, which includes a comparison to *Kindred*, also points toward concerns with Western medical discourses historically and contemporarily. Long writes, "Both Butler and Perry illustrate the way that those who insist on the less savory aspects of American history are pathologized by our culture. . . . But the turn to fantastic history and their characters' concomitant 'sickness' is not surprising when one considers the many ways that African Americans have been scripted as diseased, enfeebled, infantile, or hyperviolent by the American medical community" (247).

Each of these interpretations of Lizzie's institutionalization and pathologization gesture toward the intersectional historical relationship of Western medical discourses and the treatment of black and/or female subjects. Yet they also read Lizzie's treatment due to her disability as emblematic of racist and sexist tendencies within the history of American medicine in a way that skirts (dis)ability as an intersecting social system in that history.[13] Scholarship on *Stigmata*, therefore, tends to read the violence inflicted on Lizzie as racist and sexist rather than as ableist and racist and sexist. That is, they interpret the discourses of (dis)ability being used to institutionalize Lizzie as nonexplicit enactments of racism and sexism—as methods of oppressing black women without directly indicting blackness or femininity. Such purely metaphorical readings of disability occlude the ways discourses of (dis)ability, race, and gender are always already implicated in the others. The novel's insistence on the mutually constitutive nature of these systems is even more evident in its more literal and material critiques of the social construction of able-mindedness and the psychiatric medical-industrial complex.[14] Once again, black women's speculative fiction reimagines the possibilities of bodyminds in a fashion that changes the rules of analysis, insisting on disability as metaphorical and material and as intimately tied to race and gender.

There are numerous ways in which *Stigmata* attempts to deconstruct able-mindedness and critique the psychiatric medical-industrial complex. Throughout the novel Lizzie is critical and skeptical of the mental health professionals around her. From the start, Lizzie shows annoyance with her therapist, stating that she can recognize "that certain note in a shrink's voice that says, 'You're crazy and I'm not'" (*Stigmata* 2). She even seems to pity his smug sense of accomplishment in her release, narrating, "He is so sure he's cured my madness . . . Poor guy. He doesn't know there is no cure for what I've got" (6; original ellipsis). During her institutionalization, Lizzie initially resists the doctors' diagnoses and endures forced pharmaceutical therapies. Eventually, however, she realizes the futility of her resistance and begins to play along, stating that "all you have to do is a little pretending and bam!"— privileges result (206). This pretending is ultimately what gets Lizzie released. She gathers "up the lies necessary for [her] escape," saying, "I've polished my story of redemption and restored mental health—the one responsible for my impending freedom" (4, 5). This polished story is Lizzie's false admission that she indeed made up everything, that the rememories were just bad dreams, and that she herself had inflicted her wounds. Sievers argues that by deciding to fabricate a story that adheres to the normative expectations of the doctors, Lizzie gains some measure of control and self-protection in a situation in which her agency is severely restricted (135). This control and self-protection, however, are still limited, and the novel makes this clear to readers.

While Lizzie's lies do get her family visits, offsite privileges, and eventually her release, the chapters representing the period after her discharge remind us that the power and control of the psychiatric medical-industrial complex still loom over her life. In a postinstitutionalization therapy session, Lizzie tells the doctor that she is angry at him for taking her father's money to ask inane questions and, she continues, "because on a whim you can decide that this outburst warrants another visit to the crazy house for me" (91). Here the critique of the psychiatric medical-industrial complex is evident. Not only do mental disability labels keep Lizzie in the system and continually drain her father's money, but too much resistance to her continued follow-up treatment could be considered grounds to reinstitutionalize her and keep her isolated, drugged, and confined for good. This critique aligns both with postpsychiatry approaches to bodyminds and with the arguments against the psychiatric medical-industrial complex made by survivors, consumers, and ex-patients movements which reject the notion that pharmaceutical treatments should be the first line of treatment and insist that there should be no forced treatment of any kind. [15]

In the same moment in which Lizzie expresses anger with the doctor's ability to reinstitutionalize her "on a whim," she continues by saying, "And yes, I can still get angry without getting crazy, if you know what I mean" (91). Lizzie's insistence on the difference between being/getting angry and being/getting "crazy" is a prime example of how *Stigmata* deconstructs able-mindedness. Lizzie's emphasis on her right to sane anger also alludes to the trope of the angry black woman who is represented as outside the confines of socially sanctioned able-minded behavior and instead within "the territory of pathological resistance, embodying a lack of self-control, an unwillingness to cooperate, or an inability to be reasonable" (Taylor 186). Here *Stigmata*'s critique of the social construction of able-mindedness, therefore, includes reference to its racialized and gendered nature. That is, the novel highlights the ways in which certain emotions and behaviors—here anger—are represented as pathological and dangerous, yet also inherent and natural among particular populations such as black women.

Throughout the novel Lizzie refers to herself and her situations as "crazy" in wry and ironic ways. For example, when questioning the intentions of Anthony Paul, a man who wants to date her, Lizzie thinks, "Perhaps the crazy girl is a novelty to him" (*Stigmata* 108). Adult Lizzie takes up the term *crazy* throughout the novel, but never in a way that seems defeatist or compliant to psychiatric norms. It is only young Lizzie and young Grace who, when first experiencing and trying to understand their rememories from Ayo, question their experiences of reality (119, 38). Through ironic self-uses of the term *crazy*, Lizzie challenges the meaning of the word and disidentifies with it. When her mother won't say the word, Lizzie completes the sentence for her, saying, "Crazy? You can say that if you want, Mother. Of course, just because I know you think I'm crazy doesn't mean *I* think I'm crazy" (67; original emphasis). Here Lizzie reveals her nonplussed awareness of others' perceptions of her as well as her own rejection of such views.

The novel's critique of the social construction of able-mindedness comes to the fore in a moment between Lizzie and her cousin Ruth, the first person whom Lizzie tells about her multiple consciousnesses. After listening to Lizzie recount her rememories and question her own sanity, Ruth says that sanity "is a mutual agreement between folks trying to control their world" (192). She further elaborates, "Men used to lock up women in asylums because the woman wanted to wear trousers or because they decided they didn't want to be good Christian matrons anymore. The definitions of sanity change every day" (192). Here the novel clearly indicates that it is not only Lizzie who challenges the definition of able-mindedness and mental disability. Others in the text also insist that able-mindedness is socially constructed by hegemonic powers of race and gender as well as (dis)ability.

Eventually, Lizzie performs a socially acceptable version of able-mindedness in order to get out of the institution, but she is still disabled because she still experiences multiple consciousnesses; she has simply learned how to live with her acquired nonrealist disability. As Lizzie states at the beginning of the novel, "I'm acutely aware of having made it to the end. I'm at the end of the pain and the yelling, the crying and the cringing. The voices no longer hound me. My world is neat and unstained. There is no more blood, but there are scars" (2). This quotation illustrates that Lizzie is still disabled, still marked by her bodymind differences, but her disability is no longer as debilitating and difficult now that she has gained control of—or perhaps created peace with—Ayo and Grace. And also, of course, now that she is no longer institutionalized against her will. At the culmination of the plotline, Lizzie is not cured, but she has adapted.

Stigmata ends, in terms of the linear timeline, with a functioning disabled black woman protagonist, but the book's closing chapter indicates that perhaps life after the novel will not go so well. The last chapter of the book does not depict a present-day adult Lizzie postinstitutionalization as one might expect in a traditional linear plot. Instead, the final chapter is set in March 1988 in Birmingham, Alabama, in the middle of Lizzie's fourteen years of institutionalization. This brief final chapter depicts Lizzie in art therapy group, painting a dark picture of a brown girl standing at the railing of a ship, assumedly a young Ayo on a slave ship. This representation of Lizzie in therapy is interspersed with italicized rememories from Grace. The final chapter depicts disability in both Lizzie's and Grace's disabling experiences of multiple consciousnesses with Ayo and in the traumatic experience of Lizzie's disability being labeled as a mental disability requiring institutionalization and forced treatment. *Stigmata* closes with Lizzie still in the midst of her oppressive and frightening experiences rather than at the end of it.

Sievers suggests that the book's ending is an indication of potential negativity in Lizzie's future (138). I would argue, however, that the final institutionalization setting can be read in several ways, not all of which are negative. The scene could be interpreted as a potential return of the disabling consequences of Lizzie's multiple consciousnesses, either for Lizzie or for her descendants. It could also indicate a possible return of forced institutionalization which, as noted above, Lizzie recognizes is a real possibility if she does not continue to adhere to social expectations of able-mindedness, including attending therapy. However, I contend that, as part of the novel's critique of the psychiatric medical-industrial complex, this final scene additionally suggests alternative modes of emotional and psychic healing available to black women outside the traditional confines of the psychiatric system.

The final chapter is chronologically the latest of the chapters that take place in Lizzie's past and marks the beginning of a five-year gap in time, the largest one in the plotline, since the next chronological chapter would be the first present chapter, chapter 1, set in June of 1994. This structure gestures toward the circularity of time and experiences in the novel. The final chapter therefore marks the beginning of the largest gap or silence in the novel's timeline, and I read this particular sustained silence through Kevin Everod Quashie's concept of quiet. According to Quashie, quiet can be understood as a metonym for "the full range of one's inner life—one's desires, ambitions, hungers, vulnerabilities, [and] fears," which stands in contrast to the highly public, loud, and visibly resistant nature typically associated with black culture (6). Chapter 26 of *Stigmata* likely represents part of the two-year period in which Lizzie chooses not to speak and thereby accesses her quiet in a purposeful, conscious, and sustained way. [16] At the same time, the chapter shows Lizzie engaging in artistic practices, painting the shared rememory that she is not—within the psychiatric institution—able to speak about openly as part of her reality. I read this chapter then as primarily suggesting that part of what helped Lizzie move from a debilitating experience of multiple consciousnesses to an adapted place of peace with Grace and Ayo—and thus with her disability—is her chosen quiet and engagement with alternative forms of expression through art.

As Quashie contends, "The act of imagining is the practice and willingness to dream, speculate, or wonder, and it helps us to move beyond the limits of reality . . . imagination *is* interiority, an aspect of interiority that constitutes an essential agency of being human" (42; original emphasis). In art therapy Lizzie is able to use her interior space to process her rememories without making claims that those experiences are her own, since claims to such a reality would position her outside the boundaries of able-mindedness. It is through the quiet process of this creative medium that Lizzie is able to do her own healing and get to a place where she is prepared to effectively navigate the restrictions of the psychiatric medical-industrial complex through her performance of socially sanctioned able-mindedness. This final scene then not only indicates the possibility of negativity in Lizzie's future, but also suggests that black women's need to deal with the reality of their bodyminds and social circumstances might be alternatively satisfied through quiet and art rather than through the psychiatric medical-industrial complex. The relationship of art/craft/imagination and healing is further apparent in the fact that both Ayo and Grace also use artistic expression—journal writing/storytelling and quilting, respectively—to process their experiences. [17] Lizzie herself uses quilting to help heal the relationship between herself and her mother and between her mother and Grace. This point about alternative methods of healing and well-being outside of the medical and psychiatric industrial complexes seems particularly important for black feminist theories of (dis)ability. Ann Folwell Stanford writes that authors such as Toni Cade Bambara, Paule Marshall, and Gloria Naylor depict what she calls "unnamed," and what I would call nonrealist, illnesses and diseases among black women characters in order to "challenge medicine to look at the context in which patients live and from which their illnesses may spring, and . . . raise the question of medicine's limits and of its place in the healing enterprise" ("Mechanisms of Disease" 41). I argue that

Stigmata is an additional example of how black women writers of speculative fiction address the "socially bound nature of" (dis)ability, disease, medicine, health, and healing (29). This closing with art therapy is additionally important from a disability studies perspective because it suggests a way of operating outside of the medical or disease models of disability by presenting an ending that does not cure or eradicate disability, but rather comes to find peace, balance, and acceptance within it—suggesting that representations of healing are not inherently ableist.

Conclusion

Stigmata uses nonrealist conventions of speculative fiction, such as time travel, and theories and concepts from a genealogy of black women's writing, such as rememory, to critique the social construction of able-mindedness and the psychiatric medical-industrial complex in direct connection to the legacies of slavery. *Stigmata* demonstrates how able-mindedness is constructed through racial and gendered norms and the resulting effect of this construction on black people, especially black women. Additionally, by insisting that experiences of reality are impacted by (dis)ability, race, and gender and also revealing how discourses of able-mindedness are used to discount disabled, racialized, gendered experiences of the world with often damaging material results, *Stigmata* engages with issues deeply important to our time. In 2012, after the murder of Trayvon Martin, a black teenage boy in Florida, the Black Lives Matter movement began, which was at first primarily represented by the hashtag #BlackLivesMatter on Twitter. The movement then became active in more-public demonstrations, including marches, protests, and die-ins, in 2014 after the highly public murders of Michael Brown in Missouri and Eric Garner in New York and the lack of indictments or guilty verdicts in their, and Martin's, cases.

Although the Black Lives Matter movement responds to the general lack of respect for and valuing of black lives in America, it has been particularly focused on police violence. While many mainstream and conservative media outlets wish to dismiss recent events as singular and unrelated, many people of color recognize that this violence is learned, systemic, and indicative of the racism still alive in this country. Black people, especially black men, are regularly represented and perceived as threats, as inherently existing outside or on the boundaries of able-mindedness because they are somehow dangerously lacking in self-control. In his 2015 grand jury testimony, police officer Darren Wilson, who shot and killed eighteen-year-old Michael Brown, stated that Brown "looked like a demon" before Wilson shot him (quoted in Cave). Also, in 2014, twelve-year-old Tamir Rice, who was shot and killed by Cleveland police within seconds of their arrival on the scene, was later described as "menacing" by Steve Loomis, president of Cleveland's police union (quoted in Schultz). Black people's positioning outside and on the borders of able-mindedness allows for violence justified through recourse to these often dehumanizing discourses of apparent danger and threat. Not unlike how discourses of disability were used to justify slavery and its related violence.

Black people's positioning outside of able-mindedness also allows for us to be disbelieved about our experiences of oppression, violence, and even of our own bodyminds. For example, in 2015, fifty-seven-year-old Barbara Dawson died outside of a hospital after medical professionals inside, unable to find the source of Dawson's pain and breathing difficulties, called the police to have her forcibly removed from the hospital despite her continued insistence that she was sick and unable to breathe (Gast et al.). Dawson collapsed on the ground in police custody due to, it was later determined, a blood clot in her lung; yet for twenty minutes police assumed she was faking and being "non-compliant" so they continued to order her get up and threatened her with jail as she slowly died before them (Gast et al.). The bulk of the encounter, including Dawson's heart-wrenching plea "Please don't let me die," was caught on the dashboard camera audio. Here, police and the medical-industrial complex come together in their biopolitical authority and in their interpretation of black people as being on the boundary of able-mindedness and thus not to be believed, again with deadly consequences.

While not all black Americans are directly, physically, impacted by police and medical violence in such extreme and deadly ways—though far too many of us are—the impact of violence against black people and its justification through discourses of able-mindedness and mental disability impacts even those of us whose class, skin tone, education, and other privileges might otherwise provide some semblance of protection. That is, as social media and other internet sites allow for the intense documentation and sharing of violence against black people by police and others, the emotional and psychic toll these events have on black people across the country and the world is material and real. As Venetria K. Patton writes, "A distinguishing component of cultural trauma is that one need not directly experience an event that induces trauma" (116). We have all seen and heard too many images—from the widely shared and viewed videos of the choking death of Eric Garner to the body-slamming of a black female student by school security at Spring Valley High School in South Carolina; from the audio of Barbara Dawson's death to the video of Philando Castile bleeding to death in his car after being shot by police in Minneapolis as his girlfriend and her four-year-old daughter watched. In our contemporary moment, smartphones, dashboard cameras, body cameras, and more allow for video and audio recording of violence against black people in exceptional, yet also quotidian ways. These video and audio recordings are then quickly shared and viewed widely via twenty-four-hour news stations and social media, making the concept of "direct" experience of cultural trauma more difficult to define when we can see and hear so clearly what has occurred (again and again). I remember clearly sitting in the Indianapolis airport on a four-hour weather delay a few days after the Castile murder. I sat charging my phone near an airport television on which CNN was playing. They played and replayed the video, showed and reshowed still images, again and again as a summer storm outside grounded all flights for hours. I had already seen the video. So each time, I turned my head and pumped up the music in my earbuds because I did not need to experience that trauma again. Not again. Yet even having to turn my head, having to look around to see so many people around me unmoved, either not even paying attention to the death on-screen or looking at it casually—even these things made me want to despair. There is the trauma of violence against black people—often justified through discourses of (dis)ability—the trauma of witnessing violence against black people, and the trauma of witnessing people not care about, be dismissive of, or shift the blame back onto us for violence against black people. Our contemporary age brings trauma in layers upon reverberating layers for black people.

The traumatic rememories of the murders of Martin, Brown, Garner, Rice, Dawson, Castile, and others whose names pile up faster than I can revise this conclusion each impact how contemporary black Americans experience reality. We have now all lived it and relived it. We live in various levels of fear of it. These rememories catch me whenever I see a police car behind me on the road or another black person pulled over or stopped on the street by police. Each time I wonder if it is about to happen again. Unlike Lizzie's reality, which was highly individual and difficult to show to or share with others, this reality of mine, of ours, is one that is readily evident in the news and on social media. Black fear of violence, especially police violence, is real, valid, and justified. Black anger about the implicitly sanctioned violence against black bodyminds in the United States is real, valid, and justified. As the Black Poets Speak Out members repeatedly insist in their videos and performances, we have a right to be angry.[18] But our cultural position outside or on the border of able-mindedness allows our fear and anger to be discounted and ignored. *You're just being paranoid. You're overreacting.*

Denials of systemic violence and dismissal of black fear and anger serve to deny the reality of black people and to continue to position us outside of able-mindedness through accusations of paranoia, overreaction, and unreasonableness. Ableism against those positioned outside of able-mindedness—people with mental disabilities—is therefore used to dismiss our reality as false and allow for the continuation of racist violence. In order to resist this racist dismissal of black realities, we must also challenge the ableism inherent in it. To be clear, I am not saying that black people's realities are equivalent to the realities of people with mental disabilities, but rather that some of the discourses used to discount and disbelieve both black people and mentally disabled people are based in ableism. As Metzl writes, "In unintended and often invisible ways, psychiatric definitions of insanity continue to police racial hierarchies, tensions, and unspoken codes in addition to separating normal from abnormal behavior. Sometimes, the boundaries of sanity align closely with the perceived borders of the racial status quo" (ix). Ableism and the social construction of able-mindedness have been and continue to be used as weapons of racist violence. A similar argument could be made in regards to contemporary rape culture and the constant questioning of the mental stability of sexual assault survivors before, during, and after their experiences of sexual violence in order to discount or dismiss their realities. Ableism and the social construction of able-mindedness are used here in the continuation of patriarchal sexual violence. Like *Stigmata,* these real-life examples demonstrate how ableism, racism, and sexism not only can intersect, but also can be deployed in service of one another. To interpret and respond to these overlapping, intersecting, and mutually constitutive oppressions, we must change the rules of academic and activist approaches to better include anti-ableism in antiracist and antisexist movements.

Perry's speculative fictional neo–slave narrative, *Stigmata,* highlights the role of (dis)ability, race, and gender in experiences of reality and critiques the discursive and material consequences of the social construction of able-mindedness. The novel engages how able-mindedness is upheld through racial and gendered norms and how such norms impact practices within the psychiatric medical-industrial complex. By representing (dis)ability, race, and gender in realities distinctly different from general expectations of the rules of reality, black women's speculative fiction demonstrates how ableism, racism, and sexism can not only interact in the lives of those multiply marginalized by these systems, but can also support, supplement, or act in place of one another in the lives of those typically oppressed by one system, but not another—as my discussion of contemporary violence against black people indicates. It is through reimagining the possibilities and meanings of bodyminds in nonrealist contexts that black women's speculative fiction highlights the mutual constitution of (dis)ability, race, and gender and its impact on so many of us in often oppressive and violent ways. In the next chapter, I shift the temporal focus from how black women's speculative fiction represents the relationship of (dis)ability, race, and gender in the past and present to how black women's speculative fiction imagines the ways these systems might operate in the future, requiring us to change how we interpret representations of future worlds.

3

THE FUTURE OF BODYMINDS, BODYMINDS OF THE FUTURE

The futures we imagine reveal the biases of the present; it seems entirely possible that imagining different futures and temporalities might help us see, and do, the present differently. —ALISON KAFER, *Feminist, Queer, Crip*

In response to a series of questions about writing, including the question, "Is there a particular picture of the world which you wish to develop in your writing?," Octavia E. Butler wrote, "Only the picture of a world, past, present, or future, that contains different races, sexes, and cultures. All too often in the past, sf writers made things easy for themselves by portraying a white, middle class, male dominated universe, even attributing white, middle class, male values to their 'alien' races. I am not comfortable writing about such a universe, behaving as though it represented the one true way . . . I want to portray human variety" (Octavia E. Butler Papers, "OEB 2390," 1978). Butler is known for her ability throughout her corpus of novels and short stories to address social issues in explicit and material ways. Patricia Melzer writes that within "Butler's work, difference is used as a tool of creativity to question multiple forms of repression and dominance . . . She always remains critical of unambiguous and seemingly unproblematic approaches to dealing with difference and power" (*Alien Constructions* 69). In Butler's futuristic and fantastical worlds, such as that of the *Parable* series, difference is not erased, but addressed directly. Since Butler is one of the most prominent black science fiction writers, one who also mentored and inspired many other writers from marginalized groups, her work is an important place to explore how black women writers of speculative fiction represent a diversity of bodyminds in the future.

By explicitly representing issues of (dis)ability, race, and gender in the future, Butler's work diverges greatly from many speculative fictional—and especially science fictional—representations of the future. In speculative fiction, visions of the future have traditionally been hopeful and positive, particularly when produced by early writers in the field, most of whom were male and almost all of whom were white. In an early critical study of science fiction, Robert Scholes and Eric S. Rabkin write that "because of their orientation toward the future, science fiction writers frequently assumed that America's major problem in this area—black/white relations—would improve or even wither away" (188). Mark Bould critiques this statement, claiming that by presenting racism as a problem of the past, nonapplicable to the genre's constructed futures, speculative fiction both excludes "people of color as full subjects" and "avoids confronting the structures of racism and its own complicity in them" (177, 80). Similarly, s. e. smith argues that, in "imagining a world that is better for humanity or hypothesizing about the grim consequences of our current society's misdeeds[, speculative fiction writers] can't seem to find a place in their framework for disability rights and dodge the issues by avoiding disability at all" (95). Absence of marginalized people has been common in the history of the genre and has been widely critiqued.

When speculative fiction has addressed issues of privilege and oppression in the imagined future, this has typically occurred in one of two ways. The first is by creating future worlds in which difference is not entirely erased; however, explicit issues of (dis)ability, race, gender, class, sexuality, and nation get displaced onto aliens, robots, and other nonhuman creatures who stand in allegorically for the Other without acting as a direct representation of any specific marginalized group.[1] The second way in which speculative fiction has traditionally addressed privilege and oppression in the future is through stories that take place not in the midst of struggling with the complexity of ableist, sexist, racist, classist, and homophobic oppressions, but rather after such problems have been resolved. For example, in Marge Piercy's much celebrated feminist, speculative-fictional utopian novel, *Woman on the Edge of Time,* sexism is eradicated by eliminating sex and gender roles, racism is solved by mixing all the races into one, classism is solved by a socialist structure of shared, equal resources, and ableism is erased by removing or curing all people with disabilities.[2] Discrimination and oppression based on difference is resolved here and in many speculative fictional futures through the erasure of difference altogether, or what smith refers to as an "eliminationist ideal" (89). This supposed solution to oppression, De Witt Douglas Kilgore argues, "enshrines white [nondisabled, heterosexual] masculinity, unmarked or troubled by culture . . . as the norm to which all 'difference' must assimilate" (231). While multiple forms of difference are erased in much speculative-fictional visions of the future, disability is perhaps the most unquestioned erasure.

In the contemporary United States, the cultural impetus when thinking about the future is to assume that technology will allow people to live longer while remaining stronger, healthier, and simply more (if not hyper-) able. A disability-free future, it seems, is a better future. Feminist disability studies theorist Alison Kafer argues that while this vision of the future is generally understood as positive and hopeful, underlying it are the ableist assumptions "that disability destroys quality of life, that a better life precludes disability, and that disability can and should be 'fixed' through technological intervention" ("Debating Feminist Futures" 234). The acceptance of the positive nature of a disability-free future, therefore, stems from the fact that many people cannot imagine the benefits or value of disability to society nor the benefits, value, or possible social contributions of disabled people.

New Wave and contemporary speculative fiction writers, particularly feminist writers and writers of color, have increasingly challenged traditional genre conventions of representing the future as one of sameness by insisting on the presence of marginalized people. These contemporary representations of the future by feminists, people of color, and, increasingly, disabled people tend to be dystopian, or at least less hopeful, than their earlier white male counterparts. This dystopian tendency of marginalized speculative fiction writers is connected to the history of technological, medical, and other scientific abuses of poor, female, nonwhite, and disabled people's bodyminds, knowledges, and lands. Writers from these groups have less reason to assume a utopian tomorrow and more reason to contemplate the many possible ways that power will be dispersed in our imagined futures.

In this chapter I argue that Butler's *Parable* series actively resists the concept of a technologically created, disability-free future and its assumed inherent value through the representation of a nonrealist disability called hyperempathy. Unlike representations of a disability-free future which understand disability as incompatible with a desirable or livable future, the *Parable* books represent a black disabled future heroine and theorize alternative possibilities of bodyminds that have important implications for scholars of (dis)ability, race, and gender collectively.

The *Parable* series (also referred to as the Earthseed novels) includes two texts, *Parable of the Sower* and *Parable of the Talents*. These books represent the life of Lauren Olamina, a black woman with hyperempathy, and her family and friends. *Parable of the Sower* depicts Lauren as a teenager between the years 2024 and 2027 through her first-person narrative journal entries. During this time Lauren is living in a dystopic California as America's social infrastructure is in decline and her walled-in community is destroyed, causing her to flee with a few other survivors and move north. The book details how Lauren, in the midst of this crisis, develops a belief system she calls Earthseed. She uses this belief system to ground and guide herself and others as they travel in an uncertain and dangerous environment. *Parable of the Sower* ends with Lauren and her small group of companions beginning a new community in northern California called Acorn. *Parable of the Talents* picks up on Lauren's story, but the structure of the novel disperses the narrative voice. In this second novel, Lauren's journals are interspersed with the first-person narratives of her husband, Bankole, her brother, Marc, and her daughter, Asha, depicting their experiences as well as the development of the Acorn community and Earthseed between 2032 and 2090.

Throughout the novels hyperempathy is experienced as disabling and understood as a disability by those characters who have it. Hyperempathy is also mostly understood as a disability by medical professionals and most other characters without hyperempathy. As a result, throughout this chapter I refer to Lauren's hyperempathy as her disability even while discussing how other scholars have interpreted hyperempathy in the novels. Most of the scholars I cite here, however, do not use the term *disability* at all. Instead, they tend to refer to hyperempathy as an affliction, condition, or disease—language that resides in the medical model of disability and is counter to the work of the disability rights movement to understand disability as simultaneously social, relational, and material. I refer to hyperempathy as a disability not only because I am working from a disability studies perspective, but also because differences in bodyminds in speculative fiction must be read within the rules of reality of the text. I use *disability* and *hyperempathy* interchangeably for linguistic variety throughout the chapter and only use other terms when directly quoting an author.

On a basic level, hyperempathy is a congenital disability in which visual and auditory perceptions result in drastic sensations of pleasure or pain
without any actual touch or contact with something or someone. Or, as
Lauren explains it, "I feel what I see others feeling or what I believe they
feel" (*Parable of the Sower* 12). Although doctors in the *Parable* series refer
to hyperempathy as an "organic delusion syndrome," hyperempathy is not
exclusively mental (12). Even the term *psychosomatic* does not do this fictional disability justice because the "somatic" of hyperempathy is not singular; rather, it is Lauren viscerally responding to her visual and auditory
interpretation of another person's bodily experience. The way hyperempathy exceeds our understanding of a mental versus physical disability makes
using the term *bodymind* especially important in this chapter. As discussed
in the introduction to this book, I draw my use of *bodymind* from Margaret
Price to reference the ways in which mind and body are not distinct yet
connected components of our being, but a single entity. In particular, Price
writes that the bodymind is "a sociopolitically constituted and material entity that emerges through both structural (power- and violence-laden) contexts and also individual (specific) experience" ("The Bodymind Problem
and the Possibilities of Pain" 271). Price's emphasis on sociopolitical circumstances, individual experience, violence, and pain, as she later discusses in
the article, is especially important in understanding hyperempathy. My use
of *bodymind* here is particularly apropos because Butler's papers reveal that
she was very much aware of this concept in terms of her own life as a person
who experienced a variety of health concerns and disability.[3] In a journal
entry dated June 22, 1969, Butler used the hyphenated term "mind-body"
(Octavia E. Butler Papers, "OEB 928"). In a later journal entry dated March
17, 1999, she argued that "dichotomies that become so important to us are
false. Mind and body for instance" (Octavia E. Butler Papers, "OEB 1069").
Butler's engagement with the concept of the *bodymind*—well before it was
a theoretical term in disability studies—is clear in her representation of
hyperempathy and therefore essential to my reading of the *Parable* series.

The representation of hyperempathy in the *Parable* novels theorizes the
possibilities and meanings of bodyminds, especially disabled bodyminds, in
a number of important ways which require a change in how we read and analyze these texts and their implications. The series resists preconceived notions about disability, emphasizes the importance of context to understanding a person's experience of disability, and, finally, challenges the assumed
inherently progressive value of a technologically created, disability-free fu-

ture. As a result, this series demonstrates another way that black women's speculative fiction imagines (dis)ability differently—indeed makes us interpret (dis)ability differently—and the benefit of such reimagining to not only theories of (dis)ability, but also theories of race and gender.

In what follows, I first discuss previous scholarly interpretations of hyperempathy, which I refer to as "totalizing" approaches—meaning that these interpretations emphasize clear intelligibility over ambiguity in reading this nonrealist disability. I explain how these interpretations limit understandings of the importance of (dis)ability to both the texts and the larger political and theoretical concerns of the *Parable* series. Second, I provide a close reading of hyperempathy in context in order to underscore why this approach is so necessary in speculative fiction. This second section demonstrates how reading disability in context—within the rules of reality of the texts—opens up new modes of analysis. Having introduced these new modes in regard to the *Parable* series, I then parse out the various theoretical and thematic implications of this particular representation of disability in the future. In this third section, I additionally demonstrate how my disability-focused reading draws attention to issues of the bodymind pertinent to theorizations of race and gender as well. By doing so, I provide further evidence as to how disability studies can provide essential theories and frameworks that benefit black feminist theory and related fields of inquiry. Finally, in the conclusion, I return to the idea introduced in the epigraph of this chapter, which connects our visions of the future to the biases and behaviors of the present. I explore how black women's speculative fiction, and speculative fiction by other marginalized people, finds value and possibility in futures with diverse bodyminds and how such fictional visions of the future can have real-world implications and impact.

Interpreting Hyperempathy: The Limits of Totalizing Approaches

In most discussions of hyperempathy, scholars explain that Lauren feels or experiences the pain and/or pleasure of those around her. This basic symptom-based description of hyperempathy does little to reveal its nuances or implications. This approach also does not prioritize Lauren's personal understanding and experience of hyperempathy beyond its manifestations within her bodymind. Lauren takes a very measured and, at times, ambivalent position regarding her disability, yet critical interpretations of hyperempathy have typically taken one of four totalizing approaches that present hyperempathy as having a clear meaning and impact. Generally, critics of the *Parable* series tend to ignore hyperempathy as disability entirely, read it as primarily negative, read it as primarily positive, or read it as a metaphor for something not related to disability. Very few scholars have taken the more nuanced approach that Lauren herself seems to embrace and which, I argue, demands changing the rules of interpretation in ways that expand our conceptualization of (dis)ability, especially in regard to its practical, political, and theoretical relationships to race and gender. In this section I will discuss each of the four common totalizing approaches to hyperempathy in order to demonstrate how they reduce the complexity and importance of disability in the series. This will thereby set the stage for my own argument that the texts insist on the contextualized nature of disability and reject cultural assumptions about the value of a technologically created, disability-free future.

The first totalizing approach is to ignore or erase hyperempathy as a disability entirely. There are different ways this occurs. First is when scholars do not mention Lauren's hyperempathy at all.[4] Second is when critics mention hyperempathy in passing as a character trait of Lauren, but do not include discussion of her disability in their interpretation of the texts. In both cases hyperempathy is understood by the critic to be of minor importance to Lauren's character and to the text as a whole, so much so that it's hardly worth mentioning. Another manifestation of the critical erasure of hyperempathy appears when critics do not register hyperempathy as a disability or outright deny Lauren being disabled. An example of this version of ignoring hyperempathy occurs in an interview with Butler by Juan Williams on National Public Radio's *Talk of the Nation*. In the interview Butler speaks about the smart pills in *Parable of the Sower*, explaining that Lauren's "mother was addicted to them, and as a result [Lauren] has a birth defect" (quoted in O. E. Butler, *Conversations with Octavia Butler* 163).[5] Williams responds in a fashion that reveals his ableist perspective. He retorts, "Well, hang on a second. What do you mean a birth defect? I think, in fact, she's very smart" (163). Butler replies. "Yes. Oh, I didn't say that she wasn't smart" (163). Here Williams denies that hyperempathy is a disability or "birth defect" because Lauren is smart. I understand such a denial of hyperempathy as disability to be part of the totalizing approach of ignoring hyperempathy because it operates from a related perspective. If, as I contend above, those who do not discuss hyperempathy much or at all understand Lauren's disability as an unimportant detail, then those who refuse to recognize hyperempathy as a disability do so because Lauren does not fit stereotypical notions of disabled people and therefore assume she cannot actually be disabled or, more colloquially, readers do not *think* of her as disabled. In both cases, disability is not viewed as a critical part of Lauren's character or essential to our understanding of the series as a whole. As a result, in these interpretations hyperempathy is essentially ignored.

A second approach scholars often take toward hyperempathy is to read it as a disability, which is primarily negative. In this approach scholars either read hyperempathy itself as mostly negative, painful, or burdensome for Lauren or they read Butler's inclusion of disability negatively. Those who view Lauren's disability as primarily negative includes scholars like Melzer, who refers to hyperempathy as an "affliction"; Jeff Menne, who refers to it as a "pathology" and "psychological delusion"; and Teri Ann Doerksen, who reads Lauren as a martyr due to her disability (Melzer, *Alien Constructions* 98; Menne 731, 32; Doerksen 22). Those who read Butler's use or creation of disability as negative include Trudier Harris, who claims that Butler makes Lauren disabled in order to force the reader to sympathize with or pity her, thereby coercing the reader into being forgiving of the fact that Lauren has to kill and does so, according to Harris, in an emotionally detached way (159–61). Collectively, these negative readings of hyperempathy reveal an entrenchment in hegemonic cultural narratives of disability as inherently bad, negative, painful, and difficult, whether the critic is making such claims directly or claiming, like Harris does, that Butler is attempting to play on the affective results of such stereotypes for pragmatic purposes. Either way, negative readings of Lauren's disability tend to do little to confront the stereotypes of disability that the novels actively resist. These negative readings also often do not engage with the ways in which Lauren's particular dystopian context impacts her experience of hyperempathy by increasing exposure to pain—something I will discuss in more detail in my own analysis.

The above types of negative readings of hyperempathy are generally fewer than the positive readings of Lauren's disability. This is likely because Butler is considered a progressive political writer and critics are invested in locating and revealing her work's liberatory potential. The tendency toward positive readings of Lauren's hyperempathy may also stem from what I would call a subtle or passive ableism. Representations of disability tend to provoke emotion, particularly pity or inspiration, and the positive readings of the *Parable* series may be influenced by a liberal compensatory desire to recast disability as "specialness," to incorporate it without actually grappling with the challenges of inclusion or the negative aspects that can accompany some experiences of disability. Many scholars have read Lauren's disability as something primarily positive. Benjamin Robertson refers to Lauren's hyperempathy as "otherwise enhanced physical abilities," while Kate Schaefer calls it "an odd psychic gift" (Robertson 370; Schaefer 184). Marlene D. Allen refers to hyperempathy as both a "gift" and the "ultimate power" because it is an "innate biological and psychological propensity for sharing and empathy" (1363). Gregory Jerome Hampton positions hyperempathy as an ability rather than a disability, writing, "Although Lauren initially views her ability as a disease, she does learn to appreciate her difference and uses it to help her become a more efficient leader and matriarch by the end of the narrative" (104). Scholars take this primarily positive approach despite the fact that Lauren insists that hyperempathy "isn't some magic or ESP" (*Parable of the Sower* 11). In *Parable of the Talents,* Lauren writes, "It is incomprehensible to me that some people think of sharing as an ability or a power" (33). Later in the second book, when Lauren meets Len, another sharer, this sentiment is repeated when Len says, "Some people think sharing is a power—like some kind of extrasensory perception," and Lauren responds, "You and I know it isn't" (341). All of these instances clearly indicate that Lauren and other sharers in the novels reject an inherently positive power/ability kind of reading of hyperempathy because such readings downplay the reality of their pain and vulnerability.

In addition to calling hyperempathy a gift and a power, scholars taking a positive totalizing approach have also emphasized how this disability supposedly makes Lauren a unique leader. Allen writes that hyperempathy makes Lauren "uniquely suited to lead her people out of bondage on Earth," while Isiah Lavender insists that hyperempathy "creates in her a profound sense of compassion . . . [which] grants her the wisdom to lead people" (Allen 1363; Lavender, *Race in American Science Fiction* 21–22). Similarly, Sandra Govan writes that Lauren "shows an ability to achieve difficult tasks . . . *because* of her disability," and Lauren J. Lacey argues that because Lauren "experiences the process of becoming other" through feeling others' pain and pleasure, her "'hyperempathy' makes her uniquely positioned to understand becoming, [and] creates an alternative discourse that answers to dominant power structures and that works from the concept of becoming" (Govan 116, original emphasis; Lacey 390, 91).[6] These scholarly claims that Lauren is uniquely situated to create the alternative belief system of Earthseed and lead people due to her disability ignore the fact that there are other sharers in the books who don't survive or don't become leaders like Lauren. Lauren writes that there were once tens of millions of sharers in the world, but that they generally have a "high mortality rate" (*Parable of the Talents* 13, 33). This information makes clear that hyperempathy itself is not inherently something that positions Lauren to become the shaper of the Earthseed belief system. By reading Lauren's disability as *the* reason for her life perspective and choices, these scholars reduce Lauren to her disability alone, and this approach, despite the positive spin, denies the complexity of Lauren's specific experiences which help her become a future leader in contrast to the many other sharers in the text who do not achieve such a position. On the surface, the positive readings of Lauren's hyperempathy seem useful and important for disability studies since they seem to be resistant to the stereotypes of disability to which the negative readings conform, but singularly or predominantly positive readings of hyperempathy are also problematic since they neglect important information about hyperempathy supplied by both Lauren and other sharers in the series. Some of these issues with positive totalizing readings of Lauren's disability are repeated in the metaphorical interpretations of hyperempathy as well.

Due to the nonrealist nature of hyperempathy, some scholars take a purely metaphorical approach to it, thereby obscuring the materiality of disability and its role in the plot, character development, and themes of the series. For example, Peter G. Stillman writes that Lauren "is the living embodiment of the subversion of differences; her hyperempathetic syndrome, where she feels what others feel, symbolizes the suspending of barriers and the creation of unity across them" (28). Taking a different metaphorical interpretation, Jerry Phillips argues that Lauren is "a symbolic negation of the psychopathology of atomized, corporate society" (306). Finally, using strikingly medicalized language, Jim Miller writes, "By turning profound compassion into an illness, Butler defamiliarizes our current indifference toward each other. Rather than something which needs to be healed, perhaps Lauren's 'syndrome' is the right medicine for our present 'compassion fatigue'" (357). Each of these metaphorical readings of hyperempathy understands Butler's choice to make Lauren disabled to be a pragmatic move not intended to demonstrate anything about (dis)ability or ableism, but to make readers think about other issues such as social barriers, cultural indifference, the need for connection, and the sociopolitical value of empathy. While these readings all hold important truths about the implications of Lauren's disability and Butler's authorial choices in constructing hyperempathy as she did, reducing disability to simply metaphor erases the material importance of hyperempathy to the series. As discussed in chapter 1, disability metaphors are not inherently ableist, but they function most effectively and least problematically when used to highlight the relationship of disability to other social issues, oppressions, and identities. Here, metaphorical readings of hyperempathy obscure what this speculative fictional disability might indicate to us about disability in the real world, especially in relationship to race and gender and visions of the future. As a result, this totalizing metaphorical approach to Lauren's disability tends to be reductive and to deflect from the centrality of disability to the *Parable* series.

All of the above scholarly interpretations of Lauren's disability ignore hyperempathy or overemphasize its negative, positive, or metaphorical aspects. These readings limit our understanding of disability in the novels by interpreting hyperempathy in relatively static ways that often ignore or contradict important information about this nonrealist disability provided by Lauren and other sharers in the novels. In the next section, I analyze the representation of hyperempathy in the *Parable* series within the specific context of Lauren's future dystopian world—that is, within the rules of reality of the novels. While my interpretation of the series connects to these previous approaches in various ways, it diverges greatly by insisting on the centrality of disability to the plot, character development, and thematic content of the series.

Disability in Context: A Close Reading

As we already know, hyperempathy is a nonrealist disability from a speculative fiction futuristic world. I argue that Butler's creation of hyperempathy encourages a non-, or at least less, ableist understanding of what disability entails and means particularly due to its nonrealist nature and futuristic setting. The nonrealist nature of hyperempathy, that is, the fact that it is not a disability we recognize in our current reality, disallows readers the ability to overlay preconceived notions about disabilities we recognize from our own world. In an article on the contemporary representation of autism in sentimental narratives, Stuart Murray contends that the increased cultural awareness of autism is tied to the increased representation of autism in contemporary fiction and film ("Autism and the Contemporary Sentimental"). These two cultural phenomena impact each other, creating a cycle of social knowledge in which nondisabled writers and actors supposedly know the experience of autism enough to recreate it and audience members similarly supposedly know enough about autism to recognize it in a character's behaviors and mannerisms. In the *Parable* series, readers cannot use such cultural knowledge, assumptions, or stereotypes to interpret Lauren and her disability since we have no previous knowledge of hyperempathy to apply. It is unlike anything in our reality thus far. Readers and critics are therefore forced to learn about and understand hyperempathy within the terms of the novels, which are primarily narrated by Lauren herself.

To fully understand Lauren's character and actions we must put her and her disability into the specific social, cultural, and historical context of the novels because one's experience of a disability is not only about physical and mental manifestations, but also about one's environment and the interaction between bodymind and society. Lauren is living in a dystopian California in the mid- to late twenty-first century where social infrastructures such as schools, police, fire services, and utilities are failing; where only the very rich living in walled-in communities can afford clean water, safe food, and effective medical care; where the middle class is nearly nonexistent; and where the growing poor population lives in either dangerous, squatter settlements or in company towns, working for room and board or confined as debt slaves. This context impacts how Lauren experiences her disability and her disability impacts how she experiences and negotiates this context. In addition to the direct bodymind effects of hyperempathy, which produces pain and pleasure for Lauren and other sharers when they witness such sensations in others, hyperempathy also indirectly influences Lauren's growth, behavior, and choices throughout the series. The first portion of my analysis, therefore, relies on close reading and examines how hyperempathy impacts Lauren beyond mere symptoms. I place Lauren's hyperempathy in the context of her dystopian futuristic setting and demonstrate how disability matters both to Lauren's character development and to the plot and themes of the novel overall.

The dystopian context of the *Parable* series is important for understanding Lauren's experience of hyperempathy because, as Lauren writes, "I'm supposed to share pleasure *and* pain, but there isn't much pleasure around these days" (*Parable of the Sower* 12; original emphasis). At the beginning of *Parable of the Sower* Lauren lives "in a tiny, walled fish-bowl cul-de-sac community" where she is "the preacher's daughter" (12). In this setting Lauren is protected from the major violence that occurs outside her community, but her pleasure is also limited—primarily coming from sex, first with a friend in the community and later with her (eventual) husband, Bankole. Lauren recognizes that the walled community protects her from experiencing the extremes of her disability, and that this protection is somewhat an illusion since the community is highly unprepared to protect itself from attacks, always teetering on the edge of survival. Lauren's brother, Keith, who runs away from home and lives outside of the walled community, confirms Lauren's concern, telling her, "Out there, you wouldn't last a day. That hyperempathy shit of yours would bring you down even if nobody touched you" (110). Indeed, Lauren learns much about the effects of context on her experience of hyperempathy once her walled community is attacked and she must survive in the outside world.

Outside her walled community Lauren quickly learns the necessity of killing a person (or animal) who is in great suffering near her in order to stop sharing the pain in her own bodymind. An injured or dying person can cause Lauren severe pain to the point of unconsciousness—something which would put her in extreme danger of being robbed, raped, and/or kidnapped. The dangers of being around the injured or dying also means that when dealing with hurt friends and loved ones, Lauren knows she may not be able to provide support or protection because she can become just as incapacitated as the injured person. Lauren admits that she may only be helpful to her travel companions for a few good shots when defending from attacks by other groups and then be "useless" afterward due to the pain (251, 78). As a result, Lauren discloses her disability to those who need to know, but is otherwise secretive about it since hyperempathy is not externally visible on the bodymind, but can easily be taken advantage of by others.

An example of such potential abuse is revealed later in *Parable of the Sower* when Lauren learns that sharers, especially children with hyperempathy, are targeted by company town bosses and kidnappers because they are considered easier to control. Company towns are supposed to be safer and more stable. As a result, company towns are theoretically places where people with hyperempathy who lack the security of a walled community might want to go. The knowledge of abuse, however, confirms Lauren's belief that company towns are just revitalized versions of indentured servitude and slavery. In *Parable of the Talents*, Lauren comes to learn from personal experience that abuse can further complicate her experience of hyperempathy when she is illegally imprisoned in a Christian America "re-education camp."[7] In the camp, Lauren learns to expect high levels of pain since prisoners are frequently overworked and lashed with electronic slave collars. Thus

Lauren must endure her own pain as well as that which she shares with the prisoners around her. However, in the context of the "re-education camp" Lauren also learns that even the sharing of pleasure can take on negative and traumatic valences in a dystopian setting. Her first instance of experiencing pleasure in a negative way occurs when she recognizes the sadist pleasure of her captors, referred to as "teachers" in the camp. She writes, "There have been times where I've felt the pleasure of one of our 'teachers' when he lashed someone. The first time it happened—or rather the first time I understood what was happening, I threw up. . . . it never occurred to me that I had to protect myself from the pleasures of our 'teachers'. . . . There are a few men here, though, a few 'teachers,' who lash us until they have orgasms" (233). Here Lauren reveals how this new context has made her aware of the need to protect herself from not only pain, but also pleasure that is derived from abusing someone—pleasure that, when shared, sickens her. The particular context of the Christian American camp—an even more dangerous and violent environment within the larger dystopia—produces a new experience of hyperempathy for Lauren that shapes how she negotiates and survives this setting, ideally without revealing her disability to her captors.

Lauren's sharing of pleasure is made even more negative and traumatic in a second instance during her illegal detainment by Christian America. Not long after being imprisoned in the reeducation camp, Lauren is one of four women taken by their captors at night and raped. She writes, "Of the four of us, only I was a sharer. Of the four of us, only I endured not only my own pain and humiliation, but the wild, intense pleasure of my rapist" (234). These two moments demonstrate how the context of Lauren's dystopian environment and her specific experience of imprisonment and rape shape her experience of her disability and vice versa. Overall, as Butler succinctly stated in an interview, "This is a rough disability *for her time*" (quoted in O. E. Butler, *Conversations with Octavia Butler* 42; emphasis added). Hyperempathy could theoretically result in more positive experiences of shared pleasure than shared pain, but the context in which Lauren is living makes her experience more prone to pain, abuse, and trauma.

My discussion of hyperempathy in the context of a future dystopian California here might seem to support the negative readings of hyperempathy from the previous section. Indeed, Lauren's experience of being a sharer in this time and place is highly negative, and yet, Lauren is the heroine of the series, a black disabled woman who becomes the leader of a powerful national belief community. Reading hyperempathy closely must thus entail understanding not only how Lauren's experience of this disability is impacted by her context, but also the ways in which her disability impacts her negotiation of that context as well.

One impact of hyperempathy is that Lauren is less likely to be violent and produce pain in other people or animals because she feels each act of violence as if she had done the harm directly to herself. Lauren views this as a sort of virtue of herself and other sharers. She cannot comprehend how people without hyperempathy can so easily do violence to one another. Regarding torture specifically she writes, "It's beyond me how one human being could do that to another. If hyperempathy syndrome were a more common complaint, people couldn't do such things. They would kill if they had to, and bear the pain of it or be destroyed by it. But if everyone else could feel everyone else's pain, who would torture? Who would cause anyone unnecessary pain? . . . I wish I could give it to people. Failing that, I wish I could find other people who have it, and live among them. A biological conscience is better than no conscience at all" (*Parable of the Sower* 115). In early drafts of this series, Butler's papers reveal that she originally considered making hyperempathy a contagious disease spread by fluid or skin contact. She wrote several drafts and fragments of chapters experimenting with this idea, but ultimately chose to make the disease genetic rather than contagious.[8] As a result, the ways in which hyperempathy impacts Lauren's experience and understanding of the world cannot be transmitted to others literally via bodily contact, but only intellectually through her faith community of Earthseed.

The tenets of Earthseed are influenced by Lauren's experience of hyperempathy. Some scholars, however, have read hyperempathy as being the exclusive or dominant impetus for Earthseed's development and success. For example, Phillips, noting Lauren's idea about the possibility of giving hyperempathy to people, writes that "in a hyperempathetic world, the other would cease to exist as the ontological antithesis of the self, but would instead become a real aspect of oneself, insofar as one accepts oneself as a social being. Earthseed is the practical ethics of this heightened consciousness of what it means to experience being as, irreducibly, being-with-others" (306). Like the predominantly positive readings of hyperempathy, Phillips's interpretation reduces Lauren, and also Earthseed, to disability alone and ignores the other important influences in Lauren's individual life and larger social context, which cannot be untangled from her experience of her disability. After all, Lauren is not the only person in the text who has hyperempathy, but she is the only one to become such a clear leader. Lauren's development and leadership of Earthseed is influenced by the fact that she grew up a precocious, well-educated black girl from a middle-class background. Lauren was also the oldest child in her family, always responsible for others, including other children in the walled community. Lauren served as a teacher for the youngest children in the neighborhood while her stepmother, who ran the community school, taught the older kids. This personal history influences Lauren's development and cannot be easily or clearly separated from how she is influenced by her experience of hyperempathy. It is important to read Lauren's creation and leadership of Earthseed in the context of the totality of her life and intersectional identities as a black disabled woman from an educated middle-class background. Hyperempathy is not the sole reason for Lauren becoming such a prominent figure by the end of the novels. That said, it is possible and desirable to read Lauren's disability as strongly influencing her development of the specifics of the Earthseed faith.

The influence of hyperempathy is particularly apparent in two of the primary tenets of Earthseed: adaptation and change. Sharers are forced to adapt to the unruly sensations of their bodyminds and to change their relationship to the world in order to protect themselves from harm. As Lauren notes, "Sharers who survive learn early to take the pain and keep quiet. We keep our vulnerability as secret as we can. Sometimes we manage not to move or give any sign at all" (*Parable of the Talents* 33). Although there is no direct parallel between hyperempathy and any contemporary realist disability, there is a definite connection between hyperempathy and chronic pain. In her discussion of pain and theories of transcendence, Susan Wendell writes how she has learned to recognize her chronic pain as "meaningless" pain, that is, pain without an exact cause or problem which can be attended to or fixed (173). This is not exactly the case for hyperempathy, since witnessing severe pain can cause real injury for a sharer, but Wendell insists that by coming to understand pain as meaningless she is able to free herself from thinking about pain to pay attention to other things, to undergo "a reinterpretation of bodily sensations so as not to be overwhelmed or victimized by it" (173). In the series, Lauren has the ability to focus, pay attention, and do work while in pain, an adaptation with living *with* pain or the possibility of pain. Specifically, Lauren writes that she has learned to handle higher levels of pain than most people without visibly reacting, but as a result she is also sometimes read as seeming "grim or angry" while trying to mask pain (*Par-*

able of the Sower 13). On an individual level, therefore, hyperempathy helps Lauren recognize the value of adapting, and this then gets translated on a more communal, species, and abstract level in the values of the Earthseed communities.

Connections between the tenets of Earthseed and disability are also evident in terms of larger disability rights and disability cultural values. Concepts such as adaptation and change can be found in both the Americans with Disabilities Act and the processes of universal design.[9] The Americans with Disabilities Act, which was passed in 1990, just three years before the publication of *Parable of the Sower,* requires accommodations for people with disabilities in areas such as employment and public transportation. The law has necessitated the adaptation of many buildings to include accessible features like ramps and push buttons to open doors. Similarly, universal design—originally an architectural concept that has since expanded into areas like education—seeks to create spaces and environments that are accessible to as many people as possible. Price argues that accessibility is a process not a product, something which is never done—thus the emphasis in universal design is on frequent, contextual, and relational adaptation and change based on who is present (*Mad at School* 88–102). We see similar emphasis on contextual and relational adaptation and change within the Earthseed communities, which encourage people to contribute to the community in the ways they are most talented. Earthseed communities like Acorn also make all decisions on a communal basis, allowing everyone to express their needs, desires, and concerns before taking a vote.

My interpretation of hyperempathy in the *Parable* series demonstrates the complex interaction between (dis)ability, individual lives, and social contexts. Lauren's hyperempathy impacts her in material ways. Often her dystopian context exacerbates the negative effects of her disability, and yet, there are clear ways in which hyperempathy makes Lauren an admirable person within her dystopian setting and impacts how she navigates her world, including her creation of Earthseed. One of these statements is not prior to or more important than the other; rather, Lauren's disability and her context mutually inform her experience and understanding of the other. This close reading of hyperempathy in context demonstrates that totalizing approaches that seek to understand hyperempathy as primarily positive, negative, or metaphorical do not do justice to the complexity of Lauren's experience of this nonrealist disability. Rather than simply applying our contemporary realist assumptions about what disability means or entails, the *Parable* series encourages readers and critics alike to read closely and understand this disability in its physical, mental, social, and environmental contexts. This is particularly due to the nonrealist nature of hyperempathy and the speculative fictional futuristic context of the series overall. The interactions between Lauren's experience of hyperempathy, her dystopian future world, and her behaviors and choices within that world—especially in regard to Earthseed—demonstrate the importance of disability to the texts. This contextualized reading of hyperempathy also sets the stage for my arguments about how the series resists the assumed value of a technologically created, disability-free future, a resistance that has important race, gender, and class implications as well.

Resisting a Technologically Created, Disability-Free Future

In addition to the role of disability in shaping plot and character development in the *Parable* series, there are larger thematic, political, and theoretical implications of hyperempathy that challenge the cultural assumption that a technologically created, disability-free future is an inherently desirable, positive, and achievable future. I argue that the representation of hyperempathy resists this assumption through depictions of the unpredictable nature of future technology and the possibility of disability-related pleasure. The *Parable* series is an example of what Kafer refers to as a crip vision of the future, a theory which suggests "that disability cannot ever fully disappear, that not everyone craves an able-bodied future with no place for bodies with limited, odd, or queer movements and orientations" ("Debating Feminist Futures" 236). Butler's crip vision of the future also has important implications for and intersections with issues of race, gender, and class. Yet my argument here is strongly based on a contextualized reading of hyperempathy as disability in the *Parable* series. This section therefore also demonstrates how a disability-focused analysis can lead to broader theoretical discussions concerning other social vectors of power.

Butler's construction of hyperempathy in a future dystopian California challenges the notion that a technologically created, disability-free future is an inherently good future. Recall that the notion of a technologically created, disability-free future assumes that disability prevents the possibility of a full and valuable life, that technology can and should be used to "fix" or "cure" all disabilities, and that the eradication of all disabilities (and thus all disabled people) is as an unquestionably positive aspect of what technology can do for humankind in the future. This sort of representation of disability in the future is common in speculative media and can be found in popular films such as *Avatar* and *Source Code*, as well as the acclaimed science fiction novel *The Ship Who Sang* by Anne McCaffrey, all of which represent disabled people significantly enhanced—and essentially erased as visible figures—through technology in the future. The *Parable* series resists this trend in speculative media that assumes the positive nature of a technologically created, disability-free future by representing disabled people existing in the future, particularly in the case of Lauren as a black, disabled, woman protagonist and future leader.

When analyzing the *Parable* series, it is important to note the position of these texts as critical dystopias.[10] Kafer argues that in contemporary American culture, dystopian representations of the future are often based on the proliferation of disability, understanding this proliferation as a primary sign of how the future and future uses of technology have gone awry ("Debating Feminist Futures" 223). Critical dystopias, however, present a dystopian, even apocalyptic future, in order to comment on the problematic elements of the present and to suggest that if things do not change, then such a future is possible. At the same time, critical dystopias present the hope of change, of a different, more utopian future if the present problems are addressed and behaviors altered. As a critical dystopia, the *Parable* series does not present a negative future *based* on the proliferation of disability; rather, it presents a dystopian future that *includes* the proliferation of disability, without representing disability as inherently negative. There are two keys ways that hyperempathy in particular allows the *Parable* series to include disability in its dystopian future without falling into the stereotypical traps of reading disability primarily or exclusively as loss or suffering. First, it does so by revealing the unpredictable nature of technology, and second, by insisting on the possibility of disability-derived pleasure.

In speculative fiction, technology is most often presented as something that enhances human life and produces more abilities and powers, rather than as something which produces disability or which reduces or alters ability in a way that is not ultimately understood as positive and powerful. Perhaps this is why critics tend to read Lauren's disability so positively as a "power" despite the fact that Lauren does not understand her hyperempathy that way. Melzer writes that in contrast to "paranoid rejections of post-human subjectivity" by "Marxist and feminist critiques that focus on bodies alienated by technology . . . queer sf erotica celebrates bodies and sexualites that are enabled and enhanced through technology ("'And How Many Souls Do You Have?'" 177). Melzer here takes a primarily celebratory, posthumanist approach to technology, viewing it as that which enables and enhances bodyminds, pleasures, and quality of life and understanding the representation of technology in speculative fiction as a challenge to notions of a "natural" unadulterated body. In her critique of posthumanism, Sherryl Vint makes a related argument, contending, "Technological visions of a post-embodied future are merely fantasies about transcending the material realm of social responsibility. . . . The ability to construct the body as passé is a position only available to those privileged to think of their (white, male, straight, non-working-class) bodies as the norm. This option does not exist . . . for those whose lives continue to be structured by racist, sexist, homophobic, and other bodily-based discourses of discrimination" (*Bodies of Tomorrow* 8–9). Scholars and writers of science fiction, therefore, are often divided on the radical possibilities and limits of technology. The independent documentary, *Fixed: The Science Fiction of Human Enhancement*, discusses the various ethical concerns involved in the belief in and pursuit of continuous technological enhancement of human bodyminds by posthumanists, especially in relationship to disability and the future of disabled people. These ethical issues include financial access, continually increasing competition, and reduction of individual bodymind choice when technological enhancement possibilities become requirements. As *Fixed* suggests, technology is neither benign nor objective, but rather is created and used within particular social and historical contexts of privilege and oppression.

Butler effectively demonstrates the ambivalent, unpredictable, and contextual nature of technology in the *Parable* series. In the novels, gasoline vehicles are rare and fairly useless, while water sanitation tablets and guns, including outlawed military-grade weapons, are essential for survival. The downfall of the public education system means that educated and trained doctors and nurses are few and far between. As a result, advanced medical technologies are inaccessible to all but the very rich because of both finances and the dearth of trained professionals who can operate them. The poor end up in company towns or as debt slaves with new technology like electronic slave collars used to keep them submissive and controlled, while the rich spend the bulk of their time in virtual-reality rooms, having incredible, pleasurable experiences as the real world around them collapses. Perhaps most important, however, is how Butler's representation of hyperempathy challenges the notion that technology which prevents, reduces, or cures disability provides an automatically positive move toward a disability-free future.

In the series, hyperempathy is the result of an individual's parents' (or grandparents', since hyperempathy is hereditary) abuse of the drug Paracetco, a designer "smart pill" intended for the treatment of Alzheimer's, but that has been used by college and graduate students to increase concentration and productivity (*Parable of the Talents* 13). Since new pharmaceutical creations are forms of technology, the representation of hyperempathy's origin therefore demonstrates how a technology intended to cure one known, realist disability—when misused by the public—unintentionally creates a new disability.[11] In "A Few Rules for Predicting the Future," published in *Essence* magazine in 2000, Butler shares a story about going to her doctor to discuss unwanted side effects of a new medicine he had prescribed her. The doctor responds by telling Butler that he can give her a new drug to counteract the side effects of the first drug, stating that this second drug has no side effects whatsoever. Butler writes, "I realized that I didn't believe there were any medications that had no side effects. In fact, I don't believe we can do anything at all without side effects—also known as unintended consequences" ("A Few Rules for Predicting the Future" 166). Butler then closes this portion of the essay with a quotation from *Parable of the Sower.*

Through the origins of hyperempathy, Butler demonstrates how modern technology can have unpredictable effects, particularly technologies applied to human bodyminds. Such a speculative fictional representation is not far from impossible given the incredible rate of prescription drug consumption in contemporary American culture and our increasing interest in genetic testing, selection, and manipulation of embryos. The representation of hyperempathy suggests, in its critical dystopian form, that we cannot know in advance what our widespread cultural use of pharmaceutical treatments, genetic alterations, and other disability-preventing/curing technologies might have on our bodyminds in the long run, let alone on the bodyminds of future generations. Butler's papers reveal that she planned to extend this theme in the unfinished third book in the series, often referred to as *Parable of the Trickster.* Drafts, notes, and outlines for this text show Butler was exploring the idea of having an Earthseed community travel to start a new colony on a planet in another solar system. When the community members arrive, people begin to experience different forms of disablement, which vary from draft to draft, including blindness, epilepsy, paralysis, and hallucinations. The idea that she continued to experiment with, based on these drafts, outlines, and notes, was that either the technology used to keep the Earthseed community members alive on the trip, or the toxins in the air of the new habitable planet, caused these changes, and the community must learn to live with their altered bodyminds.[12]

Butler's engagement with the effects of technology in the future is not simply limited to (dis)ability, but also has important material intersections with issues of race, gender, and class. When imagining a disability-free future perpetuated by technological advances that will supposedly prevent congenital disability and "fix" or "cure" all acquired disabilities, it is important to ask, who will have access to these advanced medical technologies and who will not? On whose bodyminds will new and experimental drugs and devices be tested? Who will perform the labor to extract raw materials for and construct these new technologies? Who will benefit the most and who will be barred from participation? If the history of medical experimentation such as the Tuskegee experiments or the work of Dr. Marion Sims tells us anything, people of color, women, working-class people, and people in poverty will benefit the least from technological advances and will be most at risk for harm in the development, production, and consumption of new technologies.[13]

In the *Parable* series, Butler emphasizes that technology is neither inherently liberatory nor destructive. In a journal entry dated April 23, 1999, Butler writes about this directly, stating, "Technology isn't good or bad. It's part of who we are, part of what we do. It's how we us[e] it is [w]hat matters, of course" (Octavia E. Butler Papers, "OEB 1069"). Technology does not have inherent value; rather, it is how we as a culture use, misuse, and make available technologies that produces technological enhancements and/or harm. Further, the line between enhancement and harm is not always clear—nor are the two mutually exclusive. Enhancement for whom and harm to whom? What kind of enhancement and how much? What kind of harm and how much? As Butler writes, "Consequences may be beneficial or harmful. They may be too slight to matter or they may be worth the risk because the potential benefits are great, but the consequences are always there" ("A Few Rules for Predicting the Future" 166).

Technology, the *Parable* series asserts in the face of the ideal of a technologically created, disability-free future, is an ambivalent cultural tool which is subject to both use and abuse, availability and unavailability, and a variety of unintended consequences. Hyperempathy is used as a primary example of this position on technology. As a result, Butler encourages readers to understand that one's critical position in relation to technology need not be either purely celebratory or, in Melzer's words, "paranoid rejection" ("And How Many Souls Do You Have?'" 177). Instead, we can evaluate particular technologies within specific contexts of creation and use. We can do so in solidarity with people with disabilities, people of color, the working class, the poor, and others who are more likely to participate in the creation and testing of such technologies while being less likely to be the beneficiaries of the results of such developments. Butler's published and unpublished writings argue that technology guarantees neither a disability-free future nor any other supposedly desired outcome since we cannot predict its long-term effects, especially when it comes to biomedical technology. In particular, the *Parable* series demonstrates how marginalized groups, especially people of color and the poor, are less likely to have access to healing/curing technologies and are much more likely to be the targets of destructive technologies of violence and war.

The suggestion that we cannot know in advance what our impulse toward a technologically created, disability-free future might lead to may seem problematically foreboding because it potentially suggests that the problem of disability-prevention technologies is that they might simply create more disability. However, the second way that the representation of hyperempathy resists our cultural idealization of a technologically created, disability-free future is through the representation of disability-related pleasure. Butler's creation of hyperempathy insists on pleasure as an inherent aspect of the experience of this disability, a type of pleasure that nonsharers can never experience. For example, Lauren states that when having sex, "I get the guy's good feeling and my own" (*Parable of the Sower* 12). During her early travels with her friends Harry and Zahra, Lauren also shares their pleasure when they have sex near her during their watch, writing, "I got caught up in their lovemaking. I couldn't escape their sensation" (200). Later, when she meets Bankole, Lauren again discusses sharing pleasure in sex, explaining, "Best of all, he took a lot of uncomplicated pleasure in my body, and I got to share it with him. It isn't often that I can enjoy the good side of my hyperempathy. I let the sensation take over, intense and wild" (266). While these moments of Lauren's shared pleasure are few in comparison to the many representations of shared pain, they are incredibly important to Butler's representation of disability in the future. The representation of disability-related pleasure in the *Parable* series shifts the ableist ways in which our culture typically understands disabled bodyminds as both nonsexual and as always more difficult and limiting than nondisabled bodyminds. Importantly, Butler does this without making Lauren come across as magical or as the perpetually overcoming, superpowered supercrip.[14]

Butler's representation of pleasures specific to hyperempathy aligns in many ways with the experience of some people with disabilities who find specific pleasures with and through their disability, such as the use of residual limbs or "stumps" for penetration or erotic stimulation. Wendell writes that if "people's genitals are numb or paralyzed, they may discover things about the nature of intimacy and sexuality that remain unknown to people who can participate in cultural obsessions with goal-oriented, genital sex" (69). Despite the fact that Lauren has few opportunities in the texts to experience the pleasurable aspects of hyperempathy—due to her context, not her disability—the representation of pleasure produced by and through disability rather than *despite* disability represents a critical aspect of Butler's crip vision of the future. This representation not only allows oppressed people the possibility of pleasure in the face of difficult circumstances and injustice, but it also suggests that pleasure may arise specifically in the context of or as a result of different bodyminds or experiences. That is, Lauren's sharing of pleasure stems on a material level from her hyperempathy, but her relishing and appreciation of that pleasure also comes from the fact that she has experienced so much pain, and she knows how precious these moments of pleasure truly are in the context of her environment. I will return to and say more about the importance of pleasure in the context of oppression in the conclusion of this book.

Through the representation of unpredictable effects of technology and the possibility of disability-related pleasure, the *Parable* series adds to a broader theoretical understanding of the limits of and problems with the uncritically accepted notion of a technologically created, disability-free future as an inherently positive goal. These disability-based theorizations have additional important implications for issues of technological (ab)use and access in relation to racial/ethnic minorities, women, and people in poverty.

Conclusion

Butler's *Parable of the Sower* and *Parable of the Talents* are prime examples of how black women's speculative fiction can create alternative possibilities and meanings of bodyminds in ways that require attention to the context and relationship of (dis)ability, race, and gender in interpretation and analysis. Lauren's hyperempathy has often been either ignored as a nonessential part of her subjectivity or read in totalizing positive, negative, and metaphorical fashions. Such readings of hyperempathy, while often attentive to important aspects of Lauren's disability and experience, tend to overemphasize its power, pain, or impact on Lauren's life trajectory. The series demands a more contextualized approach to its complex and generative representation of disability, which challenges cultural assumptions about the supposedly inherent value of a technologically created, disability-free future. Such a disability studies–grounded approach then yields a reading of the series that also has important thematic, political, and theoretical connections with issues of race, gender, and class in regard to technology and the future.

I began this chapter with an epigraph from Kafer which reads, "The futures we imagine reveal the biases of the present; it seems entirely possible that imagining different futures and temporalities might help us see, and do, the present differently" (Feminist, Queer, Crip 28). The first half of this epigraph suggests that depictions of the future can be a reflection of what we value and desire. Speculative fictional representations of the future dominated by nondisabled, white, straight men make clear what is most desirable in the mainstream. But black women writers of speculative fiction as well as other writers of color, women writers, and disabled writers often use this genre to explore how the diverse bodies oppressed people value, desire, and inhabit might continue to exist in future worlds, even as hegemonic forces attempt to literally write us out of these futures.

We see writers from marginalized groups creating diverse visions of the future in recent collections such as Accessing the Future, which features stories by disabled writers about disabled people in the future, and Octavia's Brood, which features speculative fictional stories by writers working in social justice movements. The editors of Octavia's Brood, Walidah Imarisha and adrienne maree brown, refer to this kind of writing as visionary fiction. Visionary fiction, brown explains, is that which "explores social issues through the lens of sci-fi; is conscious of identity and intersecting identities; centers those who have been marginalized; is aware of power inequalities; is realistic and hard but hopeful; shows change from the bottom up rather than the top down; highlights that change is collective; and is not neutral—its purpose is social change and societal transformation" ("Outro" 279). Butler's Parable series is an example of visionary fiction. Collectively her body of work inspired the editors of *Octavia's Brood* to work with activists, many of whom did not previously consider themselves writers, to create the collection. Imarisha and brown's concept of visionary fiction connects with the second portion of the Kafer epigraph, which suggests that imagining different futures might impact the way we behave in the present. As Imarisha writes, "Whenever we try to envision a world without war, without violence, without prisons, without capitalism, we are engaging in speculative fiction" ("Introduction" 3). Imagination, representations, and the real world influence each other cyclically. As authors and activists imagine better futures, they create representations of that future—in words, in text, in images—which influence people to not merely hope for and believe in such futures, but work for them as well. They open up for us new ways of being in the world that may not yet exist, but could.

Butler was particularly aware of how, though a disparaged genre, speculative fiction can be incredibly important for marginalized people. In response to the question "What good is science fiction to Black people?" she rhetorically asks, "What good is any literature to Black people? What good is science fiction's thinking about the present, the future and the past? What good is its tendency to warn or to consider alternative ways of thinking and doing? What good is its examination of the possible effects of science and technology, or social organization and political direction?" (*Bloodchild and Other Stories* 134–35). Butler understood that representation matters and can have real-world implications and impacts, and she sought to do that with her work. As she wrote in one of her notebooks, "I don't want to write *about* what's wrong with us. I want to help right the wrongs. Through my writing I will help. Perhaps I can leave something 'permanently' useful behind" (Octavia E. Butler Papers, "OEB 3180," 1982–83). For her many fans who mourn her far-too-early death, it is incredibly clear that she left us so much to use in our lives and imaginations.

Butler's particular influence on the imaginations, futures, and self-images of many people, especially black women, was documented on Twitter in the summer of 2016, shortly after the tenth anniversary of her death. Using the hashtag #BecauseOfOctavia, people shared what happened in their lives because of Butler's writing or influence, such as "#BecauseOfOctavia & the futures she created with her speculative fiction especially, I dared to dream bigger, aspire higher out of comfort zone," "#BecauseOfOctavia I grew up reading science fiction and always understood the genre to be a forum to produce calls to action," and "#BecauseOfOctavia I believe I have the power to sculpt and write and speak my future into being."[15] Truly, representation matters and visionary fiction can be powerful—and this is exactly what Butler hoped for and believed in as well.

On August 2, 1983, shortly after her home was robbed, Butler ended a letter to a friend with the following sentiments, "I've got to get back into my writing. All this damned reality is getting to me. I can create a better world than this!" (Octavia E. Butler Papers, "OEB 4115," 1983). For Butler, creating a better world in her writing did not mean making a perfect world. It did not mean utopia. She was far too practical and pessimistic for that. But she believed a better world was clearly possible. In the *Parable* books Lauren is a young, black, disabled woman who manages to not merely survive but to create a belief system and lead a community that brings together and helps thousands in the midst of chaos. As a result, this series is one example of how a better future can include those of us whose lives, bodyminds, and perspectives are often devalued and discounted.

More specifically, Butler's critical and contextualized representation of technology and diverse bodyminds in the future in the *Parable* series is fostered by and through her representation of hyperempathy. This nonrealist disability resists the application of contemporary disability stereotypes and emphasizes the importance of context by having no real-world equivalent. A close reading of hyperempathy in context reveals its broader thematic, political, and theoretical resistance to the notion of a technologically created, disability-free future as an obviously positive and desirable future. Through Lauren and hyperempathy, Butler suggests that technology is neither inherently good nor predictable; that disabled, poor, and racialized people are least likely to benefit from advanced technologies yet are more likely to be victims of technological abuse; and that disability itself can produce experiences, perspectives, and even pleasures that are useful and desirable. The visionary representation of the future in the *Parable* series is not a disability- or even oppression-free one. Instead, Butler represents a future in which systems of privilege and oppression continue to operate and impact bodyminds. This speculative fictional future stands in stark contrast to both traditional speculative fiction futures and to our more general contemporary cultural assumptions about the future in the United States. As a critical dystopia and visionary fiction, the *Parable* series presents readers with a worst-case-scenario future, but does so in order to critique contemporary practices, present areas of hope, and theorize possibilities for positive change. From these texts, we can further understand how black women's speculative fiction can provide new and complex representations that challenge ableist, racist, and sexist assumptions about bodyminds and societies in the future. As I have suggested above, this kind of representation, imagining a future for ourselves and people like us, also truly matters in intellectual, emotional, psychological, and material ways. In the next chapter I continue to explore how speculative fiction can challenge ableist, racist, and sexist assumptions of the bodymind, but there I shift the focus to fantasy texts and their nonhuman characters. I explore how this form of nonrealism can challenge cultural assumptions by altering the meanings and boundaries of the categories of (dis)ability, race, gender, and sexuality in the first place.

4

DEFAMILIARIZING (DIS)ABILITY, RACE, GENDER, AND SEXUALITY

Science fiction/fantasy/horror can do that kind of disorientating shifting with anything: politics, culture, race, power, sex, sexuality, gender. That's the stuff I find interesting. It's in the nature of the genre to allow one to step outside the box and examine what's in it and think about what might be excluded and why. Any literature can do that; it's just a particular hallmark of fantastical literature. — NALO HOPKINSON (quoted in Simpson)

Speculative fiction can add significantly to the continuum of meaning. By inventing alternate or futuristic worlds, such stories can suggest other ways of organizing societies — ways we have never tried — other modes in which families, religions, division of labor, and political structures can function. It does not matter if some of these imagined alternatives might still be impossible in our own world, or if they might *always* be impossible because of the circumstances of the invented world are too different from our own. These stories still make us think, make us question, make us wonder what is, and what is not, changeable. —MARIE JAKOBER, "The Continuum of Meaning"

From *Harry Potter* to the *Twilight* series, novels and films of the fantasy genre have gained incredible mainstream popularity in recent years. This area of speculative fiction is often considered nonliterary, mainstream fluff; silly escapist texts marketed toward youth, though consumed by many adults. Scholarship in popular culture and genre studies has demonstrated that such a dismissive approach to the mainstream obscures the cultural work being performed by these texts that are intimately connected to widespread social understandings of (dis)ability, race, gender, and sexuality. Currently, black feminist and disability studies scholarship on popular culture is dominated by studies of film and television (and, for black feminists, studies of music). Less attention has been paid to mainstream genre fiction, yet, as Belinda Edmondson argues in regard to black literature in particular, "the boundaries between the conventions of popular and serious black literature have always been permeable, perhaps more now than ever; to the point where the distinctions are, while still useful, not always the most salient" (193). The existing scholarship on genre fiction tends to focus more on gender and sexuality—such as feminist readings of romance narratives—with moderate attention to race and almost no attention to (dis)ability.[1] Black feminist and disability studies scholars who give this genre serious and nuanced attention are likely to find much to explore, critique, and value in mainstream genre fiction.

In this chapter I introduce the concept of defamiliarization as a major nonrealist method through which black women's speculative fiction reimagines the possibilities and meanings of the categories of (dis)ability, race, gender, and sexuality and thereby change the rules of interpretation and analysis. *Defamiliarization* is a term used by many scholars of science fiction and speculative fiction. It is a translation of the Russian Formalist word *oestranenie*.[2] Defamiliarization is related to Darko Suvin's more genre-specific term *cognitive estrangement*, which refers to the way science fiction estranges or distances readers from their knowledge and assumptions about what constitutes reality in order to move them to question those very assumptions (3–15).[3] I use *defamiliarization* to refer to the way speculative fiction texts make the familiar social concepts of (dis)ability, race, gender, and sexuality unfamiliar in order to encourage readers to question the meanings and boundaries of these categories.

Defamiliarization doesn't occur in any single fashion; rather, this term refers to the many ways that an author can make a familiar thing seem strange or different so that this familiar thing moves from mundane and predictable to surprising, interesting, and thought-provoking. My focus here is on the defamiliarization of (dis)ability, race, gender, and sexuality specifically, but these are far from the only things that speculative fiction can defamiliarize. As Nalo Hopkinson asserts, "Speculative fiction is a great place to warp the mirror, and thus impel the reader to view differently things that they've taken for granted" (Glave and Hopkinson 149). The texts in this chapter use nonhuman bodyminds and nonrealist worlds to defamiliarize social categories, thereby demonstrating how the meaning and experience of (dis)ability, race, gender, and sexuality vary based on individual bodyminds as well as social and environmental contexts. The defamiliarization of (dis)ability is particularly important because the typical representation of disability is too easily abstracted into a metaphor for issues of loss, damage, or evil *or* made too solid and steady as an easily knowable and recognizable medical/ biological fact of the bodymind. What speculative fiction does for the representation of disability is work between these polarities and, in the process, require the reader to do some imaginative labor as well. By pushing readers to read and understand (dis)ability, race, gender, and sexuality differently through defamiliarization, black women's speculative fiction allows for new understandings and experiences of these categories to emerge.

Due to the nonhuman nature of the main characters in the texts discussed in this chapter, I theorize defamiliarization in speculative fiction here under the influence of what Julie Livingston and Jasbir K. Puar refer to as *interspecies*.[4] Working in critical tension with animal studies, Livingston and Puar suggest that the term *interspecies* "offers a broader geopolitical understanding of how the human/animal/plant triad is unstable and varies across time and space," revealing how "what counts as 'human' is always under contestation" (5, 6). According to Livingston and Puar, this interspecies contestation of the category of the human in various areas of knowledge production reveals the biopolitical anthropomorphism of such productions that prioritizes not just humans, but *particular* humans within analyses, using animals and plants as "racial and sexual proxies" (4). While I doubt Livingston and Puar intended *interspecies* to refer to werewolves, demons, and half-mortals, the term is useful as a guiding concept when considering defamiliarization in speculative fiction.

An interspecies framework insists that what counts as human is always under contestation, while defamiliarization in speculative fiction challenges not only what is recognizable as human, but also what is recognizable as belonging within the human-based categories of (dis)ability, race, gender, and sexuality. Similar to how animal studies and feminist science studies scholars, such as Anne Fausto-Sterling, question the applicability of human definitions of sex, gender, and sexuality to animal behaviors, I contend that through defamiliarization, the representation of (dis)ability, race, gender, and sexuality in speculative fictional texts with nonhuman beings reveals the very contestable nature of these categories, which are based on certain types of human beings in certain types of social contexts (Fausto-Sterling 183–86, 95–232). Understanding (dis)ability, race, gender, and sexuality designations as human social constructions helps in elucidating how these fantasy texts with nonhuman characters emphasize the unstable nature of not only what it means to be recognizably human, but also what is means to be recognizably disabled, black, woman, and so on. To demonstrate these points about defamiliarization I discuss three examples of black women's fantasy fiction: N. K. Jemisin's *The Broken Kingdoms*, Shawntelle Madison's *Coveted* series, and Nalo Hopkinson's *Sister Mine*. These texts, with their nonhuman characters and fantastical settings, challenge readers' assumptions about and understandings of (dis)ability, race, gender, and sexuality through the defamiliarization of these categories.

Jemisin's *The Broken Kingdoms*, the second book in her *Inheritance* trilogy, was published in 2010. As a whole, the *Inheritance* trilogy follows the development of a non-Earth world created by three gods and populated by mortals, godlings (the immortal children of the gods), and demons. In this world, magic is real, created and used by gods and godlings, but also able to be tapped into by demons and talented mortals. The overall plot of the series follows the changes in and battles for power among the three gods and the resulting impact on the mortal realm. Each novel in the series occurs in a different time period with a different central narrating character. While some god and godling characters appear throughout the series, most mortal characters only appear in a single text. The narrator of *The Broken Kingdoms* is Oree Shoth, a blind woman artist who can see magic as well as utilize it in her art—though Oree does not understand or know how to control the magic until later in the text. Readers eventually learn that Oree can see magic because she is a demon, the progeny of mortal and god/godling mixing. Prior to this revelation, Oree is simply a young, blind woman artist who ends up in the middle of a mortal and demon plot to kill godlings and overthrow the gods. The main plot of *The Broken Kingdoms* follows Oree's story as it fits within the overall series' coverage of the battle for power in this magical world.

Madison's *Coveted* series includes two prequel novellas, *Collected* and *Bitter Disenchantment*, the titular novel *Coveted*, the sequels *Kept* and *Compelled*, and a short story collection, *Cursed*, which contains stories set both before and after the events of the main series.[5] Published between 2012 and

2016, the *Coveted* series focuses on Natalya Stravinsky, a female werewolf with obsessive-compulsive disorder (OCD) living in New Jersey. Natalya's disability manifests through her attention to detail and order, her dislike of dirt and germs, and her extensive hoarding of holiday collectables. Readers learn that due to her disability Natalya has been exiled from her local werewolf pack. This ousting from the pack is hurtful to her on multiple levels. Not only is the exile embarrassing for Natalya and her family, but it also means a lack of community connection and protection for Natalya; other werewolves look down on her and treat her poorly. The pack exile is made worse by the fact that Natalya was formerly romantically involved with the pack leader's son, Thorn, and their relationship remains complicated throughout most of the series. Each of the texts that focus on Natalya's story includes the development of three interrelated plots central to the series: Natalya's role in the pack, her management of her disability, and her relationship with Thorn. Additionally, each text deals with a different immediate challenge such as the kidnappings of Natalya's brother and father and attacks from enemy werewolves and other nonhuman beings.

Finally, Hopkinson's *Sister Mine*, published in 2013, is set in a contemporary, fantastical Toronto, Canada. In this setting, immortal deities of Caribbean and African influence not only help regulate things such as death and the environment in the mortal world, but they also take on mortal bodies and occasionally mate with mortals as well. One pair of children from such immortal/mortal mixing is Makeda and Abby, formerly conjoined twin sisters. When the sisters were separated shortly after their birth, only Abby retained "mojo," the magic abilities of immortals. In addition, both women have disabilities—Abby has a shortened leg and Makeda has seizures. *Sister Mine* follows narrator Makeda as she tries to become more independent from her sister, but is forced back into relationship with Abby when their elderly father goes missing. In attempting to find her father with Abby, Makeda discovers long-kept family secrets and learns about herself in the process.

In this chapter I first detail how these example texts defamiliarize (dis)-ability through nonhuman bodyminds and fantastical environments and social contexts. In the second section, I demonstrate how these texts also defamiliarize race, gender, and sexuality. Throughout, I emphasize the importance of defamiliarization to how black women's speculative fiction changes the rules of reality and the rules of interpretation and analysis, concluding with a reflection on the theoretical and political value of studying mainstream genre fiction.

Making Familiar Disabilities Unfamiliar

When reading fantastical representations of (dis)ability, the line and connections between ability and disability become, at times, quite blurred. Speculative fiction can challenge assumptions about the definitions of and boundaries between disability and ability through defamiliarization. In particular, *The Broken Kingdoms,* the *Coveted* series, and *Sister Mine* defamiliarize realist disabilities—that is, disabilities we recognize from our current reality—through the nonrealist bodyminds of demons, werewolves, and half-mortals and their fantastical physical and social environments. Unlike previous chapters where speculative fiction novels have depicted nonrealist disabilities, such as multiple consciousnesses and hyperempathy, the texts in this chapter represent OCD, blindness, conjoined twins, and other realist disabilities in highly nonrealist settings. While this is a different representational approach to (dis)ability in speculative fiction, these authors' representation of realist disabilities in fantasy texts with nonhuman characters have a similar effect in that they too refuse to adhere to readers' expectations about disability.

In the last chapter, I explained how the representation of a nonrealist disability in the *Parable* books refuses to give readers the opportunity to use any preformed cultural knowledge, assumptions, or stereotypes to understand Lauren's disability because hyperempathy does not exist in our reality. In the case of the work of Jemisin, Madison, and Hopkinson here, blindness, OCD, and conjoinment are realist disabilities. Readers recognize these disabilities and therefore are inclined to read through the lens of previous cultural knowledge and assumptions about what these disabilities entail. For example, OCD is marked by what Lennard Davis calls a "sociology of disease recognition" in which "the stream of information about the disease entity swirls through the media, self-help books, memoirs, and word of mouth so that a recognizable symptom pool develops. Individuals, family, and friends can 'know' these symptoms," recognize them in themselves or others, and then informally diagnose by placing "the simplified and streamlined disease entity within a confident and knowing treatment regimen" (*Obsession* 219, 29). In the case of OCD, various fictional and nonfictional media representations have resulted in a culturally recognizable version of this disability that includes particular verbal and behavioral cues such as ritualized and repeated hand-washing or frequent attention to organization or schedule.[6] Blindness has similarly been overdetermined in fiction, film, and television as an experience of total darkness in which other senses become supernaturally attuned.[7] Representations of conjoined twins, though less common than OCD and blindness, tend to be more spectacular, engaging in discourses of enfreakment and the supercrip.[8] The nonhuman bodyminds and nonrealist worlds of the texts, however, make these realist disabilities less clearly knowable or predictable than expected, thus defamiliarizing them.

By representing realist disabilities in nonrealist contexts, these fantasy texts push readers to understand disability from the perspective of the main character, not from our preconceived notions and stereotypes. While representations of nonrealist disabilities reject the possibility of applying preconceived notions about disability entirely, representations of realist disabilities in nonrealist and nonhuman contexts play with reader expectations and twist them. The defamiliarization of realist disabilities in these fantasy texts challenges readers' assumptions about the meanings, manifestations, and effects of a particular disability on physical, mental, social, and environmental levels alike, forcing readers to reconsider what they know or think they know about what it means to be disabled. This challenge to reader assumptions about what it means to be disabled is a key part of the important political potential of these texts. In each example text below I will discuss how the work defamiliarizes realist disabilities first through nonhuman bodyminds and second through their fantastical nonrealist environments and social contexts. As a result of defamiliarization in these texts, readers must come to understand blindness, OCD, and conjoined twins differently than they might imagine such disabilities for a character in a realist text.

In *The Broken Kingdoms,* Oree is blind, yet she can see magic because she is a demon. This means that she can see gods and godlings who embody magic, and she can also see words written or spoken in the gods' magical language, whether the words are used by gods, godlings, or mortals. Oree's demon bodymind defamiliarizes blindness by making her experience distinctly different from supposedly realist representations of blindness, which often focus on total darkness and the enhancement of other senses (often to nonrealist, hyperbolic degrees). While Oree does often lavishly describe things in nonvisual terms, she also uses color and shapes to describe the things she feels, smells, sees, or senses around her. Often, sense-based terms are blurred in Oree's narration, but it is never stated that this blurring is specifically due to her disability. For example, when speaking of the color of her godling lover Madding's eyes, she refers to it as that which "I would never be able to fully describe, even if I someday learn the words. The best I can do is compare it to things I do know: the heavy thickness of red gold, the smell of brass on a hot day, desire and pride" (*The Broken Kingdoms* 16). Here it is unclear if this indescribable color is hard for Oree to explain because of her blindness or because Madding is a magical godling (another nonhuman bodymind) who may truly have eyes which mortal language cannot describe in purely visual terms. Oree's demon bodymind disallows readers the ability to overlay typical realist assumptions about what blindness does or does not entail—a key aspect of the defamiliarization of disability.

The Broken Kingdom further defamiliarizes (dis)ability in the text by emphasizing how Oree's experience of the world changes dramatically based on her environment. While discussion of the social construction of disability is ever-present in disability studies, *The Broken Kingdoms* demonstrates how ability is also context-dependent by making Oree's ability to see magic contingent on being in places where magic exists, such as in the city of Shadow. In other nonmagical spaces, such as the town where she grew up, there is no magic to see at all. There, Oree is blind without any magic to help navigate the space. The mediating presence of magic in Oree's experience of her blindness is most apparent when she visits the magical floating castle called Sky where she can see almost everything. Oree explains, "All my life I had heard arcane terms like *depth perception* and *panorama,* yet never fully understood. Now I felt like a seeing person—or how I had always imagined they must feel. I could see *everything,* except for the man-shaped shadow that was Hado at my side and the occasional shadows of other people passing by, most of them briskly and not speaking. I stared at them shamelessly, even when the shadows turned their heads to stare back" (297; original emphasis). This quote's depiction of amazement demonstrates the particularity of this space for Oree, allowing for a representation of seeing not after a cure or other alterations to the bodymind, but rather through a change in context to a particularly magic-filled location. The representation of how Oree's experiences of sight vary by location also reflects realist issues in contesting other representations of blindness that portray this disability as a monolithic experience of darkness rather than as a spectrum of experiences in which quality and types of vision vary widely. By making Oree's ability to see magic environmentally contextual, Jemisin defamiliarizes disability *and* ability, making them both contingent on a variety of physical, mental, social, and environmental factors. Oree's experience of blindness is neither predictable nor stereotypical, requiring readers to resist their preconceived notions and understand Oree's disability within its nonhuman and fantasy contexts.

Madison's *Coveted* series defamiliarizes a realist disability by centering on a main character with OCD, whose werewolf bodymind dramatically impacts her experience of this disability. In the prequel novella, *Collected*, there is no mention of Natalya using any sort of pharmaceutical treatment for her disability. In the first full novel, *Coveted*, however, Natalya specifically mentions how she previously used prescription drugs to help control her behaviors and impulses, but that this method did not work. She states that due to her fast werewolf metabolism, medications hit her too quickly, causing strange, werewolf-specific side effects. When her best friend, Aggie, suggests Natalya take a pill before her first date since breaking up with Thorn, Natalya says that "the side effects don't agree with the wolf," causing her to shake "wildly as the wolf tried to escape the calm the pills forced on [her] body" (*Coveted* 59). Later in the book, when Natalya's brother Alex is kidnapped and she is not allowed to help with the hunt to find him, she repeats that drugs are not a good solution for managing her disability as a werewolf. She states, "I didn't want to escape into the haze of my medications. I didn't want all those side effects the wolf hated. Who in their right mind would want to have fits or experience strange random patches of fur?" (160). From the perspective of the first two texts then, the *Coveted* series makes OCD, or at least the management of this disability, unfamiliar by making pharmaceutical intervention a physical impossibility for Natalya.

While readers may recognize the realist cues for OCD in Natalya's behavior, the early texts in the series align with the disability rights assertion that medication need not be the first or primary method for living well with a disability, particularly a mental disability. Although *Coveted* and *Collected* do not approach this topic directly by having Natalya outright reject pharmaceutical intervention—Natalya does take half a pill before her date—Madison's series nonetheless uses the speculative fictional context of a werewolf's nonhuman bodymind to gesture toward two realist issues of the medical-industrial complex. First, Natalya's difficulty with medication illustrates how, for some people, the effects of medication may be far worse than any symptoms of their disability and only nonpharmaceutical treatments (if any at all) are acceptable. This is initially implied to be the case for Natalya in *Coveted* when she chooses to go to therapy with Dr. Frank, a wizard psychologist who places her in a cognitive-behavioral therapy group with other supernatural beings with mental disabilities. Second, Natalya's negative reaction as a werewolf to taking human medication gestures toward concerns with how pharmaceuticals are developed in the first place.

Natalya's experience of werewolf side effects from medication made for and by humans draws attention to how pharmaceuticals are created and tested on the basis of certain beings and yet dispensed under the assumption that they will work for all or most bodyminds.

The defamiliarization of disability through Natalya's relationship to pharmaceutical treatment becomes even more complicated in the third and fourth books in the series, *Kept* and *Compelled,* in which there is an important and unexplained shift.[9] In *Kept,* Natalya is represented multiple times taking medication for her obsessive-compulsive behaviors with apparently no fits, patches of fur, or any of the other side effects mentioned in *Coveted.* This change is not explicitly accounted for and seems to have only a minor impact on the narrative. In *Compelled,* Natalya impulsively travels to Russia in an attempt to find a magical cure for Thorn, whose lifespan was shortened by a wizard. Due to the unplanned nature of the trip, she forgets her self-proclaimed "happy pills" back in the United States; so although she mentions wishing she had them, she is not actually represented taking medication during the majority of the novel (92). Readers are not given any explicit explanation as to why Natalya is suddenly, in books set less than a year after the end of *Coveted,* able to take medication without any of the complications or side effects previously mentioned in the series. This shift in Natalya's relationship to pharmaceutical treatment further defamiliarizes disability because the change keeps the reader from believing, after two books, that they fully know and understand Natalya's experience of OCD. Defamiliarization here highlights the changing nature of disability in a character's life, not just in the typically discussed movement from nondisabled to disabled, but also the change within one's relationship to disability as a category of experience and identity.

From a disability studies perspective, we can also read the shift in the use of pharmaceuticals and the narrative silence around this change as purposeful on the part of Natalya as a narrator. It is possible that she found a medication that works for her and feels no need to explain her choice in managing her disability to the reader. Reading Natalya's silence regarding her use of medication as strategic is generative from a disability studies standpoint because it connects with realist issues in the field. While the disability rights movement rejects forced treatment, its members and allies simultaneously recognize that some people with disabilities might choose to use some forms of pharmaceutical treatment nonetheless. This choice is understandable, yet ought to be one of many options made available, financially and socially. There is one moment in *Compelled* which particularly opens the series up to such an interpretation. As Natalya socializes among a new group of werewolves in Russia, she states to the reader, "My medication, which I hadn't taken since I'd left home, only did so much. I'd never be normal, and, in a way, I'd come to accept that. It was making others accept it that was far more difficult" (197). Here Natalya reveals that her medication has a limited impact on the manifestations of her OCD, and although she does not seem to have the negative werewolf-specific side effects discussed in *Coveted,* she also is not suddenly cured or completely normalized by her use of pharmaceutical treatment. Instead, she asserts that she has accepted herself as being outside of the norm—even with medication—and that it is others' inability to accept her and her disability that represents the larger concern.

In addition to defamiliarizing OCD through Natalya's werewolf bodymind, the *Coveted* series also defamiliarizes Natalya's disability at the social level. In a realist context, OCD is generally understood as a nonapparent mental disability that is not visually marked on the bodymind or via disability accoutrements such as a wheelchair, hearing aid, or cane. Through the proliferation of representations of OCD, however, this disability has become more recognizable or, as Margaret Price might phrase it, "intermittently apparent" and familiar to the general public, despite its lack of perpetually visible bodymind markers or accoutrements ("The Bodymind Problem and the Possibilities of Pain" 272). In the *Coveted* series, Natalya performs many of the expected indicators of OCD, allowing most contemporary readers to easily recognize her disability. Understanding OCD as an intermittently apparent mental disability, from a realist perspective, one would assume that when Natalya is not engaging in these recognizable behaviors she would appear nondisabled to those around her. This is not the case, however, in the context of her werewolf social environment. In the series, Natalya is said to *smell* inferior to other werewolves due to her constant nervousness and heightened anxiety. She states, "My inferior scent was the one thing I couldn't scrub off. Worry, doubt, and fear clung to me and alienated me from others" (*Kept* 44). Although this scent does not directly indicate OCD or even necessarily disability to other werewolves, it nonetheless marks her as a nonnormative, low-ranking werewolf. This scent is part of the reason why Natalya is exiled from her pack and mistreated by other werewolves in the community. The *Coveted* series's werewolf social context then constitutes a representational shift in which an otherwise intermittently apparent disability is defamiliarized into a readily and regularly apparent disability.

I use *nonapparent, intermittently apparent,* and *apparent* here rather than *visible* and *invisible* for several reasons. First and foremost I use these terms because they are increasingly becoming the preferred terms within disability rights and disability studies communities.[10] Terms of apparency move away from the ocular-centric nature of visibility and shift the onus for noticing or not noticing disability onto the perceiving person rather than onto the visibility of disability via a person's bodymind, accoutrements, or behaviors. Apparency is particularly appropriate to use in this context because for Natalya her disability is not made visible through sight, but is apparent through scent. Here OCD, typically defined as a mental disability, has important physical components for Natalya. Werewolves prioritize scent for understanding the world because of their heightened sense of smell, which remains active even while they are in human form. The emphasis on scent as a means of reading Natalya as disabled, therefore, draws attention to the limits of the human "fantasy of identification," to borrow from Ellen Samuels, which positions disability as a static category that can be easily identified, particularly through visual means (*Fantasies of Identification*). As a result of this defamiliarization of OCD, which makes it readily apparent to other werewolves, Natalya's disability becomes more actively present in her social interactions than her OCD might otherwise have been in a realist context. As a result, once again, what readers already know or expect about a realist disability is made less predictable through fantastical settings, here the social and bodymind context of a community of werewolves.

Finally, Hopkinson's *Sister Mine* defamiliarizes disability through the non-human bodyminds of half-mortal, half-celestial sisters Makeda and Abby and their experiences in the mortal versus celestial realms, two very different environmental contexts. Toward the beginning of the novel, Makeda states that she and Abby "could have lived as we were, conjoined. Between us, we had what we needed," but instead the conjoined twins were separated as infants (Hopkinson 29). The novel first, therefore, defamiliarizes the normative assumption that separation is the best and most ideal route for conjoined twins. This defamiliarization of this common perception of conjoined twins is achieved through both Makeda's insistence on their ability to live conjoined and by the fact that the women are not nondisabled after the separation surgery. Rather, they are still both disabled, just differently disabled than they were when conjoined. Though they now have separate bodies, the separation surgery left Abby with scoliosis and a shortened leg, which requires her to use crutches or a cane for mobility, and left Makeda with a liver problem that requires regular medication and occasionally causes seizures severe enough that she does not drive. The notion that separation surgery will allow conjoined twins to live "normal"—meaning nondisabled—lives is thereby questioned in the novel.

The defamiliarization of conjoined twins is further articulated through Makeda's affinity for representations of conjoined twins. She collects images, texts, and memorabilia representing Chang and Eng, Millie and Christine, and other conjoined twins from various places and historical periods, signaling an identification with these people and even a desire for the particular disability she lost through separation. This desire for and identification with conjoinment defamiliarizes (dis)ability because it inverts the trope of disability as loss and instead represents the separation surgery's attempt to "cure" disability as loss for Makeda. Her identification with conjoined twins is made most clear in Makeda's conversation with love interest, Brie, as she shows him her collection. When he asks, "You got a thing for freaks?," Makeda gets upset and asks him to leave (148). When Brie asks what he said wrong, Makeda compares his question to a white person saying "nigger," insisting that it's okay for black people to use such a term, but not white people. Not quite understanding, Brie says, "Oh. I'm sorry. But it's not like I said it to anyone's face," to which Makeda replies, "You said it to me," revealing her formerly conjoined status (148). Here Makeda's identification with "freak" as a disability community insider term reflects her disability identity even as the disability she most strongly identifies with is no longer apparent on her bodymind. This moment also underscores the importance of understanding (dis)ability, race, and gender to simultaneously operate as social constructs, systems of privilege and oppression, discourses, experiences, and identities. While Makeda is no longer conjoined and in fact cannot even remember when she was conjoined, she still strongly identifies with that particular disability experience.

Similar to Natalya's sudden change in use of medication, however, less than halfway through the text Makeda learns the truth about her and Abby's birth and separation surgery, resulting in a new defamiliarization of her disability. What seemed to be a realist disability is shifted to a new combination of realist and nonrealist. Makeda shares with the reader what her uncle tells her:

Abby had been fine when we were born. Only that shorter leg. Whereas I was all but an empty shell. A living body with a near-inert mind, and a tiny undifferentiated nubbin of aetheric where there should have been the psychic organelle of mojo that all living creatures possess to one degree or another. Whereas Abby's has been working a-okay. And it was Abby's blood and breath that had been sustaining me in the womb. . . . Dad's kin cut me away from Abby in order to keep her alive. They sliced me off my precious sister, neatly as paring a hangnail, and left me in my crib to die. (Hopkinson 114–15)

Abby and Makeda's mortal mother begged for their father to save Makeda's life and he did so by confining himself to a mortal body and giving Makeda his mojo (the magical abilities of celestials), which provided her the ability to live, grow, and develop, but also resulted in her occasional seizures. Here the text again subverts a realist linear teleology of (dis)ability in which one moves from nondisabled to disabled and supposedly forever desires to "return" to a nondisabled state. As Makeda's celestial uncle tells her, "Time's not linear, no matter what your senses tell you" (265). Makeda was born severely disabled, then she was provided her father's mojo to become differently disabled (with seizures and no mojo of her own to work with). Now with her father's mortal body's death impending, she is presented with the possibility of her own death or reversion to the disabled bodymind with which she was born, which is a differently disabled bodymind than she thought she had been born with and with which she had previously identified and desired through her conjoined twin memorabilia collection. There is no linear progress of disability and loss to be cleanly traced here.

The defamiliarization of (dis)ability in *Sister Mine* is also highly dependent on environmental context. Abby and Makeda's experiences of their bodyminds as disabled or nondisabled or something shifting in between varies dramatically depending on whether they are in the mortal or celestial realm, referred to as "palais space" in the novel. As the above quotations about Abby and Makeda's separation surgery suggest, Abby was born with mojo while Makeda had hardly any at all. The differences in the sisters' mojo and bodyminds makes Makeda primarily disabled within the context of the celestial world and Abby primarily disabled within the context of the mortal world. Like blindness and OCD in *The Broken Kingdoms* and the *Coveted* series, therefore, (dis)ability in *Sister Mine* is represented as both contextual and relational.

At the start of the novel Makeda half-jokingly refers to herself as "a crippled deity half-breed" because in the context of her celestial, immortal family, her lack of mojo is read as an impairment (2). Her deity relatives look down on her, and her lack of mojo makes visiting and operating in the palais space of the immortal realm difficult for her. In contrast, Abby, who uses crutches or a cane in the mortal realm, "could move quicker than thought" in palais space and is comfortable, accepted, and valued among their celestial relatives (98–99). In the immortal world then Makeda is marked by a nonrealist disability (lack of mojo), and Abby is essentially nondisabled, whereas in the mortal realm Abby's disability is far more apparent and prominent than Makeda's seizure condition. In particular, stress due to the situation with their missing father is represented as decreasing Abby's mobility in the mortal realm. However, she is still depicted as a fierce disabled woman who, at one point in the text, curses the "bastard [who] took the last disabled space" without a disabled parking license plate or hangtag and then shatters the person's brake light with her crutch (79–80). In speculative fiction, it is possible to move between varying states of ability and disability due to changes in bodyminds and/or spaces. While those in disability studies would say that we all vary in our abilities over time and people with chronic illnesses particularly demonstrate in realist contexts how one's relationship to (dis)ability can move in multidirectional, nonlinear ways, speculative fiction can depict such movement in ways that possibly prevent individual blame/shame and resist the necessity of medical/psychological explanations by placing individual oscillation of (dis)ability in nonrealist, nonhuman contexts. Such defamiliarization of (dis)ability discourages readers from applying their realist assumptions and prejudices to these representations as they might, for example, to a memoir of chronic pain.

In *The Broken Kingdoms,* the *Coveted* series, and *Sister Mine,* the realist disabilities of blindness, OCD, and conjoinment are central material aspects of the main characters' lives. However, the characters' nonhuman bodyminds and fantastical environmental and social contexts make understanding the physical, mental, and social manifestations of disability—as well as the impact of potential treatment or cure of disability in the *Coveted* series and *Sister Mine*—not an easily knowable and recognizable process. Due to defamiliarization, readers cannot apply realist expectations to werewolf, demon, and half-mortal bodyminds or their fantasy worlds. Instead, readers must do the imaginative labor of understanding and following the development of these characters and their disabilities from within the bodymind, environmental, and social contexts created in each text. This particularly distinguishes speculative fiction of the fantasy genre from speculative fiction of the science fiction genre. The latter tends to rely on the "hard" sciences to explain nonrealist aspects of a text; even if the speculative fictional science is nonexistent in our current reality, it tends to be based on realist scientific theories and experiments.[11] Such works rely on intellectual or rationalist explanations, whereas speculative fiction in the fantasy genre can create magical and nonhuman rationales for events which cannot and do not need to be explained otherwise. This difference makes speculative fiction with fantastical contexts well positioned to imagine (dis)ability outside the context of medical, biological, and other scientific explanations. In addition to the defamiliarization of (dis)ability, *Sister Mine*, the *Coveted* series, and *The Broken Kingdoms* also defamiliarize other prominent systems of privilege and oppression. By defamiliarizing multiple social categories in nonhuman contexts, these texts reveal the ways (dis)ability, race, gender, and sexuality are all unstable, mutually constitutive human social constructions.

Defamiliarization of Race, Gender, and Sexuality

The use of defamiliarization in black women's speculative fiction is not limited to (dis)ability alone. The additional defamiliarization of race, gender, and sexuality in these texts reveals how this speculative-fictional method of representation is integral to the texts' social critiques. The collective defamiliarization of multiple social categories emphasizes that (dis)ability, race, gender, and sexuality are distinctly human, socially constructed concepts that rely on particular notions of bodyminds, senses, behaviors, and abilities, often in mutually constitutive or intersecting ways. Defamiliarization is therefore a key nonrealist technique through which black women's speculative fiction reimagines bodyminds in ways that change the rules of interpretation and analysis, emphasizing the importance of the contexts in which categories of (dis)ability, race, and gender exist.

Race in *The Broken Kingdoms* is defamiliarized through the relative absence of realist racial and ethnic categories as well as the move away from visual clues for race in Oree's narration. The mortal realm in the series is made up of races, ethnicities, and royal family lines, such as Amn, Maro, and Arameri, which have no direct correspondence to contemporary Western racial and ethnic categories, though they are clearly influenced by such categories. For example, Jemisin refers on her blog to a character from the first book in the series as "half white, half (something like) Inka" ("Why Is Oree Shoth Blind?"). The people in the series are sometimes described as having light or dark skin or straight or curly hair, thereby making some—such as Oree, who is clearly meant to be read as black—recognizable to readers as racially marked.[12] Phenotype information does not, however, always correspond to social power or differential treatment in the text's society as it might in contemporary American society. The defamiliarization of race here means readers cannot assume that characters who are physically described in ways we would associate with a particular realist racial category are treated in the same way as one would expect of treatment for those within that racial category in a realist setting. Racial signifiers that depend on phenotype and other visual markers thus become less critical to understanding social relations throughout the series, especially in *The Broken Kingdoms,* where narrator Oree cannot generally see other mortals' features. Instead, Oree focuses on people's voices, accents, or scents, which indicate their gender, class, and, sometimes, place of origin. This demonstrates how the use of other senses can indicate race or ethnicity in ways not typically prioritized in realist contexts. Blindness combined with the new racial and ethnic categories of the text further defamiliarizes race, revealing our dependence on visual cues to determine racial categories.

In the *Coveted* series, race is defamiliarized through the differential power relationships of various nonhuman groups. The books encourage readers to understand werewolves in particular as a marginalized racial group. In *Kept,* when Natalya tells her wizard friend and romantic interest, Nick, that she does not want to be with him because he's a wizard, Nick responds, "I never took you for a person who only saw someone's race, instead of who they truly are" (*Kept* 225). In this moment, race is used to describe different nonhuman groups. These groups are not, in the context of the novels, different species altogether; rather, they are different races that typically live and mate among themselves. Although Natalya ultimately chooses to be with someone of her same race, Natalya's brother, Alex, accidentally impregnates a wood nymph and decides to marry her and help raise what could therefore be considered their mixed-race, half-nymph, half-werewolf baby.

As Natalya's refusal to be romantically involved with a wizard suggests, in this fantasy world nonhuman races have different relationships to one another. Evelyn Brooks Higginbotham asserts that race is a metalanguage, a "trope of difference, arbitrarily contrived to produce and maintain *relations* of power and subordination" (255; emphasis added). When Natalya tells Nick she doesn't want to be with him because he's a wizard, she is responding to a history of unequal relations of power between werewolves and wizards. In the series, wizards sometimes kidnap shape-shifting beings like werewolves in order to extract their life force to create powerful magic. This extraction process diminishes the lifespan of the shape-shifters involved and can even kill them.[13] In the supernatural racial hierarchy then, werewolves are below wizards in terms of power and prestige. While werewolves are not direct stand-ins for any particular marginalized group, their representation as being between animal and human and their vulnerability to abuse by spellcasters allows them to be read as a disempowered racial group.

The defamiliarization of race in the *Coveted* series is furthered by the fact that Natalya's family is Russian and she appears white in her human form, including in the cover illustrations of all the books. This appearance of racial privilege within a human context potentially obscures for readers the racialization of werewolves that occurs in the supernatural context. There is no denying, however, the derogatory and condescending ways other supernatural beings sometimes speak to Natalya, calling her "wolf" even while she is in human form. The defamiliarization of race here therefore also suggests the importance of context to one's racial identity and experience as Natalya's racial privileges and oppression vary depending on whether she is in a space with humans, werewolves, or other supernatural beings. While Natalya passes as a white human to humans, other supernatural beings in the series read her exclusively as a werewolf no matter what her form. In these ways then—the categorization of supernatural beings as different races, the racialization of werewolves as an oppressed group, and Natalya's appearance as racially white in human form—race is defamiliarized in the fantasy nonhuman context of the *Coveted* series as something similar to, yet quite different from how we understand race, racialization, and race relations in our contemporary reality.

The defamiliarization of social categories in black women's speculative fiction also occurs in regard to gender. In *Sister Mine,* Makeda explains that in the celestial world gender does not exist as it does in the mortal realm, though gendered terms are used in the books to refer to most celestial characters. Immortals, such as Makeda's uncle Death, at times take over the bodies of humans when in the moral realm, but do not identify with human concepts of gender. In celestial space, immortals can change their appearance at will. This is made most explicit in discussions of Makeda's twin cousins, the

Benjis, who, although supposedly different sexes, are so indistinguishable that Makeda can never tell them apart. The text highlights how, as in my earlier discussion of race, gender categories are also often quite dependent on visual cues and a static or predictable external bodymind presentation. Additionally, with the assistance of celestial mojo, sometimes inanimate objects can take on human form. This is represented in the character Lars, Abby's new friend and lover, who was formerly Jimi Hendrix's guitar. Though Lars is referred to with masculine pronouns due to his bodymind presentation, typical understandings of sex and gender are again defamiliarized in regard to this nonhuman character since gender identity terms seem ill-fitting or nonapplicable to a guitar-turned–human being (Hopkinson 66).

In a similar fashion, in the *Inheritance* trilogy to which *Broken Kingdom* belongs, it is explicitly stated that gods and godlings do not have a sex, gender, or even flesh in their true states. However, when visiting the mortal realm, immortals appear in fairly conventionally gendered forms for the sake and comfort of mortals. In the third book in the trilogy, the narrator, Sieh, one of the oldest godlings, states to the reader that gender "is only a game for us, an affectation, like names and flesh. We employ such things because you need them, not because we do" (*The Kingdom of Gods* 99–100). In addition, since gods and godlings have no sex or gender, and since procreation in speculative fiction need not follow realist conventions, in the *Inheritance* trilogy gods and godlings can reproduce with each other in any combination (gods with gods, gods with godlings, godlings with godlings, gods or godlings with mortals). In both *Sister Mine* and the *Inheritance* trilogy, the defamiliarization, or even outright rejection, of sex/gender contributes to an additional defamiliarization of sexuality.

In *Sister Mine*, although procreation between celestials is not explicitly explained, the text does note that due to the lack of concepts of gender as well as the limited pool of celestial beings with whom to mate, what humans would term *incest* is quite common among immortals. Makeda explains that, though relationships among family members is common for celestials, as half-immortals, dating is hard for her and Abby because many celestials look down on them—especially Makeda. Indeed, Makeda feels that she and Abby have already dated all the family members they could tolerate, including the Benjis (Hopkinson 86). This context of the normalcy of familial sexual relationships among celestials sets the groundwork for the defamiliarization of sexuality in *Sister Mine* when Makeda reveals that she and Abby were sexual partners in their teens until she heard Abby jokingly refer to her as "the donkey" (a derogatory word in the text that refers to mortals without mojo), and they have not been sexual since then (126). The revelation of Makeda and Abby's sexual relationship in the novel is interspersed with a description of the lives of Chang and Eng, the famous conjoined twins. This portion of the novel defamiliarizes our realist notions of appropriate and inappropriate sexual interactions both within the non-realist context of celestial world norms *and* within the context of disabled bodyminds. After discussing how Chang and Eng were both married with children, Makeda, speaking directly to the reader, states, "You would have said, 'Chang and Eng's sex life,' wouldn't you? Like they were one person, Changandeng, emphasis on the second syllable. When you're a twin, the world has its ways of letting you know that you and your sib are a package deal. Everything I had, Abby either had an identical one or she and I would share one. It was like we'd never actually been separated at all. . . . Abby's body was as familiar to me as my own" (124). The intimacy of conjoined and formerly conjoined twins' bodies in regard to sexuality reveals how, even without the speculative context, (dis)ability can defamiliarize sexuality. Yet *Sister Mine* insists that readers cannot separate Makeda and Abby's statuses as twin sisters, formerly conjoined twins, and half-immortals in understanding their sexualities and their relationships, emphasizing intersectionality and the importance of the context in which categories of (dis)ability, race, gender, and sexuality exist and are given meaning.

In the *Inheritance* trilogy, sexuality is similarly defamiliarized because if god/godlings have no sex or gender and their mortal realm gender presentation is chosen and mutable, then their sexuality cannot be described in gendered-attraction sexuality terms such as hetero-, homo-, or bisexual. This is the case even if the god or godling has sex with or is attracted to a single gender of mortals, because our basic sexuality terms rely on the gender of both parties. Additionally, the sexuality of mortals is challenged by this situation because even if a mortal is typically attracted to a single gender, do gendered-attraction sexuality labels still apply when a mortal has sex with a god/godling who presents in a gendered manner, but who does not actually have a sex or gender as mortals do? And what exactly does it mean to have sex with a god whose true essence is not flesh? Can we understand this as an interspecies sexual encounter?

As these questions suggest, in defamiliarizing sexuality, speculative fiction can also defamiliarize sex and sexual pleasure. In the *Inheritance* trilogy, the sex scenes between mortals and gods/godlings indicate that the gods and godlings use both their created, gendered flesh and their immortal essence to produce intense sensations (scents, tastes, visions, etc.) into and onto the bodyminds of mortals with whom they have erotic interactions. For example, in a sex scene between Oree and Madding, she says when they kiss that she "felt him . . . all the coolness and fluid aquamarine of him, the edges and ambition. . . . [She] heard chimes again as he flowed into [her] and through [her]" (*The Broken Kingdoms* 111). After kissing, Oree and Madding move to intercourse, and because Madding is "needy" and deep in his own pleasure, he unconsciously lessens control of his magical abilities. As Oree puts it, "He took me places, showed me visions. There are some things mortals aren't meant to see. When he forgot himself, I saw some of them" (111). Here *The Broken Kingdoms* imagines different possibilities for bodymind pleasure and sex through the immortal beings of the gods and godlings.

The theorization of alternative avenues for sexual pleasure also occurs in the *Coveted* series. Although gendered sexual attractions in the series remain staunchly heterosexual in line with the traditions of the romance novel, the possibilities of sexual pleasure expand beyond the confines of human heterosexual intercourse. For example, after experiencing Nick's calming spell, Natalya thinks to herself that she wouldn't mind feeling that sensation on her "girlie bits" (*Coveted* 240). In *Kept*, Nick makes that unspoken wish come true by holding Natalya's hand and casting a spell that creates pleasure and arousal. Natalya describes the experience as follows, "The warmth flowed up my arm and settled into my chest. My breathing slowed—then quickened. The sensation raced down my legs—fast enough for my toes to curl. What the hell was he doing? . . . I was getting off on his happy magic. . . . Another surge pulsed through me, and my nipples tightened" (*Kept* 124). Once Natalya lets go of Nick's hand, the sensation stops and his smile makes clear he knew exactly what he was doing. In fact, he likely was also gaining pleasure from the experience as well because, as Nick once informed Natalya, "wizards get a thrill from the exchange too—if it's with the right person" (*Coveted* 136). In these instances the possibilities for sexual pleasure get expanded beyond normative conceptions of sex through, literally, magic. This expansion implicitly acknowledges that sexuality is more than just how a person identifies in terms of gender preferences; indeed, one's sexuality incorporates an entire range of erotic desires, expressions, and activities. In both *The Broken Kingdoms* and the *Coveted* series, magic is used as a form of erotic interaction.

The defamiliarization of race, gender, and sexuality in black women's speculative fiction is important because it demonstrates that (dis)ability is not an exceptional category in these texts and is therefore not merely metaphoric or symbolic. Instead, (dis)ability represents an integral part of the collective defamiliarization of multiple social categories of privilege and oppression, which encourages readers to imagine each of them differently. The defamiliarization of (dis)ability, race, gender, and sexuality encourages us to question our assumptions about the definitions, meanings, and boundaries of these categories. Not all speculative fiction, however, works to explore and question social systems of privilege and oppression. As feminist and critical race scholars of speculative fiction have demonstrated, some texts reify social categories and their related stereotypes, even in nonhuman contexts. This is most apparent in representations of the racialized Other through the figure of the alien, robot, or cyborg.[14] It is important then that these contemporary black women writers challenge readers to think about the social construction of (dis)ability, race, gender, and sexuality through defamiliarization. This creative destabilization and challenging of the norms and stereotypes of multiple social categories is influenced by black feminist theory, which insists on the intersectional and mutually constitutive nature of social categories and oppressions. Defamiliarization in these texts also demonstrate Barbara Christian's argument that creative texts can be a form of theorizing about world. While authors do not need to identify their political positions or personal identities in order for critics to interpret the political implications of their texts, it is nonetheless useful to note that Hopkinson has explicitly identified as both feminist and queer, while Jemisin's blog certainly suggests strong antiracist, feminist politics (Batty 189; N. Johnston 204). While politicized creative work is clearly not exclusive to black women, Madison's, Jemisin's, and Hopkinson's defamiliarization of major social categories are examples of black feminist theorizing through speculative fiction. All three authors, in different ways, refuse certain expectations of (dis)ability, race, gender, and sexuality while still prioritizing those who are multiply marginalized. These texts therefore provide new and creative ways for readers to question such social categories, not only within these fantastical worlds, but also in their own realist contexts.

THE FANTASY FICTION of N. K. Jemisin, Shawntelle Madison, and Nalo Hopkinson demonstrates that defamiliarization is a major way in which black women authors of speculative fiction are able to reimagine bodyminds and change the rules of representation and interpretation. Through the defamiliarizing contexts of nonhuman characters and fantasy worlds, the meanings of (dis)ability, race, gender, and sexuality are shifted and challenged from realist definitions and boundaries. Indeed, in these fantasy texts, Jemisin, Madison, and Hopkinson create entirely new rules for representing these categories. Through defamiliarization black women's speculative fiction can make readers aware of their assumptions regarding (dis)ability, race, gender, and sexuality, possibly leading them to question these assumptions as well.

Mainstream speculative fiction, particularly fantasy fiction, represents a critical area through which disability studies and black feminist scholars can understand how political interventions and representational shifts can be made in a cultural arena typically associated with apolitical juvenility and escapism. Such scholarly work is essential to not only understanding but also changing majoritarian cultural ideologies of (dis)ability, race, gender, and sexuality. I consider it important therefore to include the work of these newer black women authors of speculative fiction alongside the work of literary legend Octavia E. Butler from previous chapters in order to demonstrate how both mainstream and literary fiction can engage similar concepts and concerns in differing, yet nonetheless productive ways.

I was first exposed to the books in this chapter not in university classrooms or academic conferences, but in online forums, Facebook groups, blogs, and other fan spaces. I read these books because people from around the world who are invested in increasing the diversity of speculative fiction have drawn attention to them as exemplars of the possibilities of nonrealism for representing issues of (dis)ability, race, gender, and sexuality. Through fiction, art, film, cosplay, blogs, and more, artists and fans from marginalized groups are not merely insisting on the tokenized presence of people of color, women, disabled people, and other marginalized groups in the worlds of speculative fiction, but demonstrating how their presence changes the rules of the genre and alters the possibilities of fan spaces as well. Mainstream texts, such as the fantasy fiction discussed in this chapter, say a lot about contemporary cultural understandings of the social systems of (dis)ability, race, gender, and sexuality. As a result, analysis of this type of work has substantial value for black feminist and disability studies scholars.

CONCLUSION

Neither black nor disabled people have any reason to be enamored of the status quo. As disabled black SF authors we have the opportunity to re-vision the dominant culture's narrative. —NISI SHAWL, "Invisible Inks"

I began this book with the concern that black feminist and disability stud-ies scholars do not communicate or engage enough with each other's work. I asserted that each field would benefit by interacting more with the other. While it is important that I have identified representations of (dis)ability in black women's speculative fiction, especially representations of disabled women protagonists, this search-and-find approach means little if the re-sulting analyses don't implicate social, cultural, intellectual, and political concerns within broader fields and society at large. My intention has been to demonstrate how a combined black feminist disability studies frame-work can help scholars of (dis)ability, race, and gender better trace and un-derstand the mutually constitutive nature of these categories as identities, experiences, systems of privilege and oppression, and historical constructs. This project is about the representation of (dis)ability, race, and gender in black women's speculative fiction, yet I hope it has meaning for so many spaces beyond these texts. However, before I talk more about the larger im-plications of my work and suggest next steps in black feminist and disability studies scholarship, let me first go back and trace some of the central claims I have made here in *Bodyminds Reimagined.*

I have insisted throughout this work that speculative fictional texts by Octavia E. Butler, Phyllis Alesia Perry, N. K. Jemisin, Shawntelle Madison, and Nalo Hopkinson are not merely imaginative escapes into alternative worlds. Instead, these works are theorizations of the possibilities and meanings of bodyminds that change the rules of interpretation and require modes of analysis that take into account both the relationships between (dis)ability, race, and gender and the contexts in which these categories exist. In the case of Butler's *Kindred,* disability is ever-present as both metaphor and materiality. Rather than being either the outcome of racist violence or a metaphor for the impact of the history of slavery, disability is simultaneously a justification for the enslavement of black people and a material effect of this racist institution. Perry's *Stigmata* demonstrates how concepts of able-mindedness are deeply dependent on racial and gender norms that impact how individuals' behaviors are interpreted and how people are then treated within the psychiatric medical-industrial complex and the wider world. Butler's *Parable* series imagines (dis)ability, race, and gender as important parts of our future. The series insists on a holistic and contextualized approach to the nonrealist disability of hyperempathy that takes into account not only how this disability impacts Lauren's bodymind, but also how her other identities, life experience, and physical and social environments shape the way she experiences her disability as well. Further, the representation of hyperempathy rejects cultural assumptions about the inherent value of a technologically created, disability-free future in ways that directly implicate issues of race, gender, and class, thereby insisting on diversity in visions of the future. Finally, Jemisin's *The Broken Kingdoms,* Madison's *Coveted* series, and Hopkinson's *Sister Mine* each use nonhuman bodyminds and fantastical environmental and social contexts to defamiliarize (dis)ability, race, gender, and sexuality. In doing so, Jemisin, Madison, and Hopkinson each provide alternative meanings to these categories within their fantastical worlds so that readers might question their assumptions about these terms in the realist world as well.

Collectively, the reimagining of the possibilities and meanings of bodyminds in contemporary black women's speculative fiction challenges our assumptions about (dis)ability, race, and gender and thereby changes the rules of how we read and interpret representations of these categories. By having racialized, disabled women protagonists who narrate their own texts and who live in future or alternative worlds in which the rules of reality are different, these books force readers to understand the experience of their intersectional identities from the main character's perspective, from within their bodyminds, their lives, and their societies. The tendency in disability studies toward life writing, documentary, and other realist representations of disability is undergirded by a desire to challenge negative understandings of people with disabilities. A similar leaning toward authenticity and realism has historically occurred among black writers, intellectuals, and activists. As my discussions of these texts demonstrate, however, such challenges to limited, problematic, or oppressive representations of marginalized people can also occur through speculative fiction, through nonrealist, fantastical, and nonhuman contexts that change the rules of reality, making us think more critically about how our current rules and assumptions about (dis)ability, race, and gender have come into being in the first place. This is not to say that speculative fiction can replace or is better than realist fiction, but, rather, that it offers important alternative avenues of representation that should not be dismissed. By altering what bodyminds can and cannot do and the worlds in which these bodyminds exist and are given meaning, black women's speculative fiction alters the categories of (dis)ability, race, and gender in ways that can be productive, instructional, and thought-provoking. The nonrealism of the texts takes us outside of our rules of reality in order to draw attention to how these rules, which eventually become naturalized assumptions and understandings, are mutable and contextual, rather than fixed. I have examined the interactions of these social categories in specific places in specific texts in order to demonstrate how such an intersectional analysis of (dis)ability, race, and gender might be performed on different sites of analysis, literary or otherwise.

This brings us then to the larger implications of this work beyond the realm of literary criticism and even, I hope, beyond the walls of the academy. I have attempted to demonstrate throughout this work how, by altering and defamiliarizing (dis)ability, race, and gender, black women's speculative fiction also highlights the ways oppressions resulting from these systems can overlap, intersect, support, and sustain one another in real-world power dynamics and interactions. I would like to particularly emphasize this point and its application beyond the covers of this book. Too often disability discourse and representation is evacuated of meaning in the work of antiracist and feminist scholars and activists as being *actually* about race or gender. As I discussed in chapter 1, this is typically due to a desire to distance certain marginalized groups from disability as a form of stigma management. At the same time, disability studies scholars have often performed the reverse move and documented the ways disability has been used as a master trope of disqualification and discrimination for most marginalized groups, therefore essentially arguing that all oppression is, at its root, ableism. The attempt to prove a master status or master oppression assumes that one category, system, or oppression is somehow prior to the others when, in fact, they are constantly shifting and shaping each other.

I find it more useful, therefore, to identify the multiple discursive systems at play even when certain identity groups do not seem to be present. This is the kind of intersectional approach that I hope this book can foster in scholars and activists alike. As I explained in the introduction, my approach to *intersectionality* takes critiques of this concept into account without leaving the term behind. I have therefore provided close and intimate tracings of the relationships of various oppressions in specific texts and textual moments. This tracing of the relationships of oppressions operates outside of the traditional metaphorical frames of intersectionality as a matrix, a highway intersection, or a Venn diagram. Unfortunately, the workings of power are not something we can simplistically visualize and chart—as useful as such static visuals may be for initially thinking about intersectionality. The kind of intersectional approach I use here, which incorporates and centers the experiences of multiply marginalized subjects but is not limited to these experiences, allow us, for example, to read enactments of medical and scientific racism as not only racist, but also as ableist toward both disabled and nondisabled people of color. These systems are so deeply entrenched and entangled that they cannot be cleanly separated. Our scholarly attempts at articulating these relationships, therefore, should be attentive to the multiple analytics of (dis)ability, race, gender, sexuality, class, and nation while still being flexible enough to decide which are most prevalent or important in a particular context. Similarly, our activist attempts to combat a particular oppression should remain aware of how these systems operate in not merely intersectional—that is, operating at the same time in the lives of multiply marginalized people—but also overlapping and mutually constitutive ways. Understanding the role of ableism in the operation of racism and the role of racism in the operation of sexism (and so on and so forth) is fundamental to effective liberation movements. Audre Lorde argues that we cannot use the master's tools to dismantle the master's house (110–14). Translating the metaphor here, we cannot take down the house of what bell hooks calls the "imperialist white supremacist capitalist patriarchy" without understanding how ableism was and is used to build, support, and reinforce that house (*We Real Cool* xiii). Without recognizing ableism as a part of the house that needs to get taken down or by continuing to participate in ableism in antiracist and feminist work, we are only further entrenching systems that are being used to oppress us.

I want to particularly emphasize that my approach to intersectionality has included identity without being limited to identity. There have been numerous critiques lately of identity politics—often by the same scholars who are critical of intersectionality—which argue that this approach to political organizing is limited, normalizing, unable to incorporate differences in experience, and easily co-opted into consumable markers of individuality within neoliberalism. In response to such critiques, Julie Avril Minich writes that "identity politics are just as easily mobilized to contest the neoliberal state as to reinforce it. Furthermore, while it is true that identity claims *can* flatten out the heterogeneous experiences and attributes of the members of an identity group, it does not logically follow that this flattening is necessary or inherent to political projects predicated on identity" (*Accessible Citizenships* 161; original emphasis). As a result, Minich argues that we cannot "know how identity will change in the absence of oppression that targets marked bodies, and we cannot know without eliminating that oppression"; therefore, rather than theorize "for a post-identity or post-national future, we need to theorize for the present we currently occupy, one in which nationalisms and identity categories—however normalizing and co-optable they may be—structure our social world in profound ways and impact people's life chances" (189). I align myself with Minich and other feminists of color who seek to destabilize and strategize uses of identity for the purposes of well-being and collective social justice action.

At the same time, I have not limited my analyses to identity alone because, as I have argued above, oppressions operate in our lives despite our identities. Ableism, racism, and sexism impact us even if we do not identify as disabled, people of color, women, trans-, or gender-nonconforming. Alison Kafer writes, "In focusing so intently on disability identity, how have disability studies and disability rights movements overlooked the crip insights of [those who do not identify as disabled] ... what can disability studies and disability movements learn from our own exclusions?" (*Feminist, Queer, Crip* 153). By taking an intersectional approach that acknowledges the role of identity, experience, social systems of privilege and oppression, and social constructions, I have sought here, and will continue to seek in future work, to find the political and personal benefits of identity politics while still remaining attentive to the ways racism, ableism, and sexism operate outside or beyond identity claims. This is particularly important in disability studies where there are often questions of who should be identified as disabled and what should and should not be included under the umbrella of disability studies as opposed to, perhaps, body studies, medical humanities, death and dying studies, or illness and health studies.

I would now like to offer a few brief suggestions for the next steps which could occur in future scholarship based on or in conversation with the work I have done here. First, my greatest hope is to see more scholarship coming from black feminist and disability studies scholars conversant in each field. For black feminist literary scholars in particular, I hope we can return to the texts we know, love, and constantly teach in order to explore how (dis)ability plays out, no longer ignoring it or reading it as purely metaphor. I believe this work, a reexamination of well-known black texts, can provoke new readings of the African American literary canon and provide us a more nuanced understanding of the relationship of (dis)ability, womanhood, and blackness over time in the United States and elsewhere. Second, I want to encourage both fields to do more work on nonrealist representations. I believe this work particularly needs to occur in regard to other writers of color, like Monique Truong, Samuel Delany, Nisi Shawl, and Jacqueline Koyanagi. There is especially much to be explored in the work of authors who engage with magical realism, vodun/voodoo, mysticism, and other culturally specific, nonrealist elements. Similarly, there is important work to be done on work by disabled writers of speculative fiction, but that work may require expanding beyond writers who actively identify as disabled to include those who publicly acknowledge having a disability, condition, or disease. For example, Butler identified as having dyslexia, but did not refer to herself as disabled.[1] As a whole then, I hope my work here encourages more scholars to explore what speculative fiction and other nonrealist modes can teach us about the relationship of (dis)ability, race, gender, and other social categories.

I opened this book with a quote from Gloria Anzaldúa which insisted on the relationship of change in the real world to change inside our minds. To close, I want to return to this notion and assert, first, that the representation of (dis)ability in black women's speculative fiction can challenge and change our understanding of (dis)ability, race, and gender (including the relationship between these terms) by providing new and unusual representations. In doing this, these texts hold opportunities for change at the individual level, as the concluding discussion in chapter 3, including the #BecauseOf Octavia hashtag, suggests. Individual change, while not sufficient enough on its own for macro-level change, is nonetheless a necessary part of changing oppressive cultures. The representational power and potential of black women's speculative fiction cannot be dismissed. Second, I assert that while black women's speculative fiction can be challenging with its frequent engagement with oppression and potential dystopian futures, these texts can also be pleasurable. This point may seem self-evident or benign, but it's incredibly important and worth elaborating on here, especially in the context of antiracist, anti-ableist, and feminist scholarship and activism.

Sometimes in the academy there is the suggestion that pleasure and intellectual work cannot combine, that our work is only recognizable as work if it is hard, if it exhausts us. Sometimes in feminism and social justice movements there is the suggestion that increased political awareness reduces one's ability to take pleasure in cultural productions, that we cannot watch a film or read a book without being critical—and that critical eye reduces or eliminates pleasure. This is something my students occasionally tell me, that my classes have "ruined" certain shows or films they used to like—before they realized how ableist, racist, or sexist they were. I tell them that if my course makes them think about issues of (dis)ability, race, and gender outside the context of class and homework, then I've done my job. Because we *should* all balk when we see a nondisabled actor playing a disabled character; we *should* all be upset when the only black character in a show is a one-dimensional stereotype; we *should* all be exasperated when the heretofore strong independent female lead ends up needing to be rescued by a man with whom she then falls in love. But that doesn't mean that recognizing problematic elements in a text or in our world negates our capacity for pleasure.

In advocating increased, nuanced engagement with speculative fiction in this book, I also want to advocate for pleasure. Pleasure does not exist outside of oppression because none of us exist outside of these systems of power, but pleasure can nonetheless arise in the midst of oppression, in the face of it, in spite of it, or sometimes even because of it. I understand pleasure here to be a broad category of positive feelings and emotions, including joy, pride, affirmation, love, and hope. For instance, I felt joy seeing Beyoncé's video for her song "Formation" (and later, her performance of the song at the Super Bowl in 2016), but the pleasure of that video for me was deeply entwined with oppression. In the "Formation" music video, there are references to Hurricane Katrina and police violence against black people, references which draw on the incredible antiblack racist violence in the United States that repeatedly marks black lives and bodyminds as less valuable. Yet for me there was pleasure in seeing those references to oppression in the music video because they were also an affirmation of the need to value black lives, and these images were coming from an incredibly popular mainstream artist who was forcing racial politics into the faces of many Americans who would prefer she keep singing and dancing about love and breakups instead. Beyoncé used that video—and the later visual album *Lemonade*—to affirm black people, her place among us, and her love for us. There can be pleasure within representations of oppression because there is joy in seeing oneself represented, even one's oppression represented, after so much denial. Seeing reflections of ourselves in representations often means feeling seen as well, knowing we are not alone.

There was a point in working on this book, however, when I started to lose sight of pleasure in any capacity. When I was working on revisions for the conclusion of chapter 2, I had recently moved for a postdoctoral fellowship and was spending the bulk of my time alone in my new apartment reading and writing about violence against black people. I started having trouble sleeping and was feeling increasingly nervous around police and police-like figures such as park rangers. I was emotionally drained at the end of each day, even though I only allowed myself to research one person per day (Tamir Rice today, Barbara Dawnson tomorrow, and so on). I took to Facebook to ask folks how they do self-care when one's work involves such continual engagement with trauma and oppression. Friends from far and wide offered advice like limiting my contact with the traumatic material, cuddling furry creatures, hugging friends, taking breaks, going for walks, yoga, meditation, prayer, and engaging with materials that bring me joy. I ended up making it a daily practice to finish my work time by standing in my hallway and reading aloud the print I have of the Lucille Clifton poem "won't you celebrate with me." This brief poem ends with the lines "come celebrate / with me that everyday / something has tried to kill me / and has failed" (Clifton 25). My daily practice became a multilayered source of pleasure for me. First, it marked the end of a work day, the end of looking at, reading about, and listening to violence against black people and justifications for that violence. Second, it affirmed that my survival is no small thing, that the failure of all those forces to kill me each day (bodily, emotionally, or otherwise) was worth appreciating. Furthermore, it reminded me that my ability to find ways to write about this violence was also important and worth celebrating. Finally, on a more meta level, it reminded me of the potential of writing and representation because of the fact that Clifton's short poem was exactly what I needed to remember pleasure, power, and purpose.

So what does all this have to do with speculative fiction by black women? As I have said before, this genre has sometimes been dismissed because it is considered juvenile, escapist, nonliterary, or even, strangely, too accessible.[2] In other words, speculative fiction is often considered too easy, too fun, and therefore too pleasurable to be serious or political. I hope that my analyses in this book have demonstrated this to be far from the case, but in arguing for the theoretical insights and political potential of these texts, I also don't want to forgo the pleasure of them because, as I have been suggesting above, pleasure is also political.

Speculative fiction can be so pleasurable to read. It can be fun, interesting, and enthralling. There were times I read texts in a single sitting, and I read more books for this study than could possibly be included. While I may have critiques of the texts I have analyzed throughout this book, I became invested in writing about the work of Butler, Perry, Jemisin, Madison, and Hopkinson not because of the moments they frustrated me, but because of how they fascinated me, how they made me think differently and imagine things I had never thought of before. They offered representations of (dis)ability I had not found elsewhere, representations that included race and gender politics and clear expressions of sexuality, representations that spoke to important realist political concerns while still being set in nonrealist worlds. I enjoyed and continue to enjoy these books (and others like them) because there is so much to say about them. I take pleasure in both reading and analyzing them. So often our work in disability studies and black feminism focuses on oppression, but for this book, I insist on acknowledging and ending with pleasure.

NOTES

Introduction

1. Contemporary here means texts produced after 1970. This temporal choice stems from Cheryl A. Wall's designation of 1970 as a watershed moment for black women's writing (2–4). However, the period after 1970 is also important for disability studies because it marks the beginning of a very activist-oriented disability rights movement inspired by the work of feminist and civil rights activists. Post-1970 is also important for the genre of science fiction, the most widely researched subset of speculative fiction. Madhu Dubey acknowledges the importance of 1970 for black speculative fiction writers, contending that "the burden of realist racial representation began to ease off only by the 1970s, or the beginning of what is commonly termed the post–Civil Rights period" ("Speculative Fictions of Slavery" 780). Similarly, Patricia Melzer writes that the 1970s introduced feminist science fiction as part of New Wave science fiction (*Alien Constructions*, 5–9). In short, the types of representations I am interested in— nonrealist black women's texts that engage (dis)ability—did not exist in significant numbers prior to 1970.

2. There are many examples of black feminist activists, theorists, and writers engaging with disability and anti-ableist politics. To take just a few: in their 1977 statement the Combahee River Collective, a black feminist group, mentions working on issues of sterilization abuse and health care, while Alondra Nelson's *Body and Soul* provides a history of health activism by the Black Panthers, the majority of whom were women who took a critical stance toward medical research and practice similar to those in disability studies and disability rights (Combahee River Collective 217). In Evelyn C. White's 1990 edition of *The Black Women's Health Book,* black women write about their experiences with and/or activism around cancer, mental health, hypertension, sickle cell anemia,

and HIV/AIDS. In particular, Vida Labrie Jones writes about black women and lupus, calling it a "complex chronic disability" well before chronic disabilities were given much attention in disability studies (V. L. Jones 156). Additionally, Ann Folwell Stanford explores how black women writers "do not simply advocate a shift from a biomedical to a biopsychosocial model (no small matter itself) but reconceptualize the nature of illness and health," while feminist disability theorist Alison Kafer locates disability in black feminist Bernice Johnson Reagon's speech "Coalition Politics" in which Reagon talks about her trouble breathing at high altitude (Stanford, *Bodies in a Broken World* 2; Kafer, *Feminist, Queer, Crip* 151–53).

3. Other scholars have discussed this lack of recognition in disability studies. See Kafer (*Feminist, Queer, Crip* 149) or Minich ("Enabling Whom?").

4. These scholars include, for example, Susan Burch, Hannah Joyner, Eli Clare, Terry Rowden, Nirmala Erevelles, Mel Chen, Cynthia Wu, Julie Avril Minich, Ellen Samuels, and Therí A. Pickens.

5. See Dovidio and Fiske; Sawyer et al.; Shavers, Klein, and Fagan; Smedley; Harrell, Burford et al.; Sternthal, Slopen and Williams; Viruell-Fuentes; Walters et al.

6. For example, Goodley uses dis/ability and Garland-Thomson ("Integrating Disability, Transforming Feminist Theory") uses ability/disability. I explain my choice around (dis)ability further in "Critical Disability Studies as Methodology."

7. See Crenshaw ("Demarginalizing the Intersection of Race and Sex"; "Mapping the Margins"). Barbara Christian argues that black feminism in particular helped validate the need for intersectional scholarship and has continued to be a major theoretical branch in this area (Christian, "Diminishing Returns" 208). See also May, *Pursuing Intersectionality*.

8. Vivian May (chapter 1) provides an extensive explanation of these elements of intersectionality.

9. For critiques of intersectionality, see Jennifer Nash, "Re-Thinking Intersectionality," "Practicing Love," and "Home Truths on Intersectionality." See also Jasbir K. Puar, "'I Would Rather Be a Cyborg Than a Goddess.'" For a robust discussion and response to a number of other critiques of intersectionality, see May.

10. Judith Butler contends that rather than comparing one or more oppressions, "what has to be thought through, is the ways in which these vectors of power require and deploy each other for the purpose of their own articulation" (18).

11. *Crip* is a term many people within disability studies and activist communities use not only in reference to people with disabilities, but also to the intellectual and art culture arising from such communities. Crip is shorthand for the word *cripple*, which has been (and is) used as an insult toward people with disabilities, but which has been reappropriated as an intragroup term of empowerment and solidarity.

12. For more on this argument see Schalk, "Interpreting Disability Metaphor and Race in Octavia E. Butler's 'The Evening and the Morning and the Night.'"

13. For example, Harriet A. Washington writes, "Blacks have dramatically higher rates of nearly every cancer, of AIDS, of heart disease, of diabetes, of liver disease, of infectious diseases, and they even suffer from higher rates of accidental death, homicide, and mental illness. . . . African Americans also suffer far more devastating but equally

preventable disease complications, such as blindness, confinement to wheelchairs, and limb loss" (20).

14. See for example Wendell 31; Fine and Asch 334; Russo and Jansen 232–33.

15. Early disability studies work to include or address race include Rosemarie Garland-Thomson's "Speaking about the Unspeakable," Martin S. Pernick's "Defining the Defective," Leonard Cassuto's *The Inhuman Race*, Rachel Adams's *Sideshow U.S.A.*, Lennard Davis's *Enforcing Normalcy*, and the essays in Garland-Thomson's edited anthology *Freakery*.

16. The film has consistently low lighting, but no other child of color is shown directly. In the final scene, in the back row of the children there appears to be one other child of color whose face is not visible.

17. We later learn that people working in the institution wear a blocker gel on their skin that hides their scent from people with the fungal disease.

18. Note this is a clearly conscious casting choice as the film is based on a novel of the same name and in the novel the protagonist is a white girl.

19. The actress who plays Melanie, Sennia Nanua, was twelve at the time of filming.

20. See Goff et al.

21. This is to say not that black women are not targets of police violence, but that the current discourse is primarily focused on black men and boys' experiences of police violence. Black women, especially black trans women and black women with mental disabilities, are also incredibly likely to be targeted by police and victims of violence in general.

22. Homosexuality was removed from the *Diagnostic and Statistical Manual of Mental Disorders* in 1973.

23. I acknowledge that contemporary scholarship on utopian literature recognizes that utopian literature is not simply about perfect or ideal futures, but about *better* futures; thus the common use of terms such as "critical utopias" (Curtis; Moylan). In some ways then, my reading of these texts might be considered utopian in that I believe they each provide a way of thinking differently about the world in ways that could improve it. That said, the legacies of exclusion of marginalized people within the utopian tradition makes me hesitant to claim this term any further (Chan; Kilgore; Stein). In particular, there is an astonishing dearth of bodymind diversity in terms of disability in utopian texts and utopian literary scholarship. I hope my work may help utopian literature scholars explore and interrogate that exclusion, both in terms of its origins, dating back to Sir Thomas More, and utopian literature's contemporary manifestations (Curtis; Gomel; Olyan; Schotland).

24. For more on sexism, feminism, and women in science fiction, see Marleen S. Barr's *Alien to Femininity*, Sarah Lefanu's *In the Chinks of the World Machine*, and Samuel Delany's "Letter to the Symposium on 'Women in Science Fiction' under the Control, for Some Deeply Suspect Reason, of One Jeff Smith" (Delany, *The Jewel-Hinged Jaw* 85–104). For more on racism, race, and people of color in relation to science fiction, see Delany's "Racism and Science Fiction," De Witt Kilgore's *Astrofuturism*, Isiah Lavender's *Race in American Science Fiction*, and Sharon DeGraw's *The Subject of Race in American Science Fiction*.

25. Tobin Siebers, for example, writes that "if social constructionism has influenced the past of disability studies, realism may well be in a position to define its future" (72).

26. Couser uses *life writing* as an umbrella term for a range of genres including auto-biography, memoir, journals, and documentary films.

27. This is also suggested by Ato Quayson when he uses nonfiction to explain the final category of "disability as normality" in his typology of disability representation, whereas he uses only fiction as an example of the other, less positive categories.

28. Virginia Bemis makes a similar argument that more realism makes for a better representation even in relation to speculative fiction. In the first paragraph alone of her discussion of Lois McMaster Bujold's nonrealist *Vorkosigan* series, Bemis focuses on realism as a determinant of quality by using the words *realistic, very authentic, so authentic, genuine*, and "fully-realized" (104).

29. For more on the limits of respectability and its manifestations in African American literature, see Morris.

30. See Barbara Christian, Hazel Carby, and Ann DuCille. I use *genealogy* here rather than *tradition* or *canon* in line with DuCille, who argues against the essentialist and static tendencies of these latter terms (147).

31. See, for example, Fox, Carmody, or Knadler.

32. Jewelle Gomez discusses the history of this concern with the purpose of black literature, as do Genre Andrew Jarrett and Kenneth Warren in their respective monographs (Gomez 950–51; Jarrett; Warren). For a discussion of related concerns in contemporary African American literature, see Richard Schur.

33. Similarly, in discussing how Ato Quayson focuses on nonfiction in his example of texts which represent disability as normality, Michael Bérubé argues that "'the real' is not a self-explanatory realm where things just are what they are. In literature and visual arts, 'realism' is an effect of protocols of representation, devices and techniques that produce the illusion of mimesis; 'the real' is what appears when a master artificer has deployed those devices with an art that conceals art" (*The Secret Life of Stories* 54).

34. Derek Newman-Stille makes a similar argument, writing, "Disability studies theorists often situate realism as most appropriate for discussing social change because it portrays the real world, but science fiction and speculative fiction offer a similar opportunity because these genres depict *possible* worlds and opportunities for changes that a society could make" (44; original emphasis).

35. For more on the history of the demands of racial realism, authenticity, and social protest within African American literature see Gene Andrew Jarrett's *Deans and Truants*.

36. Michael Bérubé, Tobin Siebers, Alison Kafer, and Ria Cheyne have all made reference to the importance of (dis)ability to science fiction narratives (Bérubé, "Disability and Narrative" 568; Siebers 7; Kafer, *Feminist, Queer, Crip* 20; Cheyne, "'She Was Born a Thing' 148). Examples of scholars who have written on disability in speculative fiction include Kathryn Allan, JoSelle Vanderhooft, Nickianne Moody, Patricia Melzer, Katrina Arndt and Maia Van Beuren, and Bérubé (Allan; Vanderhooft; Moody; Melzer "And How Many Souls Do You Have?"; Arndt and Van Beuren; Bérubé, *The Secret Life of Stories* 85–103). There is far more work on disability in speculative film, television and comics. Examples of scholarship on nonliterary, nonrealist representations of disability

includes the work of José Alaniz, Hanley E. Kanar, Johnson Cheu, Jeffrey A. Weinstock, Patrick D. Hopkins, and Ramona Ilea (Alaniz; Kanar; Cheu; Weinstock; Hopkins; Ilea).

37. See Lavender, *Race in American Science Fiction*, or Leonard.

38. For more on conflicting stereotypes, see Schalk, "Happily Ever after for Whom?" or Wanzo.

39. See, for example, Erevelles, *Disability and Difference in Global Contexts*; Mollow; or Jarman.

40. Tobin Siebers proposes the theory of complex embodiment, which "raises awareness of the effects of disabling environments on people's lived experience of the body" and emphasizes "that some factors affecting disability, such as chronic pain, secondary health effects, and aging, derive from the body. . . . Complex embodiment theorizes the body and its representations as mutually transformative" (25).

41. Similarly, Elisabeth Leonard argues that even in texts "in which there has been substantial racial mingling and the characters all have ancestry of multiple races . . . [many authors avoid] wrestling with the difficult questions of how a non-racist society comes into being and how members of minority cultures or ethnic groups preserve their culture" (354).

42. Scholars such as Ato Quayson and Lennard Davis similarly argue that when studying representations of disability one should not just focus on disabled characters, but instead read texts in their totality to consider how (dis)ability as a social system operates within them (Quayson 34; Davis, *Enforcing Normalcy* 41–48).

43. For more on the problem with universal categories, see Chandra Talpade Mohanty's *Feminism without Borders* or Robert McRuer's "Disability Nationalism in Crip Times."

44. I have argued elsewhere that some nonrealist elements of speculative fiction can be easily interpreted as representing multiple social categories and engaging multiple discourses and oppressions (Schalk, "Resisting Erasure"; Schalk, "Interpreting Disability Metaphor and Race in Octavia E. Butler's 'The Evening and the Morning and the Night'"). I do my best throughout to indicate how and why I interpret something as disability.

45. For more on the relationship between institutionalization and incarceration, see the edited collection *Disability Incarcerated*, especially the editors' introduction (Ben-Moshe and Carey).

Chapter 1. Disability and Neo–Slave Narratives

1. I write "supposedly" here because historical evidence suggests that Truth never actually spoke these words. For more on the historical evidence and myth surrounding Truth, see Nell Irvin Painter's "Representing Truth."

2. Linh U. Hua challenges Dana's assumption of a linear, predetermined future which supposedly requires that she can't alter the past in any way. Hua argues that Dana is actually complicit in a white patriarchal system by sacrificing Alice to secure her own future (395–99).

3. The term *neo–slave narrative* was originally coined by Bernard Bell in 1987 and was

later expanded on by Ashraf Rushdy. While this is a generally accepted term in literary criticism, some, such as Tim Ryan, consider the term and the previous definitions of it offered by Bell and Rushdy to be problematic and limiting (B. W. Bell 286–89; Rushdy *Neo–slave Narratives*; Ryan 187).

4. For more on traditional slave narratives, particularly their status as literature, see James Olney.

5. While one of the major contributions of contemporary neo–slave narratives is to show the impact of slavery on those who were never enslaved or those who are no longer enslaved, many early fictionalized representations of slavery prior to *Kindred* sought to use realist fiction to acknowledge slavery's horrors and resist white fictional and historical accounts that attempted to depict it as a benign or mostly benevolent institution (Dubey, "Neo–slave Narratives" 781–83). Later neo–slave narratives, however, tend to focus on the continued effect of slavery by using nonrealist narrative structures, tropes, and devices. Despite these differences, disability still appears in both realist and nonrealist neo–slave narratives as discourse and material experience.

6. For more on the role of realism in traditional slave narratives, see James Olney. For more on the role of nonrealism in neo–slave narratives, see Sherryl Vint's "'Only by Experience.'"

7. Ellen Samuels provides an additional layer to this insistence on recovery, which prevented traditional slave narratives and their subsequent scholarly commentators from engaging disability. She writes, "Discussions of literacy and illiteracy are by definition discussions of ability and disability. . . . Yet to discuss illiteracy as disability resonates with centuries of characterizations of African Americans as flawed or defective, incapable of acquiring the ability that has come to equal personhood in post-Enlightenment Western culture" (*Fantasies of Identification* 36).

8. Nirmala Erevelles argues that disability is deployed as a political and analytical category to patrol the boundaries of citizenship (*Disability and Difference in Global Contexts* 134). Andrew Dilts and Jennifer James each write about citizenship and disability in relationship to black people historically, while Julie Avril Minich (*Accessible Citizenship*) and Jess Waggoner write about citizenship, disability, and race in contemporary contexts.

9. For more on the erasure of disability in slave and other racial uplift narratives, see Knadler or chapter 1 of Samuels's *Fantasies of Identification*.

10. See Lamp and Cleigh, May and Ferri, or Schalk, "Metaphorically Speaking."

11. A very early example of oppression analogy in disability studies is Leonard Kriegel's "Uncle Tom and Tiny Tim," published in 1969, which contains numerous oppression analogies in which the situation of people with disabilities in the United States is compared to that of black people or black men (neither black nor disabled women are mentioned). The article's comparisons eventually lead to a conclusion that people with disabilities are collectively worse off than black people and can learn from how black people achieved greater social recognition and rights. Comparisons such as this were common in early disability studies and disability rights, as evidenced by the many oppression analogies cited in Joseph Shapiro's history of the disability rights movement (14, 20, 24, 29, 34, 47, 128, 59).

12. Mitchell and Snyder were not the first to critique disability as metaphor; however, their concept of *narrative prosthesis* has become the signifying term for this sort of critique. Critiques of disability metaphors that preceded or emerged at the same time as Mitchell and Snyder's include Marilyn Dahl, Simi Linton, and Ellen L. Barton (Linton 125–26). Critiques of metaphor from within disability studies that build on Mitchell and Snyder's include G. Thomas Couser and Jamie McDaniel (Couser 110–25; McDaniel).

13. For examples of scholarship that argues for the potential and purpose of reading disability as metaphor, see Jarman; Mollow; Murray, "From Virginia's Sister to Friday's Silence"; Minich; or Hall.

14. See Alexander or Erevelles, "Crippin' Jim Crow."

15. For an example of the impact of slavery on the connections between blackness and disability today due to slave law, see Barclay.

16. Harriet A. Washington also provides an extended analysis of the racialized scientific claims of the antebellum period in *Medical Apartheid,* especially in chapters 1 and 6.

17. For a discussion of psychiatric institutionalization and imprisonment, see Jonathan Metzl's *Protest Psychosis,* especially chapter 14, "A Metaphor for Race." Harriet A. Washington's *Medical Apartheid* provides numerous examples of how understandings of black people as biologically inferior, especially the notion that black people cannot experience physical or emotional pain as much as white people, allowed for an extensive history of nontherapeutic medical experimentation on black people. Regarding insurance policy discrimination, see Ralph and, also, Alondra Nelson's discussion of how health statistics were used to discriminate against black people for insurance policies (44). Jennifer C. James writes that in some states during the Revolutionary and the Civil War, "the contention that the black body was an inherently disabled entity was used to prevent blacks from joining the military. . . . [For example,] New Hampshire refused to accept 'lunatics, idiots and Negroes,' implying blackness was a similar mental deficiency" (15).

18. Baynton provides several examples of this in his article. See also May and Ferri's "Fixated On Ability" or Lamp and Cleigh's "A Heritage of Ableist Rhetoric in American Feminism from the Eugenics Period."

19. See works by Barclay or Boster for historical discussions of disablement in slavery.

20. See Barclay's "'The Greatest Degree of Perfection'" for examples of the valuation of slave bodies and how some slave law called for physical punishment and disablement of slaves for their crimes.

21. Jim Downs argues that for disabled former slaves unable to leave the plantation or work elsewhere, enslavement essentially continued after slavery had officially ended.

22. Both Anne Donadey and Marc Steinberg use the phrase "the hold of the past on the present" (Donadey 71; Steinberg 474).

23. Anne Donadey, Marc Steinberg, Benjamin Robertson, Shari Evans, and Linh U. Hua also include this interpretation in their arguments.

24. Lisa A. Long and Stephanie S. Turner make similar arguments about Dana's disability symbolizing the impact of slavery on black kinship.

25. Carrie Sandahl discusses how nonlinear temporality works in similar ways in Lynn Mann's *Weights* ("Black Man, Blind Man").

26. Robert McRuer provides some insight on the concept of the inevitability of disability in the epilogue to *Crip Theory* in his discussion of "disability to come" and "global bodies" (203–8). See also Jasbir K. Puar, "Prognosis Time."

27. A major exception to this is Linh U. Hua, who argues that Dana is actually tied to Alice. On Dana's final return to the antebellum period Rufus's life is not in danger, but Alice has just killed herself.

28. Lennard Davis discusses the problems with narrativizing disability (*Enforcing Normalcy* 3).

Chapter 2: Deconstructing Able-Mindedness

1. My use of *mental disability* follows Margaret Price, who uses it "as an umbrella term to encompass cognitive, intellectual, and psychiatric disabilities, mental illness, m/Madness and a/Autism, as well as brain injury or psychiatric survivorship. *Mental disability* is not intended to replace any of these more specific terms or erase differences, but rather to enable coalition" ("The Bodymind Problem and the Possibilities of Pain" 280; original emphasis; See also Price, *Mad at School* 19).

2. For more on reading the X-men as representations of disability, see Ilea or Hopkins.

3. See Butler, *Kindred* 11, 16, 17, 28, 46, 57, 62, 78, 114, 136, 162, 201, and 241.

4. *Postpsychiatry*, a term originally coined by Patrick Bracken and Philip Thomas, represents an alternative vision for psychiatry that moves away from purely biological approaches that seek scientifically identifiable causes and cures and moves toward postmodern, cultural approaches that "emphasize that mental phenomena, like everything else, are richly complex and pluridimensional" (Lewis 72).

5. Metzl writes that as a result of this new understanding of schizophrenia as a black male disease not only were "racial concerns, and at times overt racism . . . written into diagnostic language in ways that are invisible to us now," but also these new "understandings of [schizophrenia] shaped American cultural fears about mental illness more broadly, particularly regarding cultural stereotypes of persons with schizophrenia as being unduly hostile or violent" (xix, xvi). In other words, racism of the past continues to influence and shape cultural interpretations and the actual lived experiences of people diagnosed with schizophrenia today.

6. For a full discussion of the concept of the borderlands, see Gloria Anzaldúa, *Borderlands*.

7. For arguments on how oppression can impact the mental health of marginalized people, see chapter 5 of Frantz Fanon's *The Wretched of the Earth*, as well as Meri Nana-Ama Danquah's memoir *Willow Weep for Me* and Anna Mollow's article analyzing Danquah's text.

8. Margaret Price discusses the need to recognize and affirm the experiences of people with mental disabilities as valid and real—even if that reality involves pain and the possibility of harm—while still being aware of the ways in which the interpretations of behaviors and treatment of individuals are determined by the identity positions of everyone involved ("The Bodymind Problem and the Possibilities of Pain" 272–79).

9. Examples of metaphorical readings of Lizzie's disability include Corinne Duboin,

who refers to the novel's use of pain, scars, and wounding as figurative, arguing that Lizzie's embodied ancestors, Ayo and Grace, "symbolize the return of the repressed, the excavation of an ineffable past that informs the present," while "Lizzie's inherited wounds are the symbolic visible marks" of the trauma of slavery (286, 88). Similarly, Venetria K. Patton argues that Lizzie's "stigmata is symbolic of the cultural trauma that Ayo's descendants must work through in order to heal the scars of slavery" (173).

10. In her article on *Stigmata*, Ana Nunes explicitly connects the text to rememory, writing, "Lizzie's stigmata work as a physical manifestation of Morrison's concept of rememory, the never-ending resurfacing of a traumatic and partially lost history" (230).

11. The details of Grace's story are fleshed out more in the prequel novel, *A Sunday in June*.

12. Those chapters are chapter 20 (April 1981. Montgomery), chapter 22 (July 1982. Montgomery), chapter 24 (November 1986. Birmingham), and chapter 26 (March 1988. Birmingham).

13. There is a history of feminist writing about psychiatric disability as a literal effect of patriarchy on women, as a metaphorical impact of patriarchy on women, or as an act of rebellion against patriarchy by women (May and Ferri 122, 28–30; Donaldson). Vivian M. May and Beth A. Ferri contend that such moves, when left purely metaphorical or unconnected to the material impact of mutually constitutive systems of power, construct "disability in opposition to the feminist subject" because disability is primarily understood as an effect of patriarchy which feminism seeks to eradicate (121). Elizabeth J. Donaldson similarly insists that feminist use of madness as a metaphor for women's resistance to patriarchy obscures the lived experiences of people with psychiatric disabilities.

14. This critique is particularly important in the context of a neo–slave narrative. While many critics have argued that neo–slave narratives challenge the discipline of history and modes of historical knowledge, the representation of disability in *Stigmata* demonstrates how neo–slave narratives can also contribute to critiques of other major cultural institutions, like psychiatry, that have both exploited and suppressed gendered and racialized knowledges with real bodymind consequences.

15. For a history of the ex-patient's movement, see Judi Chamberlin's "The Ex-Patient's Movement" and Bradley Lewis's *Moving Beyond Prozac, DSM, and the New Psychiatry*. See also, MindFreedom International's website.

16. The exact dates of Lizzie's two-year silence are not given, but since the final chapter falls in the middle of her institutionalization and she does not speak in the scene, I believe it is reasonable to read this as part of her period of quiet.

17. For an extended reading of the significance of quilting in the novel, see the second chapter of Woolfork's *Embodying American Slavery in Contemporary Culture* (51–57).

18. Black Poets Speak Out is a creative movement to use poetry to protest violence against black people. Black poets nationwide have posted videos on social media and organized readings. Each poet prefaces their reading with the statement, "I am a black poet who will not remain silent while this nation murders black people. I have a right to be angry" (see Browne; A. Johnston).

Chapter 3: Bodyminds of the Future

1. See Cheu, Weinstock, or Lavender's "Ethnoscapes" for discussions of nonhuman creatures standing in for marginalized groups.

2. See Kafer's discussion of Piercy's novel ("Debating Feminist Futures" 219, 32–33).

3. For more on Butler's personal relationship to disability, see Schalk, "Experience, Research, and Writing."

4. See, for example, Ingrid Thaler's reading of *Parable of the Sower* (69–97).

5. Throughout interviews about the Parable books, Butler refers to Lauren's disability as a defect, problem, delusion, *and* disability (O. E. Butler, *Conversations with Octavia Butler* 42, 70–71, 114, 63). Her language runs the gamut, but she generally seems to take a similar perspective to Lauren's disability as Lauren herself does in the books. Since authorial intent is not my concern here I include some reference to Butler's interviews, but do not allow her perspective to determine how I interpret the texts.

6. It's important to note how Lauren J. Lacey insists on putting *hyperempathy* in quotation marks. This occurs both in the portion I cite and each time the term appears in the article. This gesture seems to emphasize the fictional or constructed nature of Lauren's disability—both in the fact that it's not a realist disability and that it's not "real" pain or pleasure impacting her bodymind from the outside. Placing hyperempathy consistently in scare quotes, however, potentially dismisses the reality of Lauren's experience and the importance of the materiality of disability to the texts. Such a move positions Lacey's reading as primarily positive, but also verging on ignoring or erasing hyperempathy as disability as well. Although I have kept the quotation marks around *hyperempathy* in my citation of Lacey in order to remain true to her writing, I oppose this tactic myself because it runs counter to my speculative-fictional reading strategy, which reads nonrealist texts within their own rules of reality.

7. In *Parable of the Talents*, Christian America, also called CA, is a new, highly conservative Christian group that gains national power when one of its leaders is elected president. Among other abuses, CA kidnaps children from "bad" parents, sends such children far away to live with new CA families, illegally imprisons people, and, supposedly among small radical sects, burns "witches" at the stake and cuts out "bad" women's tongues.

8. See, for example, Octavia E. Butler Papers, "OEB 1757," 1989; "OEB 1766," 1989; "OEB 1767," 1989; and "OEB 3261," 1990.

9. Universal design seeks to create spaces and environments which are accessible to as many people as possible. In *Mad at School*, Margaret Price argues that accessibility is a process not a product—thus the emphasis on adaptation and change. She provides concrete suggestions for creating a universally designed classroom (88–102).

10. Jim Miller categorizes the *Parable* series as a critical dystopia, and other scholars have similarly noted the dystopian/utopian paradoxical moves within the novels. See also Stillman; Thaler; Wegner, chapter 8.

11. A similar representation of a technology intended to cure disability actually producing new disability appears in Butler's short story "The Evening, the Morning and the Night," published in her collection *Bloodchild and Other Stories*. Harriet A. Washington

provides an interesting, related historical example of medical technology's misuse resulting in disability in her discussion of how, in the 1900s to the 1920s, attempts to use X-ray treatment to whiten the skin of black people and to remove excess hair and coloration of "ethnic" whites resulted in numerous reported cancer cases by 1970 (226–27).

12. See Octavia E. Butler Papers, "OEB 2033," 1999; "OEB 2051," 2001; "OEB 2150," 2001; "OEB 2170," 2001; and "OEB 2123," 2001.

13. Sims, one of the "fathers" of gynecology, developed and practiced new gynecological procedures on black female slaves.

14. For more on superpowered supercrips, see Schalk, "Reevaluating the Supercrip."

15. Kim Love, ""#Becauseofoctavia & the Futures She Created with Her Speculative Fiction Especially, I Dared to Dream Bigger, Aspire Higher out of Comfort Zone," tweet, June 4, 2016, 9:47 p.m., https://twitter.com/kimmaytube?lang=en; Leigh B, "#Becauseofoctavia I Grew up Reading Science Fiction and Always Understood the Genre to Be a Forum to Produce Calls to Action," tweet, June 2, 2016, 9:49 p.m., accessed September 12, 2016; Starfish & Squid, "#Becauseofoctavia I Grew up Reading Science Fiction and Always Understood the Genre to Be a Forum to Produce Calls to Action," tweet, June 2, 2016, 8:42 p.m., https://twitter.com/denengethefirst?lang=en.

Chapter 4: Defamiliarizing (Dis)ability

1. Ria Cheyne writes that "in critical work on contemporary popular genres such as science fiction, romance, and crime fiction, there is little engagement with disability" ("Introduction" 117).

2. For more on the meaning and history of *oestranenie*, see Buchanan (354–55).

3. For a useful summary of and response to this concept, see Perry Nodelman's "The Cognitive Estrangement of Darko Suvin."

4. Mel Y. Chen discusses these issues using the term *transspecies* (89–126).

5. For the purposes of this chapter I do not include *Bitter Disenchantment* in my analysis since this prequel focuses on a secondary character of the series.

6. See McRuer, Davis, or Pickens (McRuer, *Crip Theory* 23–30; Davis, *Obsession*; Pickens, "'It's a Jungle Out There'").

7. See Rodas or Kleege.

8. For discussions of the spectacularization of conjoined twins, see Samuels, Wu, or Cleary (Samuels "Examining Millie and Christine McKoy"; Wu; Cleary). For discussions of enfreakment see Bogdan, Garland-Thomson, or Adams (Bogdan; Garland-Thomson *Freakery*; Adams). For discussions of the supercrip, see Schalk, "Reevaluating the Supercrip."

9. Natalya also mentions taking antianxiety pills in the short story "Contents May Have Shifted," which is set after the fourth book in the series (Madison, *Cursed*). Medication is not mentioned anywhere else in *Cursed*.

10. Cal Montgomery discusses more of the issues with the term *invisible disability* in his article, "A Hard Look at Invisible Disability."

11. See Darko Suvin's argument about the difference between science fiction and fan-

tasy and Joanna Russ's discussion of the science in science fiction (Suvin 3–36; Russ 112–16). It is important, however, to note how many writers of color, such as Nalo Hopkinson, have increasingly blurred the line between science fiction and fantasy.

12. Oree is described as having "smooth, near-black Maro skin" and a "storm of hair," and Jemisin repeatedly refers to Oree as black in her blog post on the character (*The Broken Kingdoms* 24; "Why Is Oree Shoth Blind?").

13. In *Kept,* Natalya learns that both her mother and Thorn were once victims of this kind of kidnapping and abuse by wizards, and, later in the text, in a moment of panic when he and Natalya are being attacked, Nick uses Natalya's life force to protect them both.

14. See Cheu or Lavender.

Conclusion

1. For more on Butler's personal relationship to disability, see Schalk, "Experience, Research, and Writing."

2. Butler herself complained about this perspective in a journal entry, writing *"people sneer at my stuff because it's simple and accessible!* As though accessibility were a crime" (Octavia E. Butler Papers, "OEB 1054," 1998; original emphasis).

BIBLIOGRAPHY

Adams, Rachel. *Sideshow U.S.A.: Freaks and the American Cultural Imagination*. Chicago: University of Chicago Press, 2001.

Al-Ayad, Djibril, and Kathryn Allan, eds. *Accessing the Future*. Futurefire.net Publishing, 2015. https://www.amazon.com/Accessing-Future-Djibril-Al-Ayad/dp/0957397542/ref=sr_1_1?ie=UTF8&qid=1497890476&sr=8-1&keywords=accessing+the+future.

Alaniz, José. "Death and the Superhero: The Silver Age and Beyond." *International Journal of Comic Art* 8, no. 1 (2006): 234–48.

Alexander, Michelle. *The New Jim Crow: Mass Incarceration in the Age of Colorblindness*. New York: New Press, 2010.

Allan, Kathryn. *Disability in Science Fiction: Representations of Technology as Cure*. New York: Palgrave Macmillan, 2013.

Allen, Marlene D. "Octavia Butler's Parable Novels and the 'Boomerang' of African American History." *Callaloo* 32, no. 4 (Fall 2009): 1353–65.

Anzaldúa, Gloria. *Borderlands: The New Mestiza = La Frontera*. 3rd ed. San Francisco: Aunt Lute Books, 2007.

———. "La conciencia de la mestiza: Towards a New Consciousness." In *Making Face, Making Soul: Haciendo Caras*, edited by Gloria Anzaldúa, 377–89. San Francisco: Aunt Lute Books, 1990.

Arndt, Katrina, and Maia Van Beuren. "*The Speed of Dark* and *This Alien Shore*: Representations of Cognitive Difference." *Journal of Literary and Cultural Disability Studies* 7, no. 1 (2013): 89–104.

Avatar (film). Directed by James Cameron. 20th Century Fox, 2009.

Baldys, Emily M. "Disabled Sexuality, Incorporated: The Compulsions of Popular Romance." *Journal of Literary and Cultural Disability Studies* 6, no. 2 (2012): 125–41.

Barclay, Jenifer L. "'The Greatest Degree of Perfection': Disability and the Construction of Race in American Slave Law." *South Carolina Review* 46, no. 2 (2014): 27–43.

———. "Mothering the 'Useless': Black Motherhood, Disability, and Slavery." *Women, Gender, and Families of Color* 2, no. 2 (2014): 115–40.

Barker, Clare. *Postcolonial Fiction and Disability: Exceptional Children, Metaphor and Materiality*. New York: Palgrave Macmillan, 2011.

Barr, Marleen S. *Alien to Femininity: Speculative Fiction and Feminist Theory*. Contributions to the Study of Science Fiction and Fantasy. New York: Greenwood, 1987.

———. *Lost in Space: Probing Feminist Science Fiction and Beyond*. Chapel Hill: University of North Carolina Press, 1993.

Barton, Ellen L. "Textual Practices of Erasure." *Embodied Rhetorics: Disability in Language and Culture*, edited by James C. Wilson and Cynthia Lewiecki-Wilson, 169–99. Carbondale: Southern Illinois University Press, 2001.

Batty, Nancy. "'Caught by a . . . Genre': An Interview with Nalo Hopkinson." ARIEL: *A Review of International English Literature* 33, no. 1 (2002): 175–201.

Baynton, Douglas. "Disability and the Justification of Inequality in American History." In *The New Disability History: American Perspectives*, edited by Paul Longmore and Lauri Umansky, 33–57. New York: New York University Press, 2001.

Bell, Bernard W. *The Afro-American Novel and Its Tradition*. Amherst: University of Massachusetts Press, 1987.

Bell, Chris. "Introducing White Disability Studies: A Modest Proposal." In *The Disability Studies Reader*, 2nd ed., edited by Lennard J. Davis, 275–82. New York: Routledge, 2006.

Bemis, Virginia. "Chaos and Quest: Miles Vorkosigan's Disability Narrative." In *Lois McMaster Bujold: Essays on a Modern Master of Science Fiction and Fantasy*, edited by Janet Brennan Croft, 104–15. Jefferson, NC: McFarland and Company, 2013.

Ben-Moshe, Liat, and Allison C. Carey. *Disability Incarcerated: Imprisonment and Disability in the United States and Canada*. New York: Palgrave Macmillan, 2014.

Bérubé, Michael. "Disability and Narrative." PMLA 120, no. 2 (2005): 568–76.

———. *The Secret Life of Stories: From "Don Quixote" to "Harry Potter," How Understanding Intellectual Disability Transforms the Way We Read*. New York: New York University Press, 2016.

Bogdan, Robert. *Freak Show: Presenting Human Oddities for Amusement and Profit*. Chicago: University of Chicago Press, 1988.

Boster, Dea H. *African American Slavery and Disability: Bodies, Property, and Power in the Antebellum South, 1800–1860*. Studies in African American History and Culture. New York: Routledge, 2013.

Bould, Mark. "The Ships Landed Long Ago: Afrofuturism and Black Sf." *Science Fiction Studies* 34, no. 2 (2007): 177–86.

Fixed: The Science/Fiction of Human Enhancement (film). Directed by Reagan Brashear. New Day Films, 2013.

Bracken, Patrick, and Philip Thomas. "Postpsychiatry: A New Direction for Mental Health." *Postpsychiatry* 322, no. 7288 (2001): 724–27.

brown, adrienne maree. "Outro." In *Octavia's Brood: Science Fiction Stories from Social Justice Movements*, edited by Walidah Imarisha and adrienne maree brown, 279–81. Oakland, CA: AK Press, 2015.

Browne, Mahogany L. "Black Poets Speak Out." Poetry Society of America. November 11, 2015. https://www.poetrysociety.org/psa/poetry/crossroads/black_poets_speak_out/.

Buchanan, Ian. *A Dictionary of Critical Theory.* Oxford: Oxford University Press, 2010.

Butler, Judith. *Bodies That Matter: On the Discursive Limits of "Sex."* New York: Routledge, 1993.

Butler, Octavia E. *Bloodchild and Other Stories.* 2nd ed. New York: Seven Stories, 2005.

———. *Conversations with Octavia Butler.* Jackson: University Press of Mississippi, 2010.

———. "A Few Rules for Predicting the Future." *Essence* (May 2000): 165–66, 264.

———. *Kindred.* Boston: Beacon, 2003.

———. Octavia E. Butler Papers. The Huntington Library. San Marino, CA.

———. *Parable of the Sower.* New York: Grand Central Publishing, 2007.

———. *Parable of the Talents.* New York: Warner Books, 2000.

Carby, Hazel V. *Reconstructing Womanhood: The Emergence of the Afro-American Woman Novelist.* New York: Oxford University Press, 1987.

Carmody, Todd. "In Spite of Handicaps: The Disability History of Racial Uplift." *American Literary History* 27, no. 1 (2015): 56–78.

Cassuto, Leonard. *The Inhuman Race: The Racial Grotesque in American Literature and Culture.* New York: Columbia University Press, 1997.

Cave, Damien. "Officer Darren Wilson's Grand Jury Testimony in Ferguson, Mo., Shooting." *New York Times.* November 25, 2014. https://www.nytimes.com/interactive/2014/11/25/us/darren-wilson-testimony-ferguson-shooting.html?_r=0.

Chamberlin, Judi. "The Ex-Patient's Movement: Where We've Been and Where We're Going." *Journal of Mind and Behavior* 11 (1990): 323–36.

Chan, Edward K. "Utopia and the Problem of Race: Accounting for the Remainder in the Imagination of the 1970s Utopian Subject." *Utopian Studies* 17, no. 3 (2006): 465–90.

Chen, Mel Y. *Animacies: Biopolitics, Racial Mattering, and Queer Affect.* Perverse Modernities. Durham, NC: Duke University Press, 2012.

Cheu, Johnson. "De-gene-erates, Replicants and Other Aliens: (Re)Defining Disability in Futuristic Film." In *Disability/Postmodernity: Embodying Disability Theory*, edited by Mairian Corker and Tom Shakespeare, 198–212. London: Continuum, 2002.

Cheyne, Ria. "Introduction: Popular Genres and Disability Representation." *Journal of Literary and Cultural Disability Studies* 6, no. 2 (2012): 117–23.

———. "'She Was Born a Thing': Disability, the Cyborg, and the Posthuman in Anne McCaffrey's *The Ship Who Sang.*" *Journal of Modern Literature* 36, no. 3 (2013): 138–56.

Christian, Barbara. *Black Women Novelists: The Development of a Tradition, 1892–1976.*

Contributions in Afro-American and African Studies. Westport, CT: Greenwood, 1980.

———. "The Race for Theory." *Cultural Critique* no. 6 (spring 1987): 51–63.

———. "Diminishing Returns." In *New Black Feminist Criticism, 1985–2000*, edited by Gloria Bowles, M. Giulia Fabi, and Arlene Keizer. Urbana: University of Illinois Press, 2007.

Cleary, Krystal. "Misfitting and Hater Blocking: A Feminist Disability Analysis of the Extraordinary Body on Reality Television." *Disability Studies Quarterly* 36 (2016).

Clifton, Lucille. *The Book of Light*. Port Townsend, WA: Copper Canyon, 1993.

Cohen, Cathy J. "Punks, Bulldaggers and Welfare Queens: The Radical Potential of Queer Politics?" In *Black Queer Studies: A Critical Anthology*, edited by E. Patrick Johnson and Mae G. Henderson, 21–51. Durham, NC: Duke University Press, 2005.

Combahee River Collective. "A Black Feminist Statement." In *This Bridge Called My Back: Writings by Radical Women of Color*, edited by Cherríe Moraga and Gloria Anzaldúa, 210–18. New York: Kitchen Table: Women of Color Press, 1983.

Couser, G. Thomas. *Signifying Bodies: Disability in Contemporary Life Writing*. Corporealities. Ann Arbor: University of Michigan Press, 2009.

Crenshaw, Kimberlé. "Demarginalizing the Intersection of Race and Sex: A Black Feminist Critique of Antidiscrimination Doctrine, Feminist Theory and Antiracist Politics." *University of Chicago Legal Forum* (1989): 139–67.

———. "Mapping the Margins: Intersectionality, Identity Politics, and Violence against Women of Color." *Stanford Law Review* 43, no. 6 (1991): 1241–99.

Curtis, Claire P. "Utopian Possibilities: Disability, Norms, and Eugenics in Octavia Butler's *Xenogenesis*." *Journal of Literary and Cultural Disability Studies* 9, no. 1 (2015): 19–33.

Dahl, Marilyn. "The Role of the Media in Promoting Images of Disability—Disability as Metaphor: The Evil Crip." *Canadian Journal of Communication* 18 (1993): 75–80.

Danquah, Meri Nana-Ama. *Willow Weep for Me: A Black Woman's Journey through Depression, a Memoir*. New York: Norton, 1998.

Davis, Lennard J. *The End of Normal: Identity in a Biocultural Era*. Ann Arbor: University of Michigan Press, 2013.

———. *Enforcing Normalcy: Disability, Deafness, and the Body*. London: Verso, 1995.

———. *Obsession: A History*. Chicago: University of Chicago Press, 2008.

DeGraw, Sharon. *The Subject of Race in American Science Fiction*. Literary Criticism and Cultural Theory. New York: Routledge, 2007.

Delany, Samuel R. *The Jewel-Hinged Jaw: Notes on the Language of Science Fiction*. Rev. ed. Middletown, CT: Wesleyan University Press, 2009.

———. "Racism and Science Fiction." *New York Review of Science Fiction* 1998. http://www.nyrsf.com/racism-and-science-fiction-.html.

Dery, Mark. "Black to the Future: Afro-Futurism 1.0." In *Afro-Future Females: Black Writers Chart Science Fiction's Newest New-Wave Trajectory*, edited by Marleen S. Barr, 6–13. Columbus: Ohio State University Press, 2008.

Dilts, Andrew. "Incurable Blackness: Criminal Disenfranchisement, Mental Disability, and the White Citizen." *Disability Studies Quarterly* 32, no. 3 (2012). http://dsq-sds.org/article/view/3268/3101.

Doerksen, Teri Ann. "Octavia E. Butler: Parables of Race and Difference." In *Into Darkness Peering: Race and Color in the Fantastic*, edited by Elisabeth Anne Leonard, 21–34. Westport, CT: Greenwood, 1997.

Donadey, Anne. "African American and Francophone Postcolonial Memory: Octavia Butler's *Kindred* and Assia Djebar's *La Femme Sans Sépulture*." *Research in African Literatures* 39, no. 3 (2008): 65–81.

Donaldson, Elizabeth J. "The Corpus of the Madwoman: Toward a Feminist Disability Studies Theory of Embodiment and Mental Illness." *NWSA Journal* 14, no. 3 (2002): 99–119.

Dovidio, John F., and Susan T. Fiske. "Under the Radar: How Unexamined Biases in Decision-Making Processes in Clinical Interactions Can Contribute to Health Care Disparities." *American Journal of Public Health* 102, no. 5 (2012): 945–52.

Downs, Jim. "The Continuation of Slavery: The Experience of Disabled Slaves during Emancipation." *Disability Studies Quarterly* 28, no. 3 (2008). http://www.dsq-sds .org/article/view/112/112.

Du Bois, W. E. B. "The Comet." In *Dark Matter: A Century of Speculative Fiction from the African Diaspora*, edited by Sheree R. Thomas, 5–18. New York: Grand Central Publishing, 2000.

Dubey, Madhu. *Black Women Novelists and the Nationalist Aesthetic*. Bloomington: Indiana University Press, 1994.

———. "Neo-Slave Narratives." In *A Companion to African American Literature*, edited by Gene Andrew Jarrett, 332–46. Malden, MA: Blackwell, 2010.

———. "Speculative Fictions of Slavery." *American Literature* 82, no. 4 (2010): 779–805.

Duboin, Corinne. "Trauma Narrative, Memorialization, and Mourning in Phyllis Alesia Perry's *Stigmata*." *Southern Literary Journal* 40, no. 2 (2008): 284–304.

DuCille, Ann. *The Coupling Convention: Sex, Text, and Tradition in Black Women's Fiction*. New York: Oxford University Press, 1993.

Edmondson, Belinda. "The Black Romance." *Women's Studies Quarterly* 35, nos. 1/2 (2007): 191–211.

Erevelles, Nirmala. "Crippin' Jim Crow: Disability, Dis-Location, and the School-to-Prison Pipeline." In *Disability Incarcerated: Imprisonment and Disability in the United States and Canada*, edited by Liat Ben-Moshe, Chris Chapman, and Allison C. Carey, 81–100. New York: Palgrave Macmillan, 2014.

———. *Disability and Difference in Global Contexts: Enabling a Transformative Body Politic*. New York: Palgrave Macmillan, 2011.

———. "In Search of the Disabled Subject." In *Embodied Rhetorics: Disability in Language and Culture*, edited by James C. Wilson and Cynthia Lewiecki-Wilson, 92–111. Carbondale: Southern Illinois University Press, 2001.

Evans, Shari. "From 'Hierarchical Behavior' to Strategic Amnesia: Structures of Memory and Forgetting in Octavia Butler's *Fledgling*." In *Strange Matings: Science Fiction, Feminism, African American Voices, and Octavia E. Butler*, edited by Rebecca J. Holden and Nisi Shawl, 237–62. Seattle: Aqueduct, 2013.

Ewart, Chris. "Terms of Disappropriation: Disability, Diaspora and Dionne Brand's

What We All Long For." *Journal of Literary and Cultural Disability Studies* 4, no. 2 (2010): 147–61.

Fanon, Frantz. *The Wretched of the Earth,* translated by Richard Philcox. New York: Grove, 2004.

Fausto-Sterling, Anne. *Sexing the Body: Gender Politics and the Construction of Sexuality.* New York: Basic Books, 2000.

Fine, Michelle, and Adrienne Asch. *Women with Disabilities: Essays in Psychology, Culture, and Politics.* Health, Society, and Policy. Philadelphia: Temple University Press, 1988.

Flagel, Nadine. " 'It's Almost Like Being There': Speculative Fiction, Slave Narrative, and the Crisis of Representation in Octavia Butler's *Kindred."* *Canadian Review of American Studies* 42, no. 2 (2012): 216–45.

Fox, Ann M. "A Different Integration: Race and Disability in Early-Twentieth-Century African American Drama by Women." *Legacy: A Journal of American Women Writers* 30, no. 1 (2013): 151–71.

Garland-Thomson, Rosemarie. *Extraordinary Bodies: Figuring Physical Disability in American Culture and Literature.* New York: Columbia University Press, 1997.

———., ed. *Freakery: Cultural Spectacles of the Extraordinary Body.* New York: New York University Press, 1996.

———. "Integrating Disability, Transforming Feminist Theory." In *Feminisms Redux: An Anthology of Literary Theory and Criticism,* edited by Robyn Warhol-Down and Diane Price Herndl, 487–513. New Brunswick, NJ: Rutgers University Press, 2009.

———. "Speaking about the Unspeakable: The Representation of Disability as Stigma in Toni Morrison's Novels." In *Courage and Tools: The Florence Howe Award for Feminist Scholarship, 1974–89,* edited by Joanne Glasgow and Angela Ingram, 238–51. New York: Modern Language Association of America, 1990.

Gast, Phil, Alinda Machado, Ed Danko, and Javier De Diego. "Woman Forced from Florida Hospital Dies after Arrest: Audio of Scene Released." CNN. January 8, 2016. http://www.cnn.com/2016/01/07/us/florida-woman-removed-hospital-dies/.

The Girl with All the Gifts (film). Directed by Colm McCarthy. Lionsgate, 2016.

Glave, Dianne D., and Nalo Hopkinson. "An Interview with Nalo Hopkinson." *Callaloo* 26, no. 1 (Winter 2003): 146–59.

Goff, Phillip Atiba, Matthew Christian Jackson, Brooke Allison Lewis Di Leone, Carmen Marie Culotta, and Natalie Ann DiTamasso. "The Essence of Innocence: Consequences of Dehumanizing Black Children." *Journal of Personality and Social Psychology* 104, no. 4 (2014): 526–45.

Gomel, Elana. "The Plague of Utopias: Pestilence and the Apocalyptic Body." *Twentieth Century Literature* 46, no. 4 (2000): 405–33.

Gomez, Jewelle. "Speculative Fiction and Black Lesbians." *Signs* 18, no. 4 (1993): 948–55.

Goodley, Dan. *Dis/Ability Studies: Theorising Disablism and Ableism.* New York: Routledge, 2014.

Govan, Sandra. "Disparate Spirits Yet Kindred Souls: Octavia E. Butler, 'Speech Sounds,' and Me." In *Strange Matings: Science Fiction, Feminism, African American*

Voices, and Octavia E. Butler, edited by Rebecca J. Holden and Nisi Shawl, 109–27. Seattle: Aqueduct, 2013.

Haley, Alex. Roots. Garden City, NY: Doubleday, 1976.

Hall, Alice. Disability and Modern Fiction: Faulkner, Morrison, Coetzee and the Nobel Prize for Literature. New York: Palgrave Macmillan, 2012.

Hampton, Gregory Jerome. Changing Bodies in the Fiction of Octavia Butler: Slaves, Aliens, and Vampires. Lanham, MD: Lexington, 2010.

Harrell, Camara Jules P., Tanisha I. Burford, Brandi N. Cage, Travette McNair Nelson, Sheronda Shearon, Adrian Thompson, and Steven Green. "Multiple Pathways Linking Racism to Health Outcomes." Du Bois Review: Social Science Research on Race 8, no. 1 (2011): 143–57.

Harris, Trudier. Saints, Sinners, Saviors: Strong Black Women in African American Literature. New York: Palgrave, 2001.

Henton, Jennifer E. "Close Encounters between Traditional and Nontraditional Science Fiction: Octavia E. Butler's Kindred and Gayl Jones's Corregidora Sing the Time Travel Blues." In Afro-Future Females: Black Writers Chart Science Fiction's Newest New Wave Trajectory, edited by Marleen S. Barr, 100–118. Columbus: Ohio State University Press, 2008.

Higginbotham, Evelyn Brooks. "African-American Women's History and the Metalanguage of Race." Signs 17, no. 2 (1992): 251–74.

hooks, bell. Feminist Theory: From Margin to Center. South End Press Classics. 2nd ed. Cambridge, MA: South End, 2000.

———. We Real Cool: Black Men and Masculinity. New York: Routledge, 2004.

Hopkins, Patrick D. "The Lure of the Normal: Who Wouldn't Want to Be a Mutant?" In X-Men and Philosophy: Astonishing Insight and Uncanny Argument in the Mutant X-Verse, edited by Rebecca Housel and J. Jeremy Wisnewski, 5–16. Blackwell Philosophy and Pop Culture Series. New York: John Wiley and Sons, 2009.

Hopkinson, Nalo. Sister Mine. New York: Grand Central Publishing, 2013.

Hosey, Sara. "'One of Us': Identity and Community in Contemporary Fiction." Journal of Literary and Cultural Disability Studies 1, no. 1 (2009): 35–50.

Hua, Linh U. "Reproducing Time, Reproducing History: Love and Black Feminist Sentimentality in Octavia Butler's Kindred." African American Review 44, no. 3 (2010): 391–407.

Ilea, Ramona. "The Mutant Cure of Social Change: Debating Disability." In X-Men and Philosophy: Astonishing Insight and Uncanny Argument in the Mutant X-Verse, edited by Rebecca Housel and J. Jeremy Wisnewski, 170–83. New York: John Wiley and Sons, 2009.

Imarisha, Walidah. "Introduction." In Octavia's Brood: Science Fiction Stories from Social Justice Movements, edited by Walidah Imarisha and adrienne maree brown, 3–5. Oakland, CA: AK Press, 2015.

Imarisha, Walidah, and adrienne maree brown, eds. Octavia's Brood: Science Fiction Stories from Social Justice Movements. Oakland, CA: AK Press, 2015.

Jakober, Marie. "The Continuum of Meaning: A Reflection on Speculative Fiction and Society." In The Influence of Imagination: Essays on Science Fiction and Fantasy as *Agents of Social Change*, edited by Lee Easton and Randy Schroeder, 27–31. Jefferson, NC: McFarland and Company, 2008.

James, Jennifer C. *A Freedom Bought with Blood: African American War Literature from the Civil War to World War II*. Chapel Hill: University of North Carolina Press, 2007.

Jarman, Michelle. "Coming up from Underground: Uneasy Dialogues at the Intersections of Race, Mental Illness, and Disability Studies." In *Blackness and Disability*, edited by Christopher M. Bell, 9–30. East Lansing: Michigan State University Press, 2012.

Jarrett, Gene Andrew. *Deans and Truants: Race and Realism in African American Literature*. Philadelphia: University of Pennsylvania Press, 2007.

Jemisin, N. K. *The Broken Kingdoms*. New York: Orbit, 2010.

———. *The Kingdom of Gods*. New York: Orbit, 2011.

———. "Why Is Oree Shoth Blind?". Epiphany 2.0 (blog). January 27, 2011. http://nkjemisin.com/2011/01/why-is-oree-shoth-blind/.

John, Marie-Elena. *Unburnable*. New York: Amistad, 2006.

Johnston, Amanda. "Black Poets Speak Out." Tumblr post, 2014. Accessed November 11, 2015. https://blackpoetsspeakout.tumblr.com/About.

Johnston, Nancy. "'Happy That It's Here': An Interview with Nalo Hopkinson." In *Queer Universes: Sexualities in Science Fiction*, edited by Wendy Gay Pearson, Veronica Hollinger, and Joan Gordon. 200–215. Liverpool, UK: Liverpool University Press, 2008

Jones, Duncan, dir. *Source Code* (film). Summit Entertainment, 2014.

Jones, Edward P. *The Known World*. New York: Amistad, 2003.

Jones, Vida Labrie. "Lupus and Black Women: Managing a Complex Chronic Disability." In *The Black Women's Health Book: Speaking for Ourselves*, edited by Evelyn C. White, 160–66. Seattle: Seal Press, 1994.

June, Pamela B. *The Fragmented Female Body and Identity: The Postmodern, Feminist, and Multiethnic Writings of Toni Morrison, Theresa Hak Kyung Cha, Phyllis Alesia Perry, Gayl Jones, Emma Pérez, Paula Gunn Allen, and Kathy Acker*. Modern American Literature. New York: Peter Lang, 2010.

Kafer, Alison. "Debating Feminist Futures: Slippery Slopes, Cultural Anxiety, and the Case of the Deaf Lesbians." In *Feminist Disability Studies*, edited by Kim Q. Hall, 218–42. Bloomington: Indiana University Press, 2011.

———. *Feminist, Queer, Crip*. Bloomington: Indiana University Press, 2013.

Kanar, Hanley E. "No Ramps in Space: The Inability to Imagine Accessibility in *Star Trek: Deep Space Nine*." In *Fantasy Girls: Gender in the New Universe of Science Fiction and Fantasy Television*, edited by Elyce Rae Helford, 245–64. Lanham, MD: Rowman and Littlefield, 2000.

Kilgore, De Witt Douglas. *Astrofuturism: Science, Race, and Visions of Utopia in Space*. Philadelphia: University of Pennsylvania Press, 2003.

Kleege, Georgina. "Blindness and Visual Culture: An Eyewitness Account." *Journal of Visual Culture* 4, no. 2 (2005): 179–90.

Kline, Wendy. *Building a Better Race: Gender, Sexuality, and Eugenics from the Turn of the Century to the Baby Boom*. Berkeley: University of California Press, 2001.

Knabe, Susan, and Wendy Gay Pearson. "'Gambling against History': Queer Kinship and Cruel Optimism in Octavia Butler's *Kindred*." In *Strange Matings: Science Fiction, Feminism, African American Voices, and Octavia E. Butler*, edited by Rebecca J. Holden and Nisi Shawl, 51–78. Seattle: Aqueduct, 2013.

Knadler, Stephen. "Dis-Abled Citizenship: Narrating the Extraordinary Body in Racial Uplift." *Arizona Quarterly: A Journal of American Literature, Culture, and Theory* 69, no. 3 (2013): 99–128.

Kriegel, Leonard. "Uncle Tom and Tiny Tim: Some Reflections on the Cripple as Negro." *American Scholar* 38 (1969): 412–30.

Lacey, Lauren J. "Octavia E. Butler on Coping with Power in *Parable of the Sower, Parable of the Talents*, and *Fledgling*." *Critique* 49, no. 4 (2008): 379–94.

Lamp, Sharon, and W. Carol Cleigh. "A Heritage of Ableist Rhetoric in American Feminism from the Eugenics Period." In *Feminist Disability Studies*, edited by Kim Q. Hall, 175–90. Bloomington: Indiana University Press, 2011.

Lavender, Isiah. "Ethnoscapes: Environment and Language in Ishmael Reed's *Mumbo Jumbo*, Colson Whitehead's *The Intuitionist*, and Samuel R. Delany's *Babel-17*." *Science Fiction Studies* 34, no. 2 (2007): 187–200.

———. *Race in American Science Fiction*. Bloomington: Indiana University Press, 2011.

Lefanu, Sarah. *In the Chinks of the World Machine: Feminism and Science Fiction*. London: Women's Press, 1988.

Leonard, Elisabeth Anne. *Into Darkness Peering: Race and Color in the Fantastic*. Contributions to the Study of Science Fiction and Fantasy. Westport, CT: Greenwood, 1997.

Lewis, Bradley. *Moving beyond Prozac, DSM, and the New Psychiatry: The Birth of Postpsychiatry*. Ann Arbor: University of Michigan Press, 2006.

Linton, Simi. *Claiming Disability: Knowledge and Identity*. Cultural Front. New York: New York University Press, 1998.

Livingston, Julie, and Jasbir K. Puar. "Interspecies." *Social Text* 29, no. 1 106 (2011): 3–14.

Long, Lisa A. "A Relative Pain: The Rape of History in Octavia Butler's *Kindred* and Phyllis Alesia Perry's *Stigmata*." *College English* 64, no. 4 (2002): 459–83.

Lorde, Audre. *Zami: A New Spelling of My Name*. Crossing Press Feminist Series. Trumansburg, NY: Crossing Press, 1982.

Lubiano, Wahneema. "But Compared to What? Reading Realism, Representation, and Essentialism in *School Daze, Do the Right Thing*, and the Spike Lee Discourse." *Black American Literature Forum* 25, no. 2 (1991): 253–82.

Madison, Shawntelle. *Bitter Disenchantment: A Coveted Novella*. New York: Ballantine. 2013.

———. *Collected*, edited by Jennifer Jakes. 2012.

———. *Compelled*. Self-published, 2014.

———. *Coveted*. New York: Ballantine, 2012.

———. *Cursed: A Collection of Coveted Short Stories*. Self-published, 2016.

———. *Kept*. New York: Ballantine, 2012.

May, Vivian M. *Pursuing Intersectionality, Unsettling Dominant Imaginaries*. Contemporary Sociological Perspectives. New York: Routledge, 2015.

May, Vivian M., and Beth A. Ferri. "Fixated on Ability: Questioning Ableist Metaphors in Feminist Theories of Resistance." *Prose Studies* 27, nos. 1/2 (2005): 120–40.

McBride, James. *Song Yet Sung*. New York: Riverhead Books, 2008.

McCaffrey, Anne. *The Ship Who Sang*. New York: Walker and Co., 1969.

McDaniel, Jamie. "'You Can Point a Finger at a Zombie. Sometimes They Fall Off.': Contemporary Zombie Films, Embedded Ableism, and Disability as Metaphor." *Midwest Quarterly* 57, no. 4 (2016): 423–46.

McKittrick, Katherine. *Demonic Grounds: Black Women and the Cartographies of Struggle*. Minneapolis: University of Minnesota Press, 2006.

McRuer, Robert. *Crip Theory: Cultural Signs of Queerness and Disability*. New York: New York University Press, 2006.

———. "Disability Nationalism in Crip Times." *Journal of Literary and Cultural Disability Studies* 4, no. 2 (2010): 163–78.

Melzer, Patricia. *Alien Constructions: Science Fiction and Feminist Thought*. Austin: University of Texas Press, 2006.

———. "'And How Many Souls Do You Have?': Technologies of Perverse Desire and Queer Sex in Science Fiction Erotica." In *Queer Universes: Sexualities in Science Fiction*, edited by Wendy G. Pearson, Veronica Hollinger, and Joan Gordon, 161–79. Liverpool, UK: Liverpool University Press, 2008.

Menne, Jeff. "'I Live in This World, Too': Octavia Butler and the State of Realism." *Modern Fiction Studies* 57, no. 4 (2011): 715–37.

Metzl, Jonathan. *The Protest Psychosis: How Schizophrenia Became a Black Disease*. Boston: Beacon, 2009.

Miller, Jim. "Post-Apocalyptic Hoping: Octavia Butler's Dystopian/Utopian Vision." *Science Fiction Studies* 25, no. 2 (1998): 336–60.

MindFreedom International. "MFI Wins Human Rights in Mental Health." March 24, 2013. http://www.mindfreedom.org/.

Minich, Julie Avril. *Accessible Citizenships: Disability, Nation, and the Cultural Politics of Greater Mexico*. Philadelphia: Temple University Press, 2014.

———. "Enabling Whom? Critical Disability Studies Now." *Lateral* 5, no. 1 (2016). https://doi.org/10.25158/L5.1.9.

Minister, Meredith. "Female, Black, and Able: Representations of Sojourner Truth and Theories of Embodiment." *Disability Studies Quarterly* 32, no. 1 (2012). http://dsq-sds.org/article/view/3030/3057.

Mitchell, Angelyn. "Not Enough of the Past: Feminist Revisions of Slavery in Octavia E. Butler's *Kindred*." *MELUS* 26, no. 3 (2001): 51–75.

Mitchell, David T., and Sharon L. Snyder. *Narrative Prosthesis: Disability and the Dependencies of Discourse*. Corporealities. Ann Arbor: University of Michigan Press, 2001.

Mohanty, Chandra Talpade. *Feminism without Borders: Decolonizing Theory, Practicing Solidarity*. Durham, NC: Duke University Press, 2003.

Mollow, Anna. "'When Black Women Start Going on Prozac': Race, Gender, and Mental Illness in Meri Nana-Ama Danquah's *Willow Weep for Me*." *MELUS* 31, no. 3 (2006): 67–99.

Montgomery, Cal. "A Hard Look at Invisible Disability." *Ragged Edge*, no. 2 (2001). http://www.raggededgemagazine.com/0301/0301ft1.htm.

Moody, Nickianne. "Untapped Potential: The Representation of Disability/Special Ability in the Cyberpunk Workforce." *Convergence: The International Journal of Research into New Media Technologies* 3, no. 3 (1997): 90–105.

Morris, Susana M. *Close Kin and Distant Relatives: The Paradox of Respectability in Black Women's Literature*. Charlottesville: University of Virginia Press, 2014.

Morrison, Toni. *Beloved: A Novel*. New York: Vintage International, 2004.

Moya, Paula M. L. "Introduction." In *Reclaiming Identity: Realist Theory and the Predicament of Postmodernism*, edited by Paula M. L. Moya and Michael Hames-Garcia, 1–28. Berkeley: University of California Press, 2000.

Moylan, Tom. *Demand the Impossible: Science Fiction and the Utopian Imagination*. New York: Methuen, 1986.

Murray, Stuart. "Autism and the Contemporary Sentimental: Fiction and the Narrative Fascination of the Present." *Literature and Medicine* 25, no. 1 (2006): 24–45.

———. "From Virginia's Sister to Friday's Silence: Presence, Metaphor, and the Persistence of Disability in Contemporary Writing." *Journal of Literary and Cultural Disability Studies* 6, no. 3 (2012): 241–58.

Nash, Jennifer C. "Home Truths on Intersectionality." *Yale Journal of Law and Feminism* 23, no. 2 (2011): 445–70.

———. "Practicing Love: Black Feminism, Love-Politics, and Post-Intersectionality." *Meridians: Feminism, Race, Transnationalism* 11, no. 2 (2013): 1–24.

———. "Re-Thinking Intersectionality." *Feminist Review* 89 (2008): 1–15.

Nelson, Alondra. *Body and Soul: The Black Panther Party and the Fight against Medical Discrimination*. Minneapolis: University of Minnesota Press, 2011.

Newman-Stille, Derek. "Where Blindness Is Not (?) a Disability: Alison Sinclair's *Darkborn* Trilogy." *Mosaic: A Journal for the Interdisciplinary Study of Literature* 46, no. 3 (2013): 43–58.

Nodelman, Perry. "The Cognitive Estrangement of Darko Suvin." *Children's Literature Association Quarterly* 5, no. 4 (1981): 24–27.

Nunes, Ana. "From the Fantastic to Magical Realism: The Spectral Presence in Phyllis Perry's *Stigmata*." In *Revisiting Slave Narratives II*, edited by Judith Misrahi-Barak, 223–48. Montpellier, France: Presses Universitaires de la Méditerranée, 2007.

Olney, James. "'I Was Born': Slave Narratives, Their Status as Autobiography and as Literature." *Callaloo: A Journal of African American and African Arts and Letters*, no. 20 (1984): 46–73.

Olyan, Saul M. "Disability in the Prophetic Utopian Vision." In *Disability in the Hebrew Bible*, 78–92. New York: Cambridge University Press, 2008.

Painter, Nell Irvin. "Representing Truth: Sojourner Truth's Knowing and Becoming Known." *Journal of American History* 81, no. 2 (1994): 461–92.

Parham, Marisa. "Saying 'Yes': Textual Traumas in Octavia Butler's *Kindred*." *Callaloo* 32, no. 4 (2009): 1315–31.

Passalacqua, Camille. "Witnessing to Heal the Self in Gayl Jones's *Corregidora* and Phyllis Alesia Perry's *Stigmata*." *MELUS* 35, no. 4 (2010): 139–63.

Patton, Venetria K. *The Grasp That Reaches beyond the Grave: The Ancestral Call in Black Women's Texts*. Albany: State University of New York Press, 2013.

Pernick, Martin. "Defining the Defective: Eugenics, Aesthetics, and Mass Culture in Early-Twentieth-Century America." In *The Body and Physical Difference: Discourses of Disability*, edited by David T. Mitchell and Sharon L. Snyder, 89–110. Ann Arbor: University of Michigan Press, 1997.

Perry, Phyllis Alesia. *Stigmata*. New York: Anchor Books, 1999.

———. *A Sunday in June: A Novel*. New York: Hyperion, 2004.

Phillips, Jerry. "The Intuition of the Future: Utopia and Catastrophe in Octavia Butler's *Parable of the Sower*." NOVEL: *A Forum on Fiction* 35, nos. 2/3 (2002): 299–311.

Pickens, Therí A. "'It's a Jungle Out There': Blackness and Disability in *Monk*." *Disability Studies Quarterly* 33, no. 3 (2013). http://dsq-sds.org/article/view/3391/3269.

———. "Octavia Butler and the Aesthetics of the Novel." *Hypatia* 30, no. 1 (2015): 167–80.

Piercy, Marge. *Woman on the Edge of Time*. New York: Knopf, 1976.

Price, Margaret. "The Bodymind Problem and the Possibilities of Pain." *Hypatia* 30, no. 1 (2015): 268–84.

———. *Mad at School: Rhetorics of Mental Disability and Academic Life*. Corporealities. Ann Arbor: University of Michigan Press, 2011.

Puar, Jasbir K. "'I Would Rather Be a Cyborg Than a Goddess': Becoming-Intersectional in Assemblage Theory." *philoSOPHIA: A Journal of Continental Feminism* 2, no. 1 (2012): 49–66.

———. "Prognosis Time: Towards a Geopolitics of Affect, Debility and Capacity." *Women and Performance: A Journal of Feminist Theory* 19, no. 2 (2009): 161–72.

Quashie, Kevin Everod. *The Sovereignty of Quiet: Beyond Resistance in Black Culture*. New Brunswick, NJ: Rutgers University Press, 2012.

Quayson, Ato. *Aesthetic Nervousness: Disability and the Crisis of Representation*. New York: Columbia University Press, 2007.

Ralph, Michael. "'Life . . . in the Midst of Death': Notes on the Relationship between Slave Insurance, Life Insurance, and Disability." *Disability Studies Quarterly* 32, no. 3 (2012). http://dsq-sds.org/article/view/3267/3100.

Roberts, Dorothy E. *Killing the Black Body: Race, Reproduction, and the Meaning of Liberty*. New York: Pantheon, 1997.

Robertson, Benjamin. "'Some Matching Strangeness': Biology, Politics, and the Embrace of History in Octavia Butler's *Kindred*." *Science Fiction Studies* 37, no. 3 (2010): 362–81.

Rodas, Julia Miele. "On Blindness." *Journal of Literary and Cultural Disability Studies* 1, no. 2 (2009): 115–30.

Rushdy, Ashraf H. A. *Neo-Slave Narratives: Studies in the Social Logic of a Literary Form*. Race and American Culture. New York: Oxford University Press, 1999.

———. *Remembering Generations: Race and Family in Contemporary African American Fiction*. Chapel Hill: University of North Carolina Press, 2001.

Russ, Joanna. "Towards an Aesthetic of Science Fiction." *Science Fiction Studies* 2, no. 2 (1975): 112–19.

Russo, Nancy Felipe, and Mary A. Jansen. "Women, Work, and Disability: Opportunities and Challenges." In *Women with Disabilities: Essays in Psychology, Culture and Politics*, edited by Michelle Fine and Adrienne Asch, 229–44. Philadelphia: Temple University Press, 1988.

Ryan, Tim A. *Calls and Responses: The American Novel of Slavery since "Gone with the Wind."* Southern Literary Studies. Baton Rouge: Louisiana State University Press, 2008.

Samuels, Ellen. "Examining Millie and Christine McKoy: Where Enslavement and Enfreakment Meet." *Signs* 37, no. 1 (2011): 53–81.

———. *Fantasies of Identification: Disability, Gender, Race.* New York: New York University Press, 2014.

Sandahl, Carrie. "Black Man, Blind Man: Disability Identity Politics and Performance." *Theatre Journal* 56, no. 4 (2004): 579–602.

———. "Queering the Crip or Cripping the Queer? Intersections of Queer and Crip Identities in Solo Autobiographical Performance." *GLQ: A Journal of Lesbian and Gay Studies* 9, nos. 1–2 (2003): 25–56.

Sawyer, Pamela J., Brenda Major, Bettina J. Casad, Sarah S. M. Townsend, and Wendy Berry Mendes. "Discrimination and the Stress Response: Psychological and Physiological Consequences of Anticipating Prejudice in Interethnic Interactions." *American Journal of Public Health* 102, no. 5 (2012): 1020–26.

Schaefer, Kate. "On Re-Reading *Parable of the Sower.*" In *Strange Matings: Science Fiction, Feminism, African American Voices, and Octavia E. Butler*, edited by Rebecca J. Holden and Nisi Shawl, 182–85. Seattle: Aqueduct, 2013.

Schalk, Sami. "Coming to Claim Crip: Disidentification with/in Disability Studies." *Disability Studies Quarterly* 33, no. 2 (2013). http://dsq-sds.org/article/view/3705/3240.

———. "Critical Disability Studies as Methodology." *Lateral* (2016). https://doi.org/10.25158/L6.1.13.

———. "Experience, Research, and Writing: Octavia E. Butler as Author of Disability Literature." *Palimpsest* (2017): 51–75.

———. "Happily Ever after for Whom? Blackness and Disability in Romance Narratives." *Journal of Popular Culture* 49, no. 6 (2016): 1241–60.

———. "Interpreting Disability Metaphor and Race in Octavia E. Butler's 'The Evening and the Morning and the Night.'" *African American Review* 50, no. 2 (Summer 2017): 139–51.

———. "Metaphorically Speaking: Ableist Metaphors in Feminist Writing." *Disability Studies Quarterly* 33, no. 4 (2013). http://dsq-sds.org/article/view/3874/3410.

———. "Reevaluating the Supercrip." *Journal of Literary and Cultural Disability Studies* 10, no. 1 (2016): 71–86.

———. "Resisting Erasure: Reading (Dis)Ability and Race in Speculative Media." In *Routledge Companion to Disability and Media*, edited by Beth A. Haller, Gerard Goggin, and Katie Ellis. New York: Routledge, 2018.

Schiff, Sarah Eden. "Recovering (from) the Double: Fiction as Historical Revision in Octavia E. Butler's *Kindred*." *Arizona Quarterly: A Journal of American Literature, Culture, and Theory* 65, no. 1 (2009): 107–36.

Scholes, Robert, and Eric S. Rabkin. *Science Fiction: History, Science, Vision*. New York: Oxford University Press, 1977.

Schotland, Sara Deutch. "Disability and Disease in Utopian and Dystopian Fiction: Justice and Care Perspectives." PhD diss., University of Maryland, College Park, 2013. http://drum.lib.umd.edu/handle/1903/12957.

Schultz, Connie. "A Tale of Two Cities." *Politico Magazine*, February 23, 2015. http://www.politico.com/magazine/story/2015/02/tamir-rice-cleveland-police-115401_full.html#.V8B04vmAOkr.

Schur, Richard. "The Crisis of Authenticity in Contemporary African American Literature." In *Contemporary African American Literature: The Living Canon*, edited by Lovalerie King and Shirley Moody-Turner, 235–54. Bloomington: Indiana University Press, 2013.

Schuyler, George S. *Black No More*. New York: Modern Library, 1999.

Shapiro, Joseph P. *No Pity: People with Disabilities Forging a New Civil Rights Movement*. New York: Times Books, 1994.

Shavers, Vickie L., William M. P. Klein, and Pebbles Fagan. "Research on Race/Ethnicity and Health Care Discrimination: Where We Are and Where We Need to Go." *American Journal of Public Health* 102, no. 5 (2012): 930–32.

Shawl, Nisi. "Invisible Inks: On Black Sf Authors and Disability." *WisCon Chronicles* 7 (2013): 40–46.

Sherry, Mark. "(Post)Colonising Disability." *Wagadu* 4 (2007): 10–22.

Siebers, Tobin. *Disability Theory*. Ann Arbor: University of Michigan Press, 2008.

Sievers, Stefanie. "Embodies Memories—Sharable Stories? The Legacies of Slavery as a Problem of Representation in Phyllis Alesia Perry's *Stigmata*." In *Monuments of the Black Atlantic: Slavery and Memory*, edited by Joanne M. Braxton and Maria I. Diedrich, 131–40. Piscataway, NJ: Transaction, 2004.

Simpson, Hyacinth M. "Fantastic Alternatives: Journeys into the Imagination: A Conversation with Nalo Hopkinson." *Journal of West Indian Literature* 14, nos. 1–2 (2005): 96–112.

Smedley, Brian D. "The Lived Experience of Race and Its Health Consequences." *American Journal of Public Health* 102, no. 5 (2012): 933–35.

smith, s. e. "To Go Where No Ism Has Gone Before: Disability at the Final Frontier." In *Shattering Ableist Narratives*, vol. 7, *The Wiscon Chronicles*, edited by Joselle Vanderhooft, 83–95. Seattle: Aqueduct, 2013.

Snyder, Sharon L., and David T. Mitchell. *Cultural Locations of Disability*. Chicago: University of Chicago Press, 2006.

Spaulding, A. Timothy. *Re-Forming the Past: History, the Fantastic, and the Postmodern Slave Narrative*. Columbus: Ohio State University Press, 2005.

Stallings, L. H. "Sampling the Sonics of Sex (Funk) in Paul Beatty's *Slumberland*." In *Contemporary African American Literature: The Living Canon*, edited by Lovalerie

King and Shirley Moody-Turner, 189–212. Blacks in the Diaspora. Bloomington: Indiana University Press, 2013.

Stanford, Ann Folwell. *Bodies in a Broken World: Women Novelists of Color and the Politics of Medicine.* Studies in Social Medicine. Chapel Hill: University of North Carolina Press, 2003.

———. "Mechanisms of Disease: African-American Women Writers, Social Pathologies, and the Limits of Medicine." *NWSA Journal* 6 no. 1 (1994): 28–47.

Stein, Karen F. "Inclusion and Exclusion in Some Feminist Utopian Fictions." In *Women's Utopian and Dystopian Fiction,* edited by Sharon R. Wilson, 112–32. Newcastle upon Tyne, UK: Cambridge Scholars, 2013.

Steinberg, Marc. "Inverting History in Octavia Butler's Postmodern Slave Narrative." *African American Review* 38, no. 3 (2004): 467–76.

Sternthal, Michelle J., Natalie Slopen, and David R. Williams. "Racial Disparities in Health: How Much Does Stress Really Matter?" *Du Bois Review: Social Science Research on Race* 8, no. 1 (2011): 95–113.

Stillman, Peter G. "Dystopian Critiques, Utopian Possibilities, and Human Purposes in Octavia Butler's Parables." *Utopian Studies* 14, no. 1 (2003): 15–35.

Suvin, Darko. *Metamorphoses of Science Fiction: On the Poetics and History of a Literary Genre.* New Haven, CT: Yale University Press, 1979.

Taylor, Ashley. "The Discourse of Pathology: Reproducing the Able Mind through Bodies of Color." *Hypatia* 30, no. 1 (2015): 181–98.

Thaler, Ingrid. *Black Atlantic Speculative Fictions: Octavia E. Butler, Jewelle Gomez, and Nalo Hopkinson.* Routledge Research in Atlantic Studies. New York: Routledge, 2010.

The Tomorrow People (film). Berlanti Productions, 2013–14.

Turner, Stephanie S. "'What Actually Is': The Insistence of Genre in Octavia Butler's *Kindred.*" *Femspec* 4, no. 2 (2003): 259–59.

Vanderhooft, JoSelle, ed. *Shattering Ableist Narratives.* Seattle: Aqueduct, 2013.

Vidali, Amy. "Seeing What We Know: Disability and Theories of Metaphor." *Journal of Literary and Cultural Disability Studies* 4, no. 1 (2010): 33–54.

Vint, Sherryl. *Bodies of Tomorrow: Technology, Subjectivity, Science Fiction.* Toronto: University of Toronto Press, 2007.

———. "'Only by Experience': Embodiment and the Limitations of Realism in Neo–Slave Narratives." *Science Fiction Studies* 34, no. 2 (2007): 241–61.

Viruell-Fuentes, Edna A. "'It's a Lot of Work': Racialization Processes, Ethnic Identity Formations, and Their Health Implications." *Du Bois Review: Social Science Research on Race* 8, no. 1 (2011): 37–52.

Waggoner, Jess. "'Oh Say Can You—': Race and Mental Disability in Performances of Citizenship." *Journal of Literary and Cultural Disability Studies,* 10 no. 1 (2016): 87–102.

Walker, Margaret. *Jubilee.* Boston: Houghton Mifflin, 1966.

Wall, Cheryl A. *Changing Our Own Words: Essays on Criticism, Theory, and Writing by Black Women.* New Brunswick, NJ: Rutgers University Press, 1989.

Walters, Karina L., Selina A. Mohammed, Teresa Evans-Campbell, Romona E. Bel-trán, David H. Chae, and Bonnie Buran. "Bodies Don't Just Tell Stories, They Tell Histories: Embodiment of Historical Trauma among American Indians and Alaska Natives." *Du Bois Review: Social Science Research on Race* 8, no. 1 (2011): 179–89.

Wanzo, Rebecca. "Black Love Is Not a Fairy Tale: African American Women, Ro-mance, and Rhetoric." *Poroi: An Interdisciplinary Journal of Rhetorical Analysis and Invention* 7, no. 2 (2011): 1–18.

Warren, Kenneth W. *What Was African American Literature?* Cambridge, MA: Har-vard University Press, 2011.

Washington, Harriet A. *Medical Apartheid: The Dark History of Medical Experimenta-tion on Black Americans from Colonial Times to the Present*. New York: Doubleday, 2006.

Wegner, Phillip E. *Life between Two Deaths, 1989–2001: U.S. Culture in the Long Nine-ties*. Post-Contemporary Interventions. Durham, NC: Duke University Press, 2009.

Weinstock, Jeffrey A. "Freaks in Space: 'Extraterrestrialism' and 'Deep-Space Mul-ticulturalism.'" In *Freakery: Cultural Spectacles of the Extraordinary Body*, edited by Rosemarie Garland-Thomson, 327–37. New York: New York University Press, 2006.

Wendell, Susan. *The Rejected Body: Feminist Philosophical Reflections on Disability*. New York: Routledge, 1996.

White, Evelyn C., ed. *The Black Women's Health Book: Speaking for Ourselves*. Seattle: Seal Press, 1990.

White, Hayden. "The Value of Narrativity in the Representation of Reality." *Critical Inquiry* 7, no. 1 (1980): 5–27.

Wood, Sarah. "Exorcizing the Past: The Slave Narrative as Historical Fantasy." *Femi-nist Review*, no. 85 (2007): 83–96.

Woolfork, Lisa. *Embodying American Slavery in Contemporary Culture*. Urbana: Uni-versity of Illinois Press, 2009.

Wu, Cynthia. *Chang and Eng Reconnected: The Original Siamese Twins in American Culture*. Philadelphia: Temple University Press, 2012.

Yaszek, Lisa. "'A Grim Fantasy': Remaking American History in Octavia Butler's *Kin-dred*." *Signs* 28, no. 4 (2003): 1053–66.

INDEX